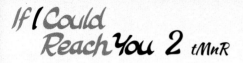

If I Could Reach You 2 tMnR

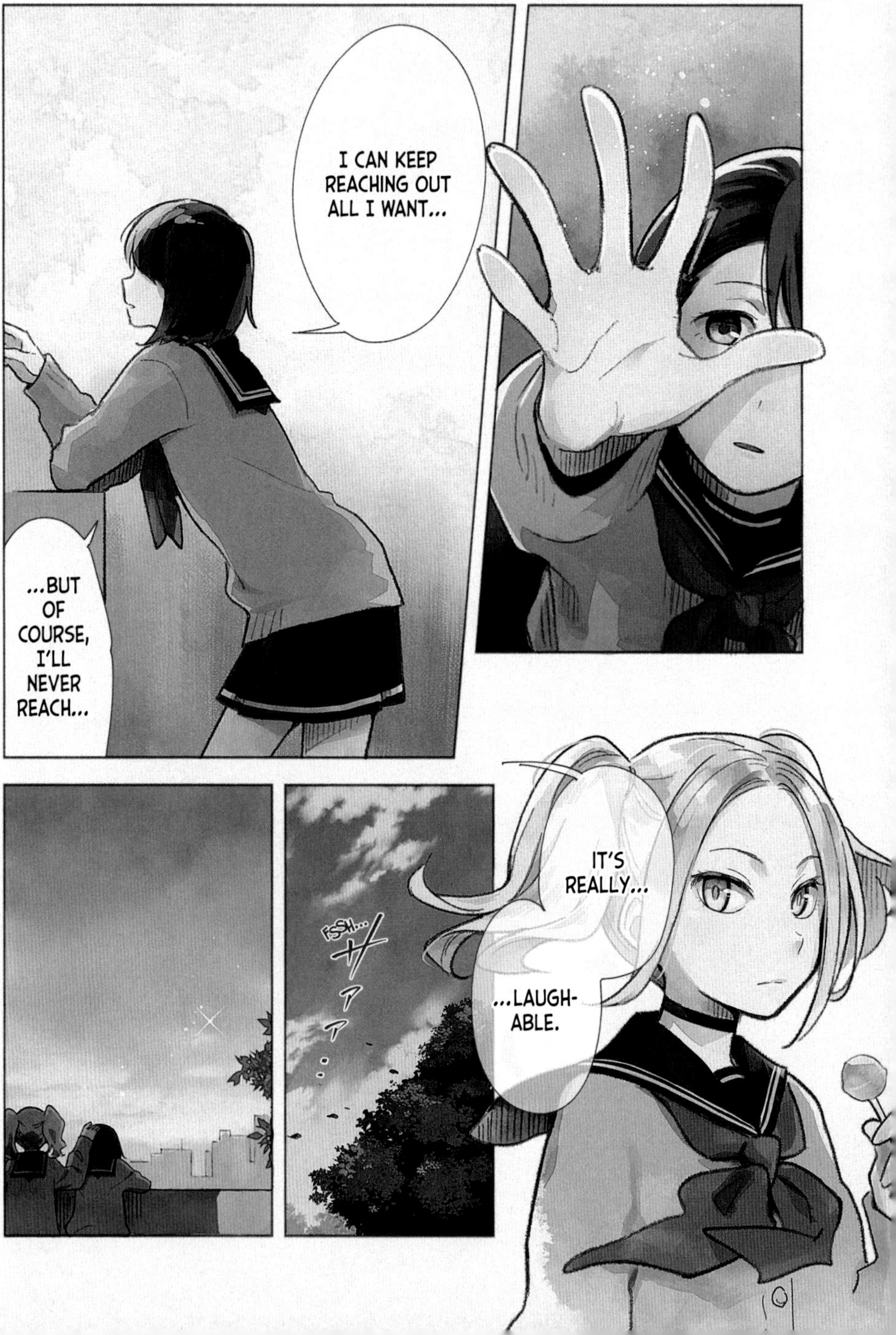
I CAN KEEP REACHING OUT ALL I WANT...
...BUT OF COURSE, I'LL NEVER REACH...
IT'S REALLY...
...LAUGHABLE.
FSSH...
ザアア‥

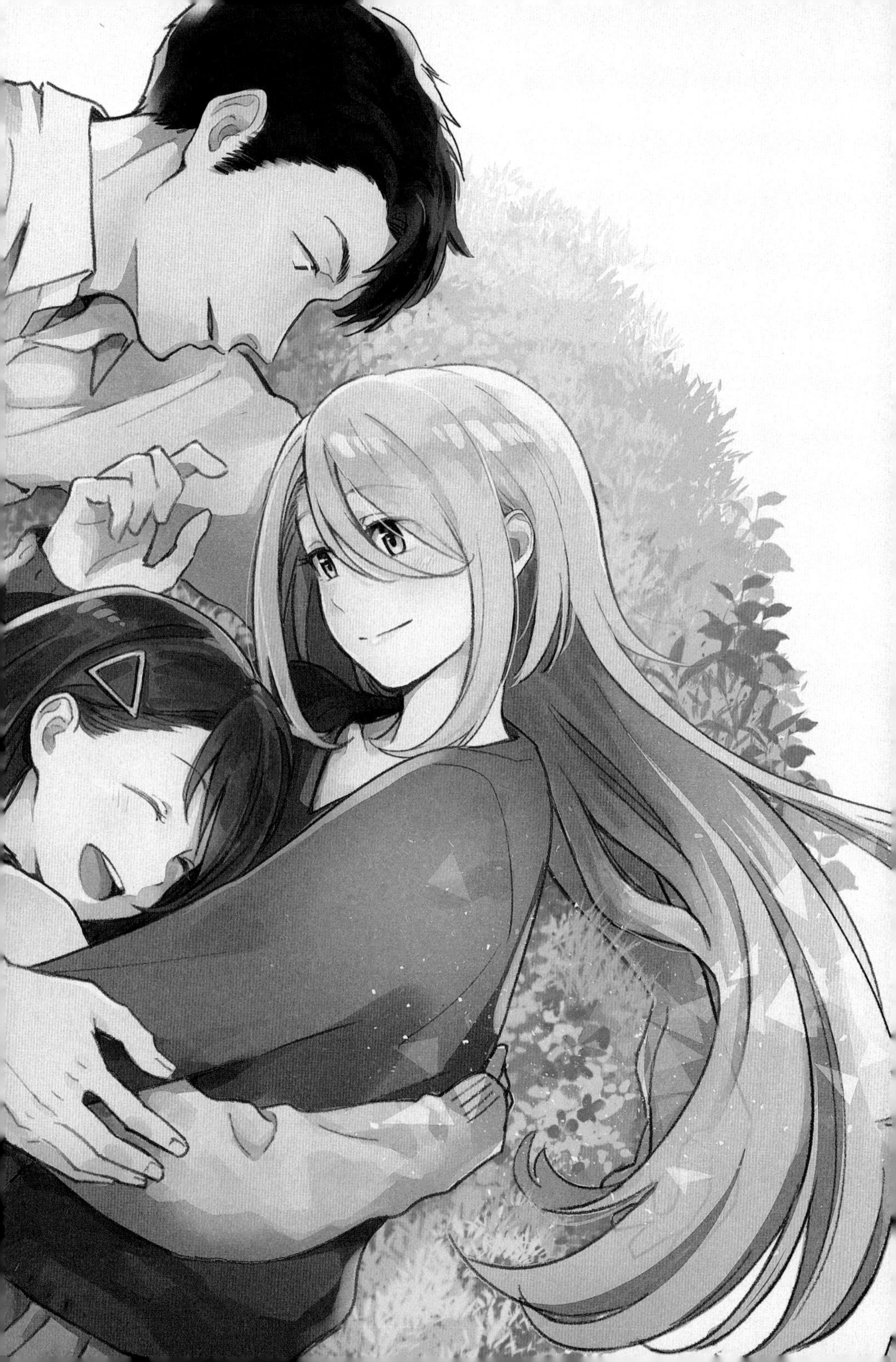

Chapter 6

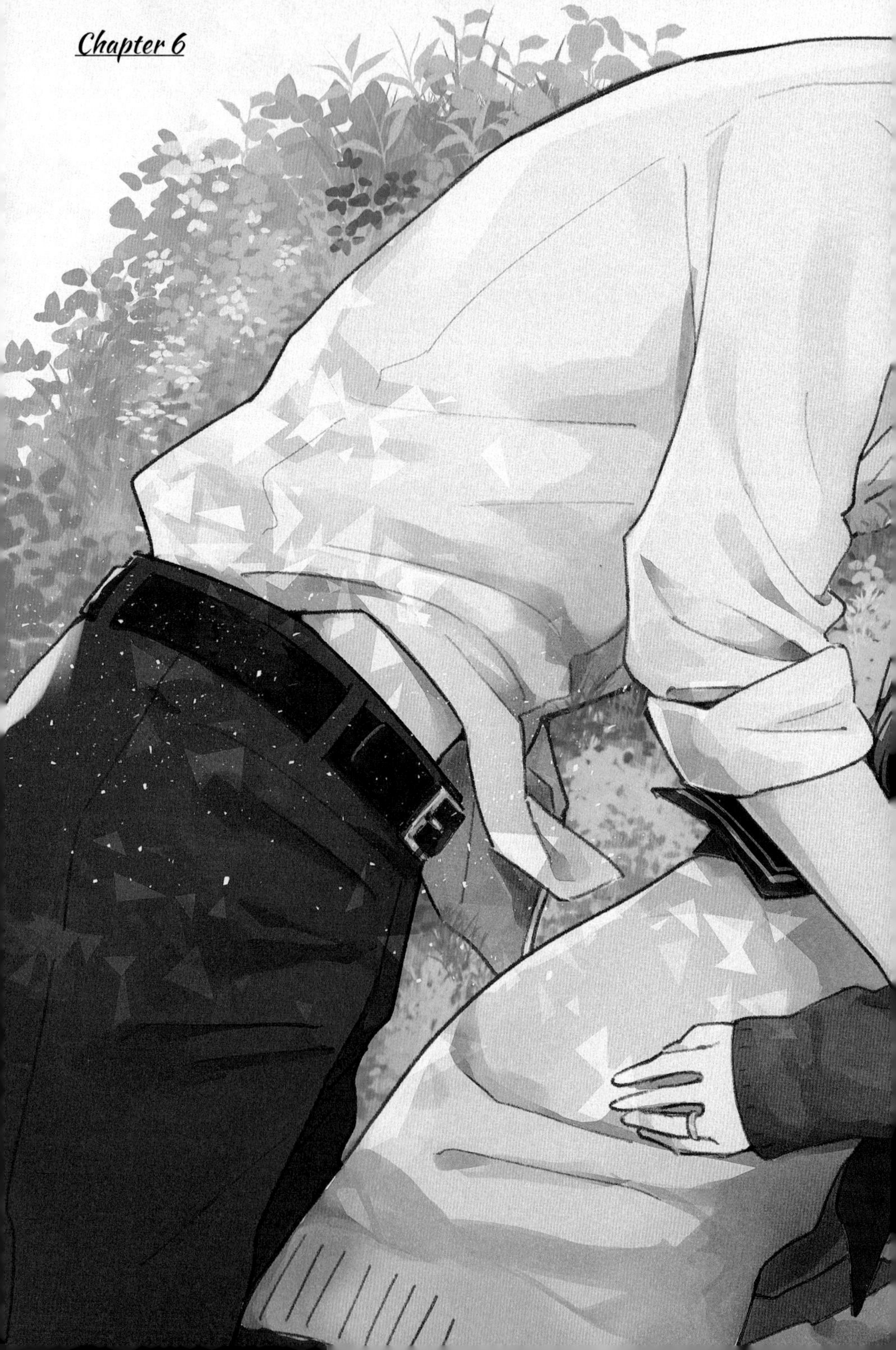

If I Could Reach You

2

C O N T E N T S

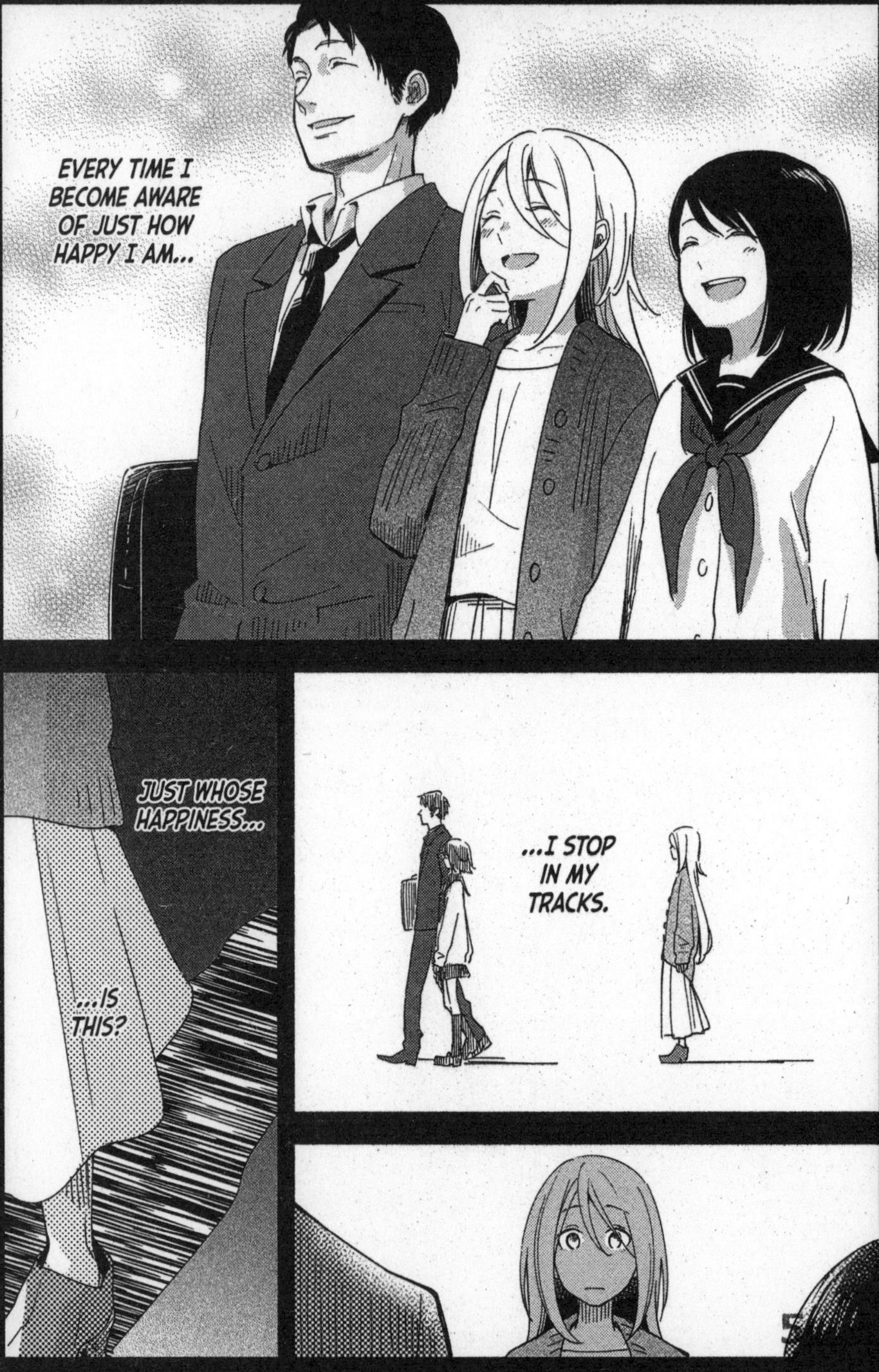
EVERY TIME I BECOME AWARE OF JUST HOW HAPPY I AM...
...I STOP IN MY TRACKS.
JUST WHOSE HAPPINESS...
...IS THIS?

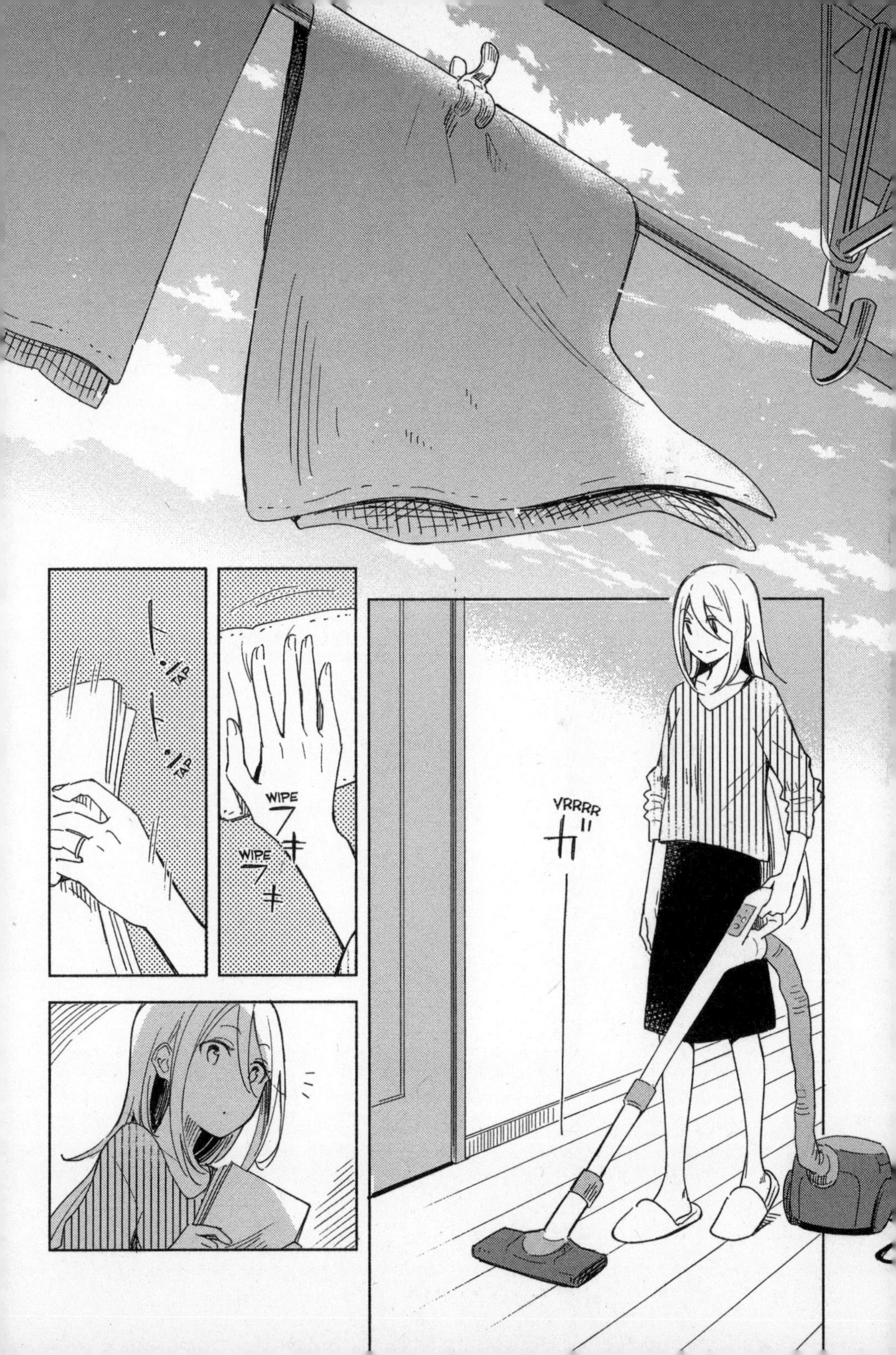

VRRRR
ガ
WIPE
フキ
WIPE
フキ
TAP
TAP

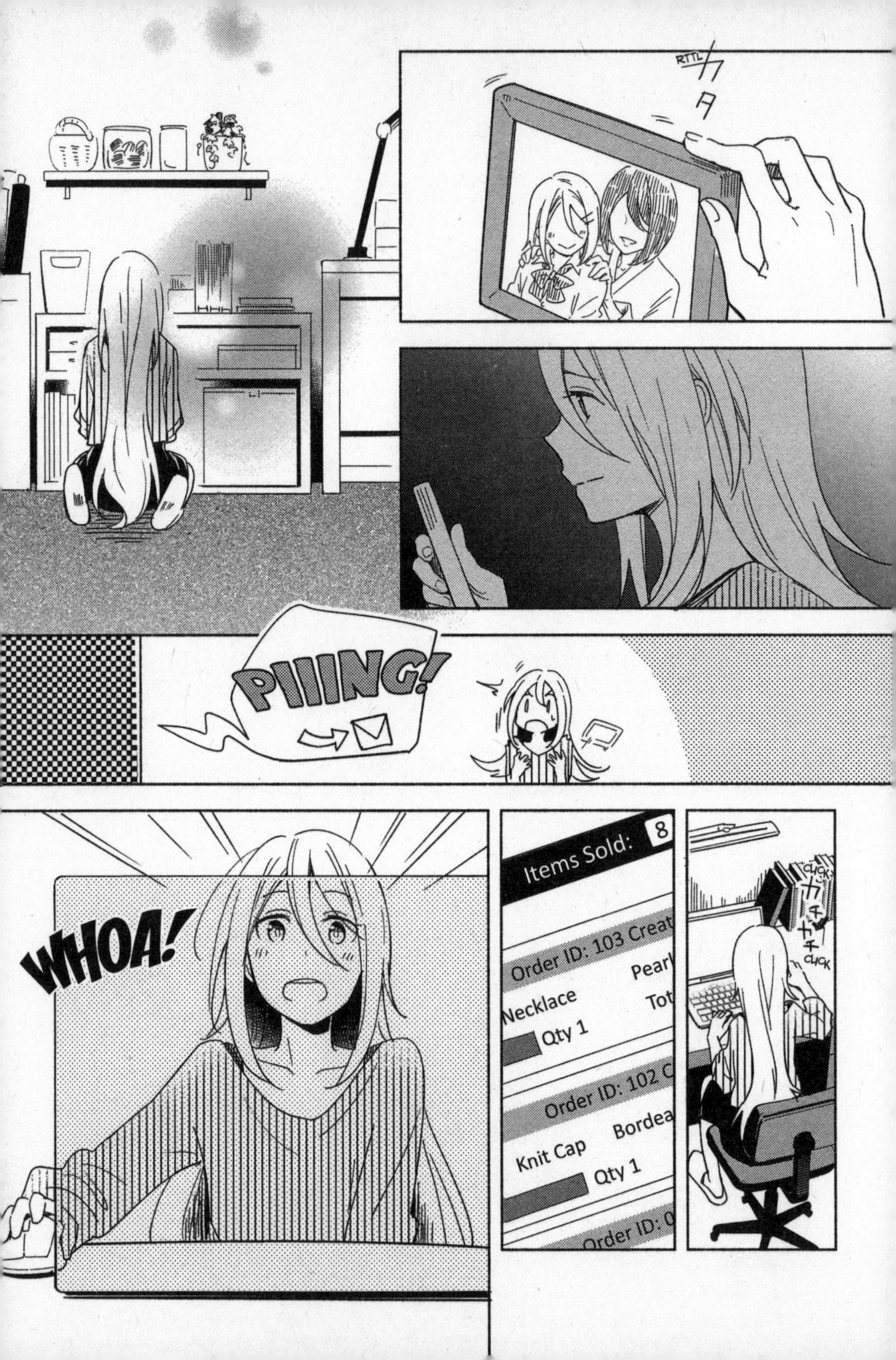
RTTL
カタ
PIIING!
CLICK
カチ
カチ
CLICK
Items Sold: 8
Order ID: 103 Creat
Pearl
Necklace
Tot
Qty 1
Order ID: 102 C
Bordea
Knit Cap
Qty 1
Order ID: 0
WHOA!

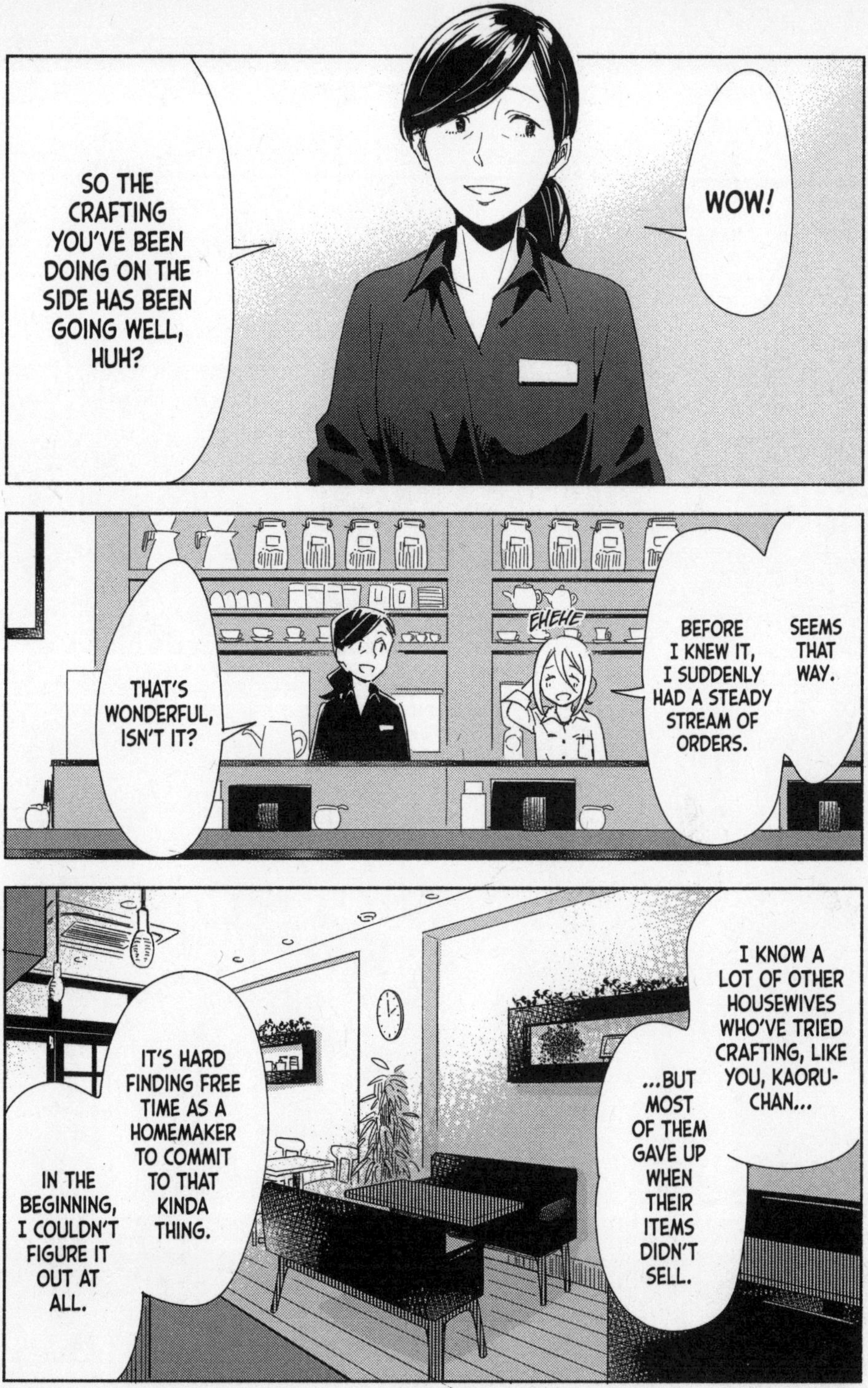
WOW!
SO THE CRAFTING YOU'VE BEEN DOING ON THE SIDE HAS BEEN GOING WELL, HUH?
SEEMS THAT WAY.
BEFORE I KNEW IT, I SUDDENLY HAD A STEADY STREAM OF ORDERS.
EHEHE
THAT'S WONDERFUL, ISN'T IT?
I KNOW A LOT OF OTHER HOUSEWIVES WHO'VE TRIED CRAFTING, LIKE YOU, KAORU-CHAN...
...BUT MOST OF THEM GAVE UP WHEN THEIR ITEMS DIDN'T SELL.
IT'S HARD FINDING FREE TIME AS A HOMEMAKER TO COMMIT TO THAT KINDA THING.
IN THE BEGINNING, I COULDN'T FIGURE IT OUT AT ALL.

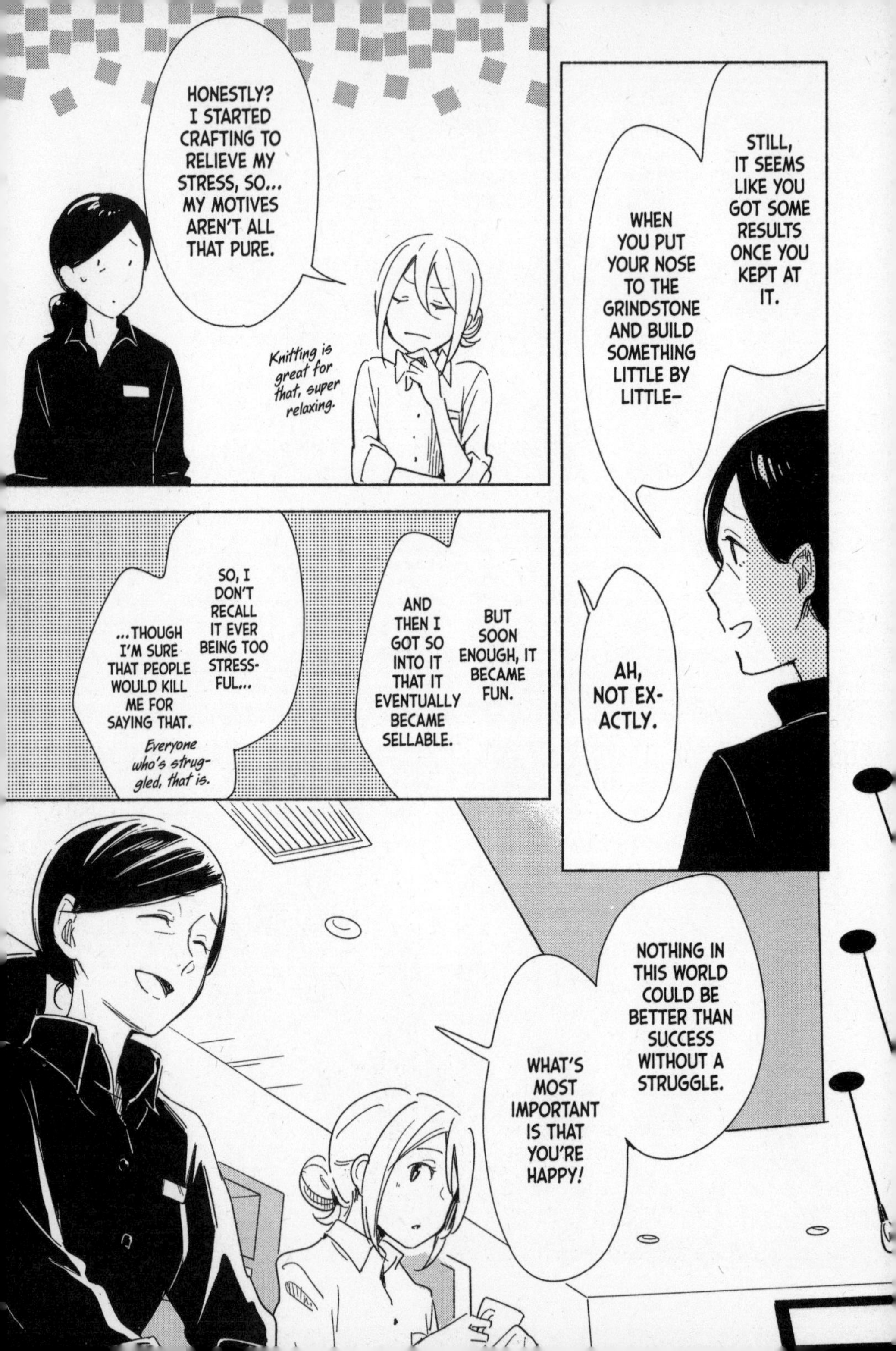
STILL, IT SEEMS LIKE YOU GOT SOME RESULTS ONCE YOU KEPT AT IT.
WHEN YOU PUT YOUR NOSE TO THE GRINDSTONE AND BUILD SOMETHING LITTLE BY LITTLE–
AH, NOT EX-ACTLY.
HONESTLY? I STARTED CRAFTING TO RELIEVE MY STRESS, SO... MY MOTIVES AREN'T ALL THAT PURE.
Knitting is great for that, super relaxing.
BUT SOON ENOUGH, IT BECAME FUN.
AND THEN I GOT SO INTO IT THAT IT EVENTUALLY BECAME SELLABLE.
SO, I DON'T RECALL IT EVER BEING TOO STRESS-FUL...
...THOUGH I'M SURE THAT PEOPLE WOULD KILL ME FOR SAYING THAT.
Everyone who's strug-gled, that is.
NOTHING IN THIS WORLD COULD BE BETTER THAN SUCCESS WITHOUT A STRUGGLE.
WHAT'S MOST IMPORTANT IS THAT YOU'RE HAPPY!

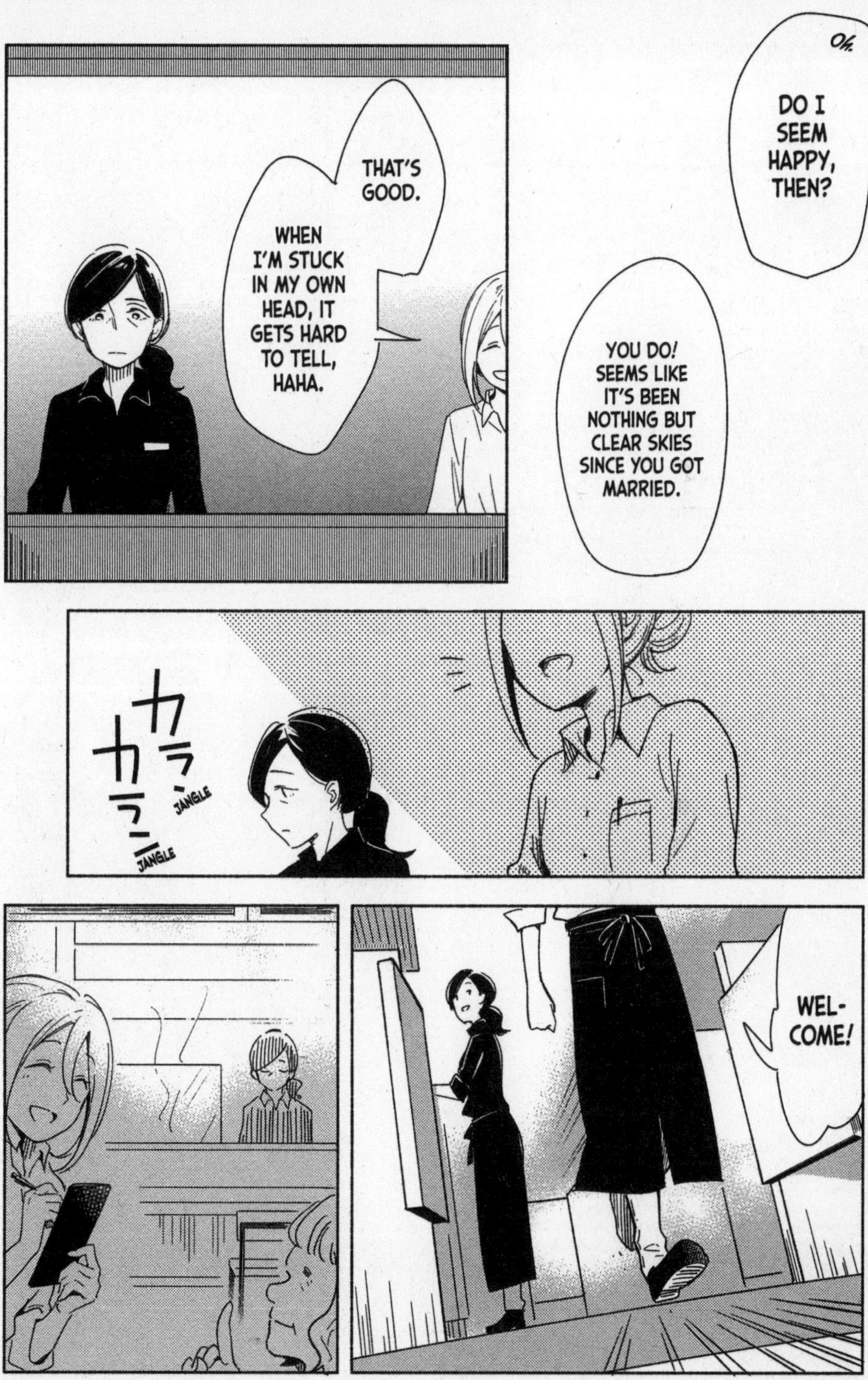
Oh.
DO I SEEM HAPPY, THEN?
YOU DO! SEEMS LIKE IT'S BEEN NOTHING BUT CLEAR SKIES SINCE YOU GOT MARRIED.
THAT'S GOOD.
WHEN I'M STUCK IN MY OWN HEAD, IT GETS HARD TO TELL, HAHA.
カラン
JANGLE
カラン
JANGLE
WEL-COME!

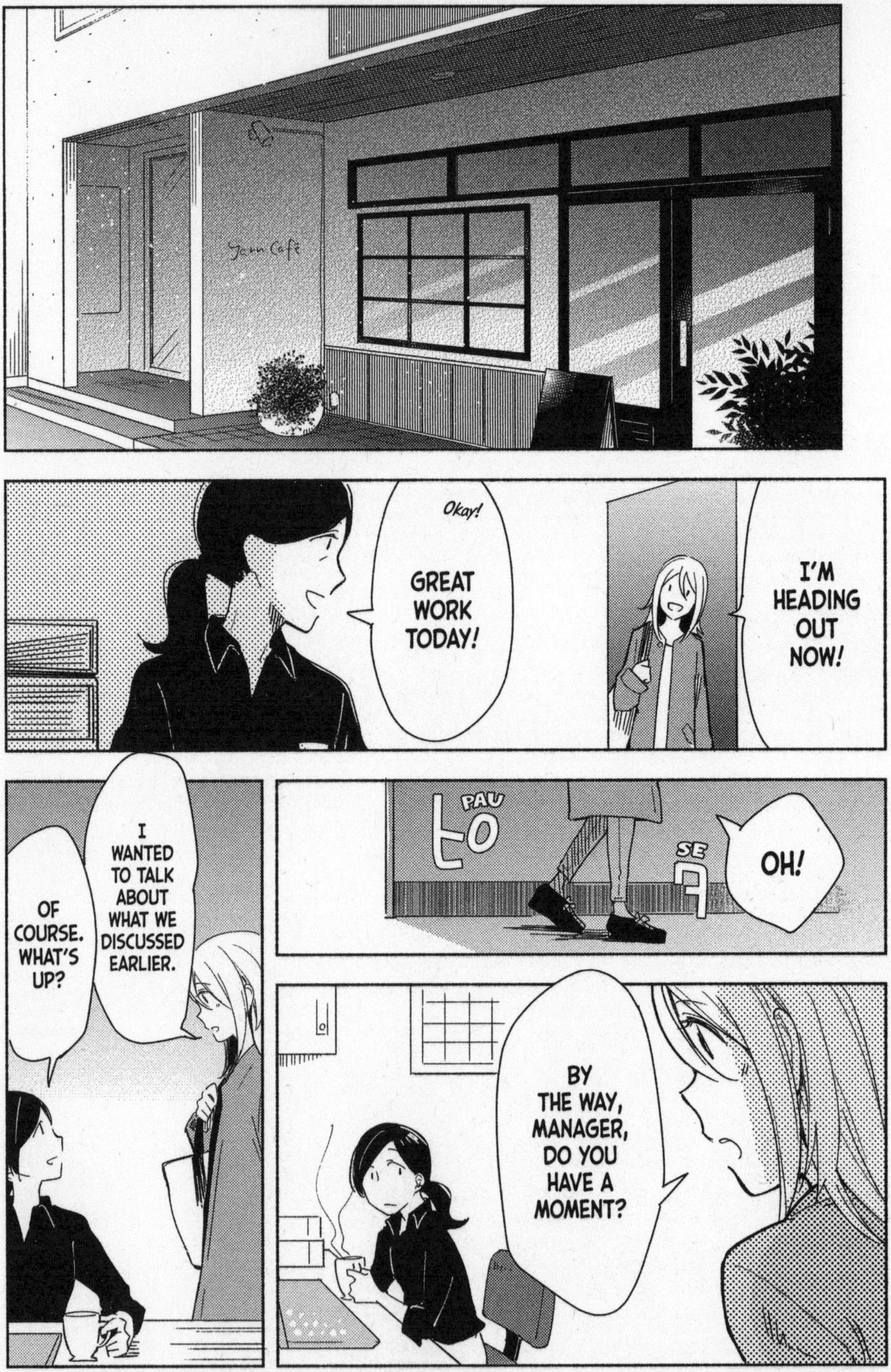
I'M HEADING OUT NOW!
Okay!
GREAT WORK TODAY!
PAU
SE
OH!
BY THE WAY, MANAGER, DO YOU HAVE A MOMENT?
I WANTED TO TALK ABOUT WHAT WE DISCUSSED EARLIER.
OF COURSE. WHAT'S UP?

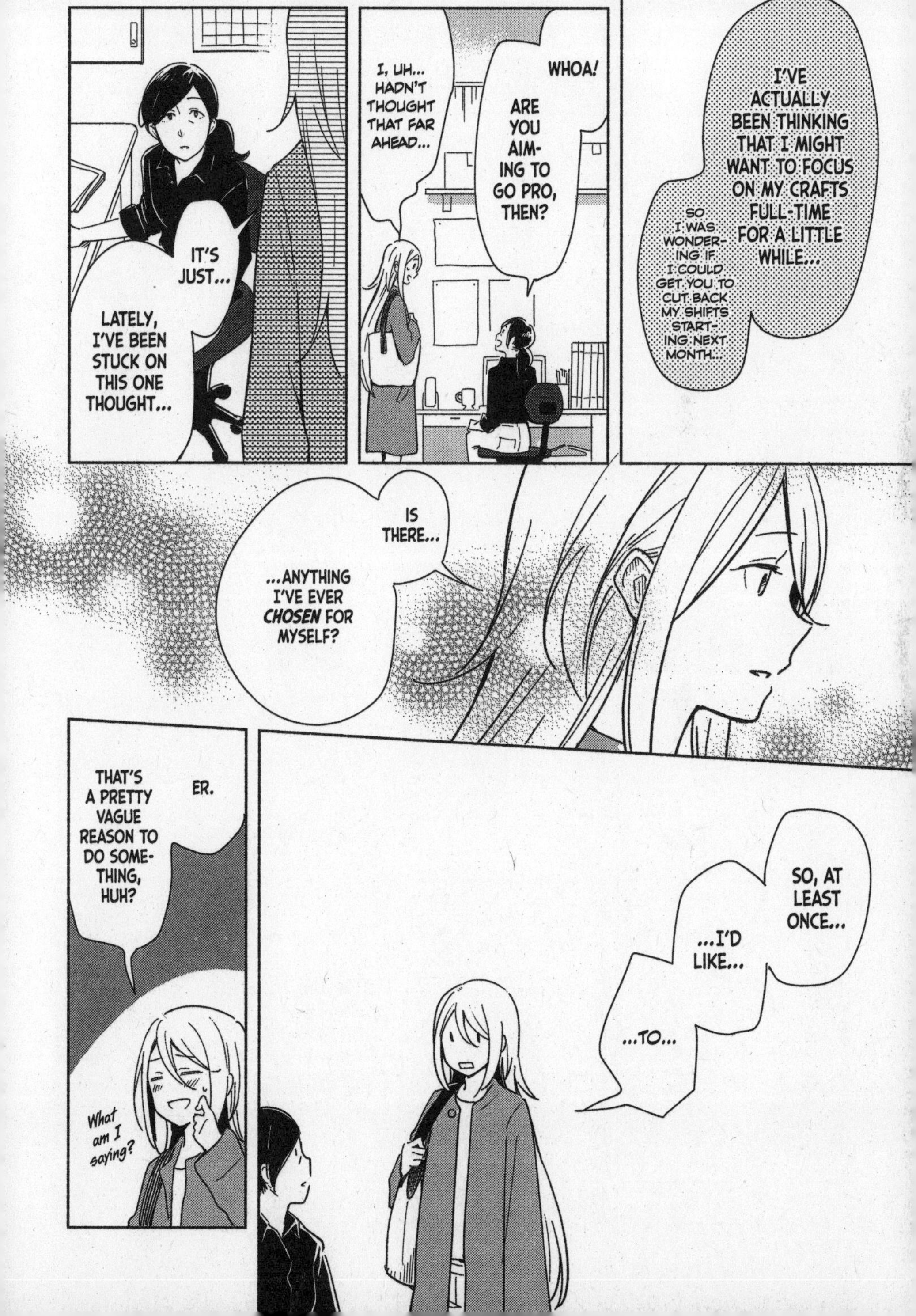
I'VE ACTUALLY BEEN THINKING THAT I MIGHT WANT TO FOCUS ON MY CRAFTS FULL-TIME FOR A LITTLE WHILE...
SO I WAS WONDERING IF I COULD GET YOU TO CUT BACK MY SHIFTS STARTING NEXT MONTH...
WHOA!
ARE YOU AIMING TO GO PRO, THEN?
I, UH... HADN'T THOUGHT THAT FAR AHEAD...
IT'S JUST...
LATELY, I'VE BEEN STUCK ON THIS ONE THOUGHT...
IS THERE...
...ANYTHING I'VE EVER *CHOSEN* FOR MYSELF?
SO, AT LEAST ONCE...
...I'D LIKE...
...TO...
ER.
THAT'S A PRETTY VAGUE REASON TO DO SOMETHING, HUH?
What am I saying?

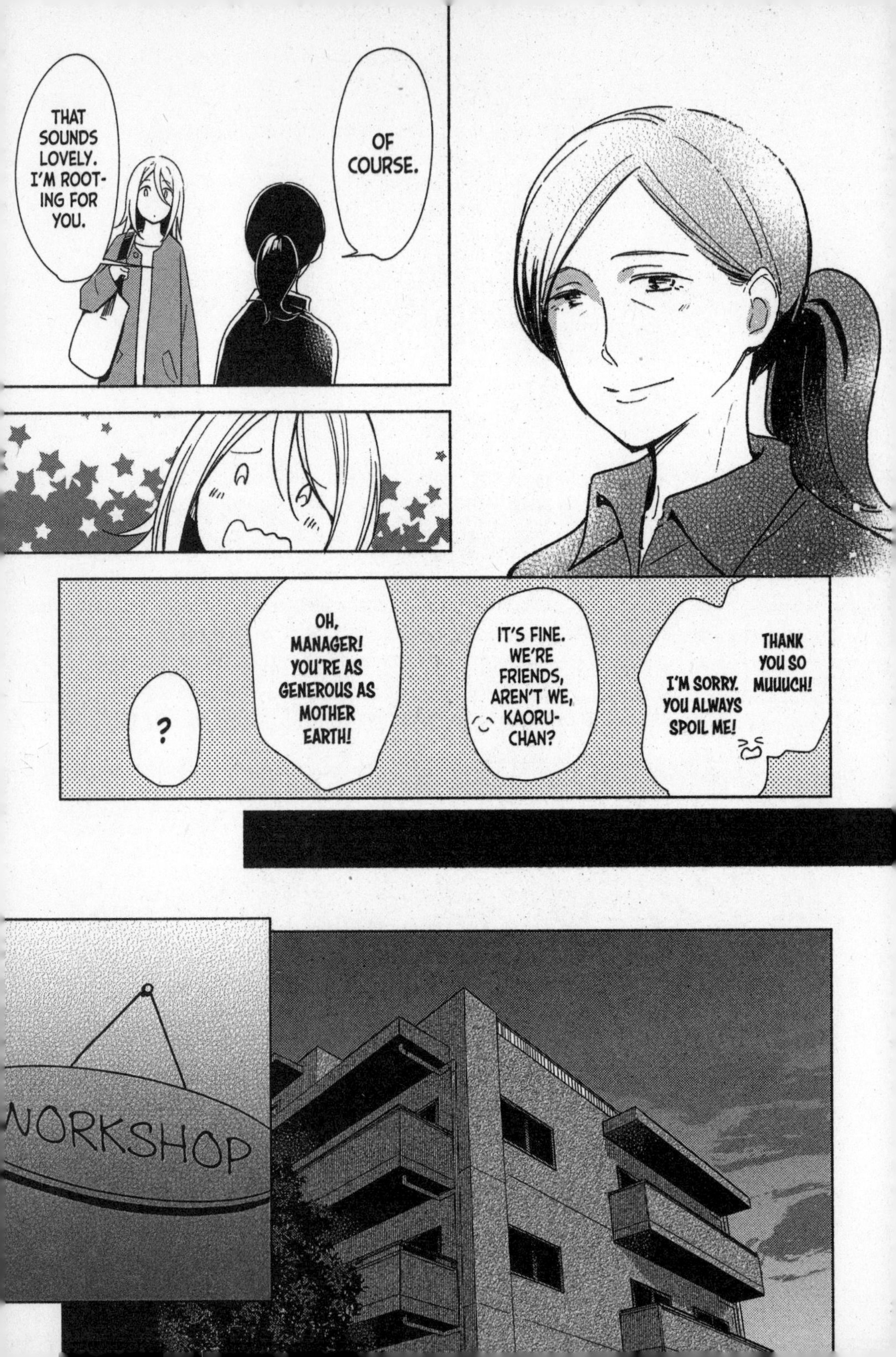
OF COURSE.
THAT SOUNDS LOVELY. I'M ROOTING FOR YOU.
THANK YOU SO MUUUCH!
I'M SORRY. YOU ALWAYS SPOIL ME!
IT'S FINE. WE'RE FRIENDS, AREN'T WE, KAORU-CHAN?
OH, MANAGER! YOU'RE AS GENEROUS AS MOTHER EARTH!
?
ORKSHOP

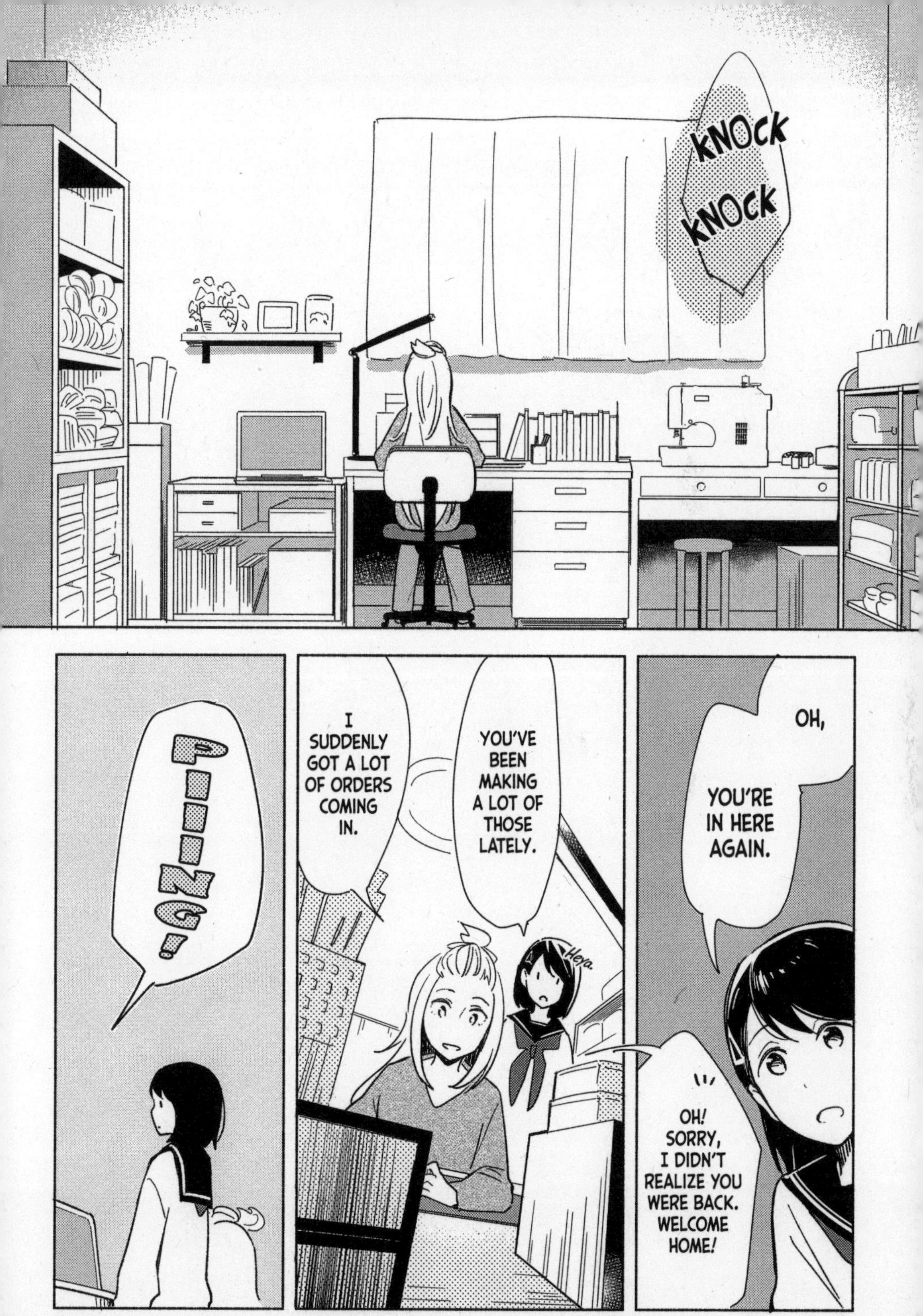
KNOCK
KNOCK
OH, YOU'RE IN HERE AGAIN.
OH! SORRY, I DIDN'T REALIZE YOU WERE BACK. WELCOME HOME!
YOU'VE BEEN MAKING A LOT OF THOSE LATELY.
I SUDDENLY GOT A LOT OF ORDERS COMING IN.
Heya.
PIIING!

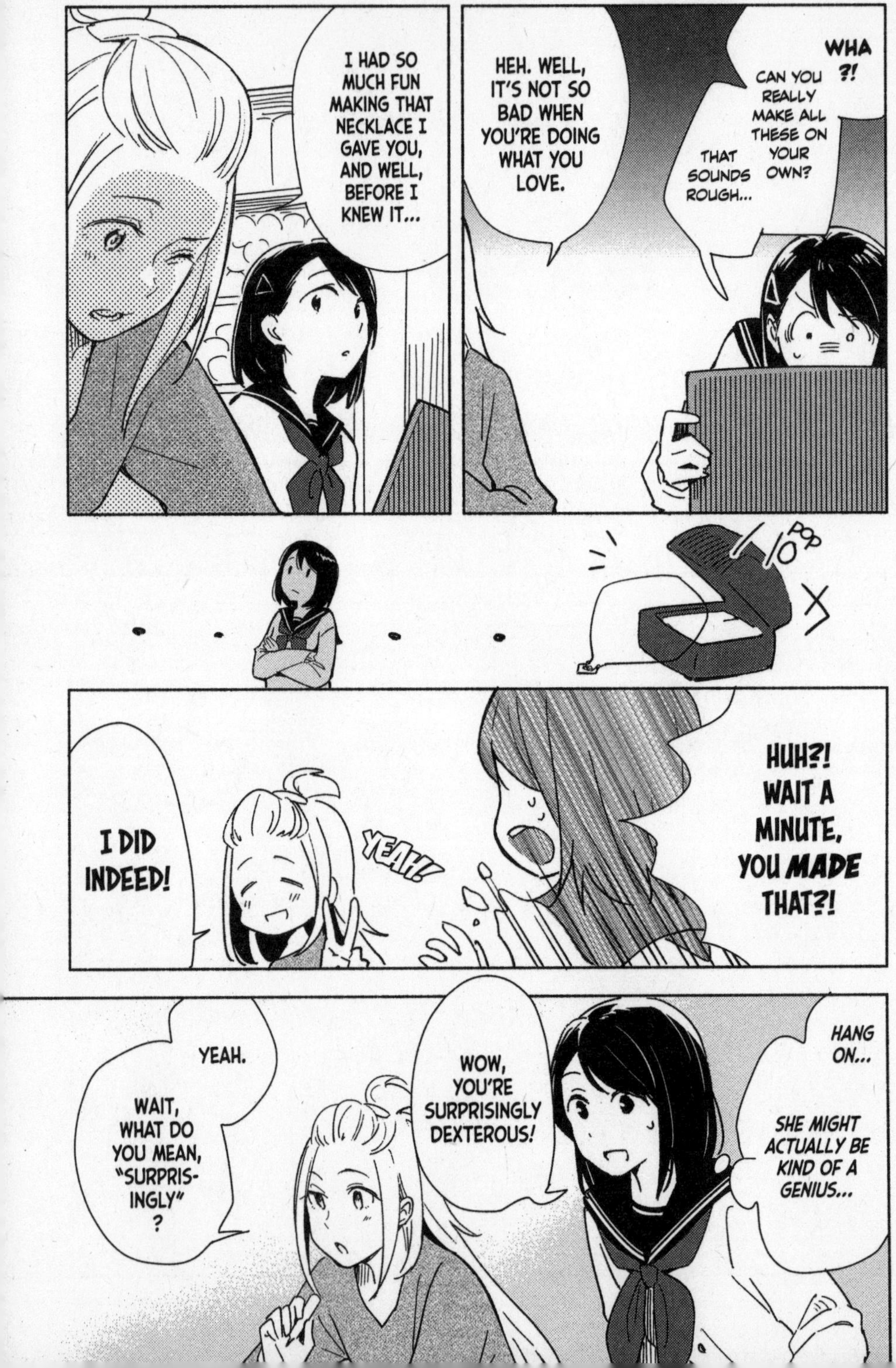
WHA ?!
CAN YOU REALLY MAKE ALL THESE ON YOUR OWN?
THAT SOUNDS ROUGH...
HEH. WELL, IT'S NOT SO BAD WHEN YOU'RE DOING WHAT YOU LOVE.
I HAD SO MUCH FUN MAKING THAT NECKLACE I GAVE YOU, AND WELL, BEFORE I KNEW IT...
POP
. . . .
HUH?! WAIT A MINUTE, YOU *MADE* THAT?!
YEAH!
I DID INDEED!
HANG ON...
SHE MIGHT ACTUALLY BE KIND OF A GENIUS...
WOW, YOU'RE SURPRISINGLY DEXTEROUS!
YEAH.
WAIT, WHAT DO YOU MEAN, "SURPRIS-INGLY"?

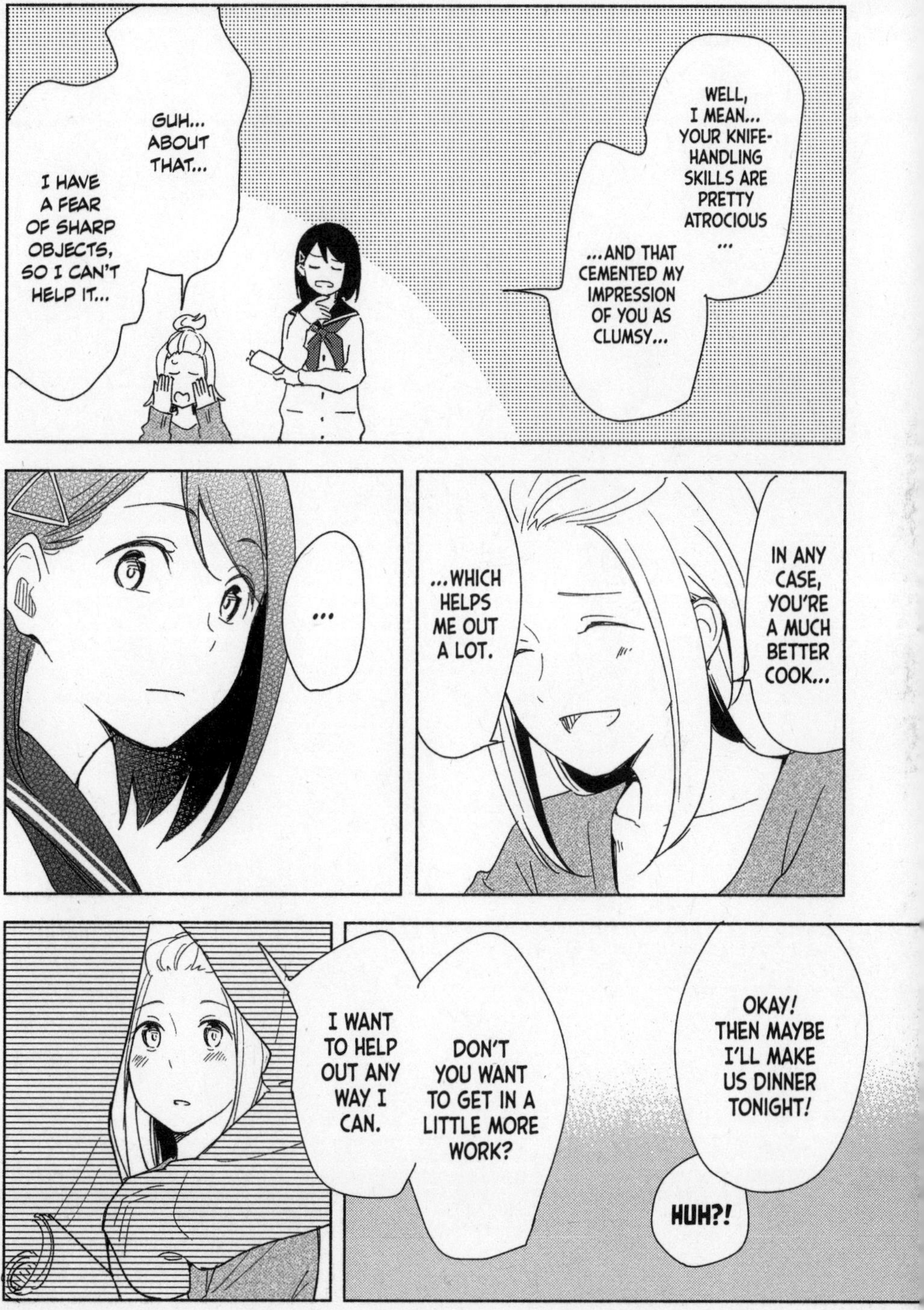

WELL, I MEAN... YOUR KNIFE-HANDLING SKILLS ARE PRETTY ATROCIOUS ...
...AND THAT CEMENTED MY IMPRESSION OF YOU AS CLUMSY...
GUH... ABOUT THAT...
I HAVE A FEAR OF SHARP OBJECTS, SO I CAN'T HELP IT...
IN ANY CASE, YOU'RE A MUCH BETTER COOK...
...WHICH HELPS ME OUT A LOT.
...
OKAY! THEN MAYBE I'LL MAKE US DINNER TONIGHT!
HUH?!
DON'T YOU WANT TO GET IN A LITTLE MORE WORK?
I WANT TO HELP OUT ANY WAY I CAN.

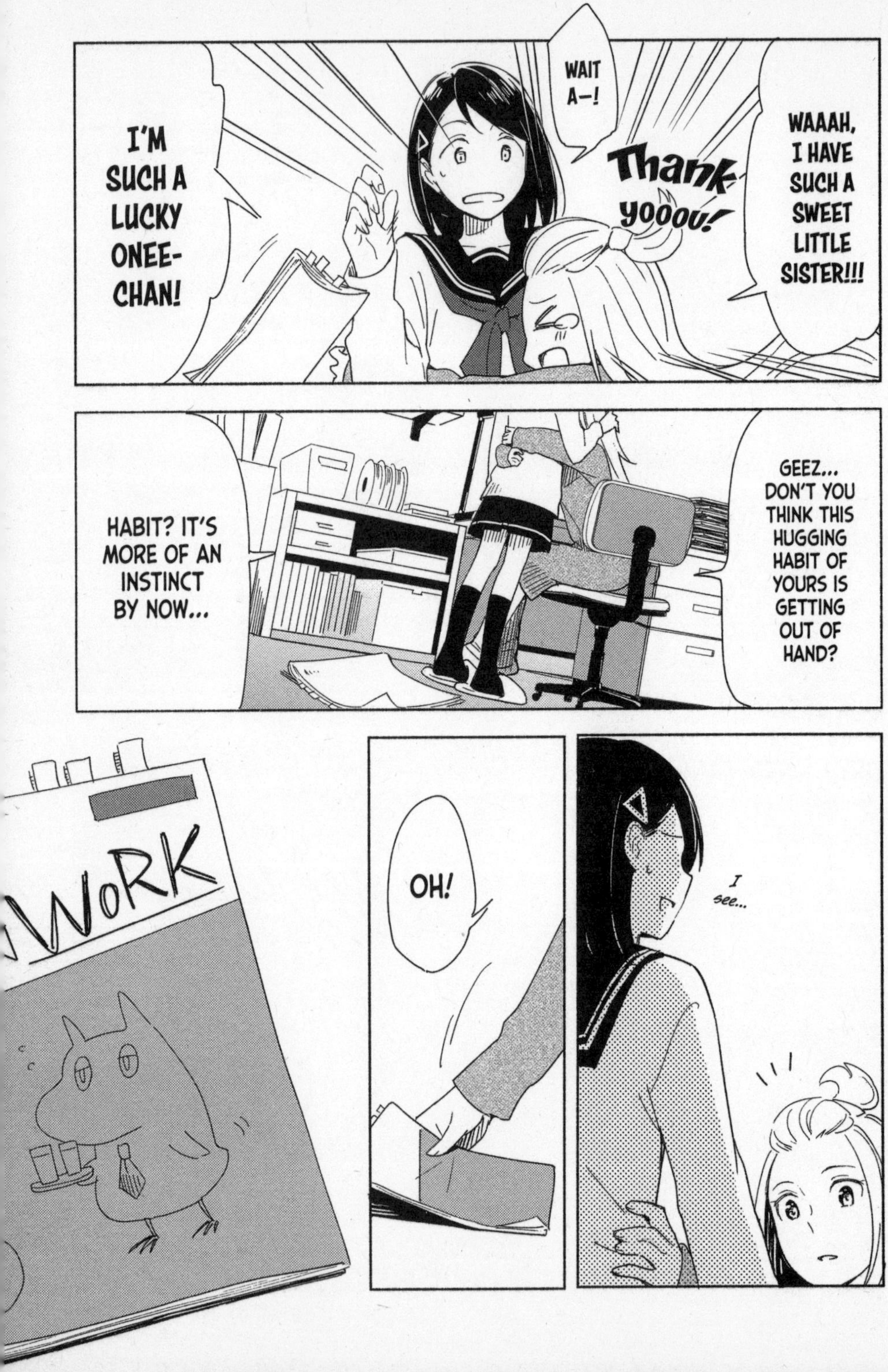
WAAAH, I HAVE SUCH A SWEET LITTLE SISTER!!!
Thank yooou!
WAIT A—!
I'M SUCH A LUCKY ONEE-CHAN!
GEEZ... DON'T YOU THINK THIS HUGGING HABIT OF YOURS IS GETTING OUT OF HAND?
HABIT? IT'S MORE OF AN INSTINCT BY NOW...
I see...
OH!
WoRK

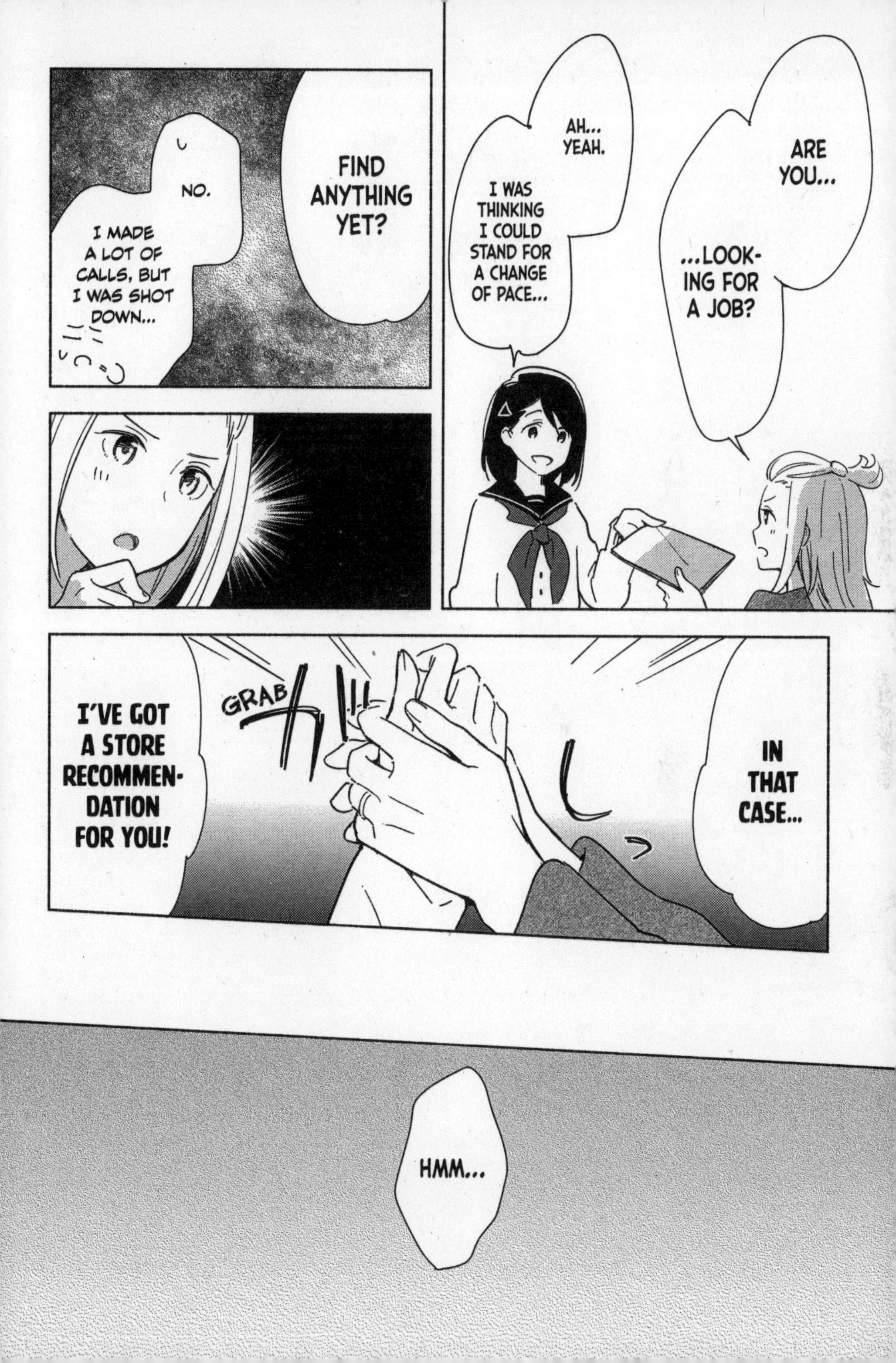
ARE YOU...
...LOOKING FOR A JOB?
AH... YEAH.
I WAS THINKING I COULD STAND FOR A CHANGE OF PACE...
FIND ANYTHING YET?
NO.
I MADE A LOT OF CALLS, BUT I WAS SHOT DOWN...
IN THAT CASE...
GRAB
I'VE GOT A STORE RECOMMENDATION FOR YOU!
HMM...

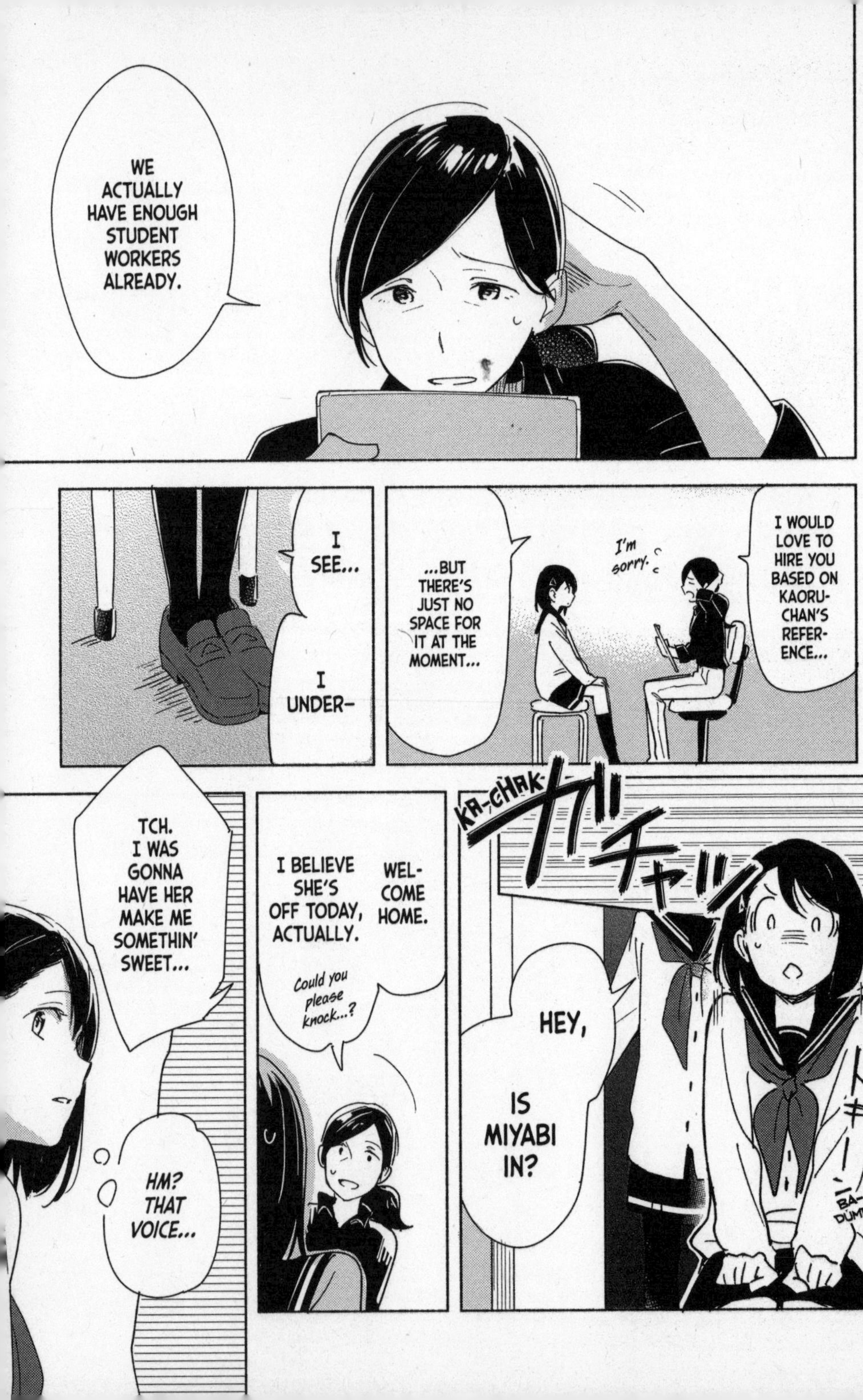
WE ACTUALLY HAVE ENOUGH STUDENT WORKERS ALREADY.
I WOULD LOVE TO HIRE YOU BASED ON KAORU-CHAN'S REFERENCE...
I'm sorry.
...BUT THERE'S JUST NO SPACE FOR IT AT THE MOMENT...
I SEE...
I UNDER–
KA-CHAK
ガチャッ
HEY,
IS MIYABI IN?
ドキー
BA-DUMP!
WELCOME HOME.
I BELIEVE SHE'S OFF TODAY, ACTUALLY.
Could you please knock...?
TCH. I WAS GONNA HAVE HER MAKE ME SOMETHIN' SWEET...
HM? THAT VOICE...

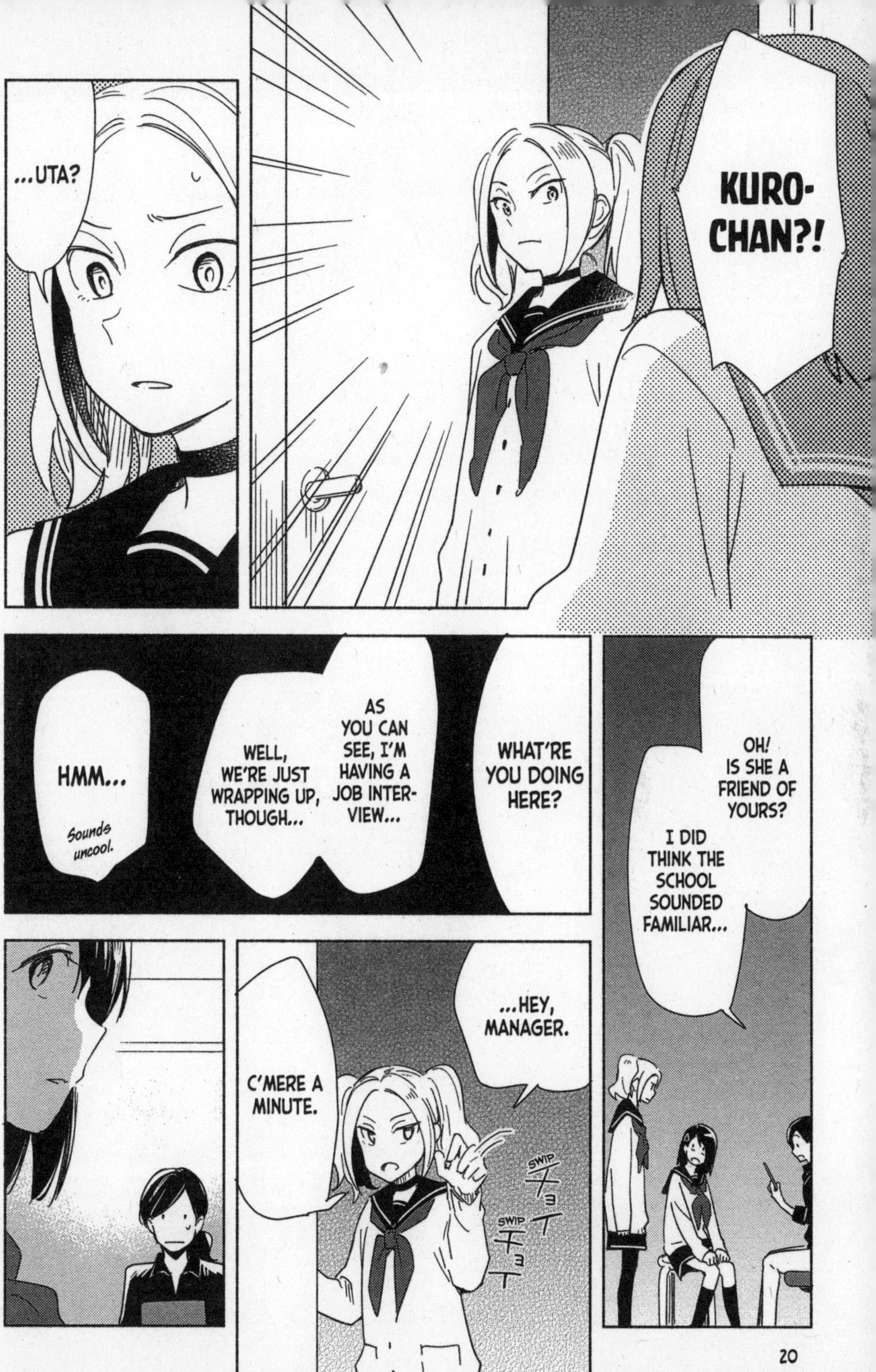
KURO-CHAN?!
...UTA?
OH! IS SHE A FRIEND OF YOURS?
I DID THINK THE SCHOOL SOUNDED FAMILIAR...
WHAT'RE YOU DOING HERE?
AS YOU CAN SEE, I'M HAVING A JOB INTER-VIEW...
WELL, WE'RE JUST WRAPPING UP, THOUGH...
HMM...
Sounds uncool.
...HEY, MANAGER.
C'MERE A MINUTE.
SWIP
SWIP

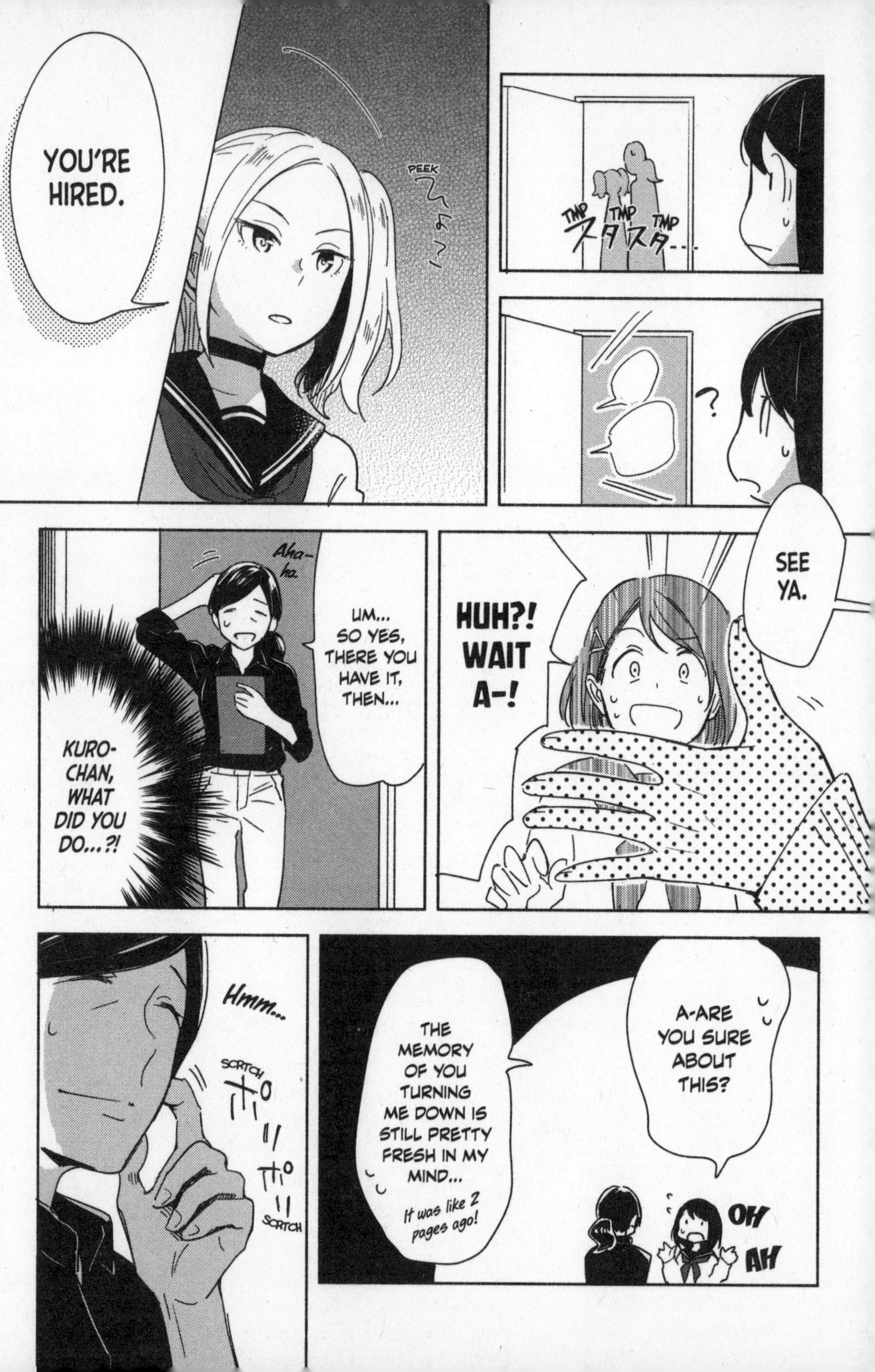

TMP
TMP
TMP
?
YOU'RE HIRED.
PEEK
SEE YA.
HUH?! WAIT A-!
Aha-ha.
UM... SO YES, THERE YOU HAVE IT, THEN...
KURO-CHAN, WHAT DID YOU DO...?!
A-ARE YOU SURE ABOUT THIS?
THE MEMORY OF YOU TURNING ME DOWN IS STILL PRETTY FRESH IN MY MIND...
It was like 2 pages ago!
OH
AH
Hmm...
SCRTCH
SCRTCH

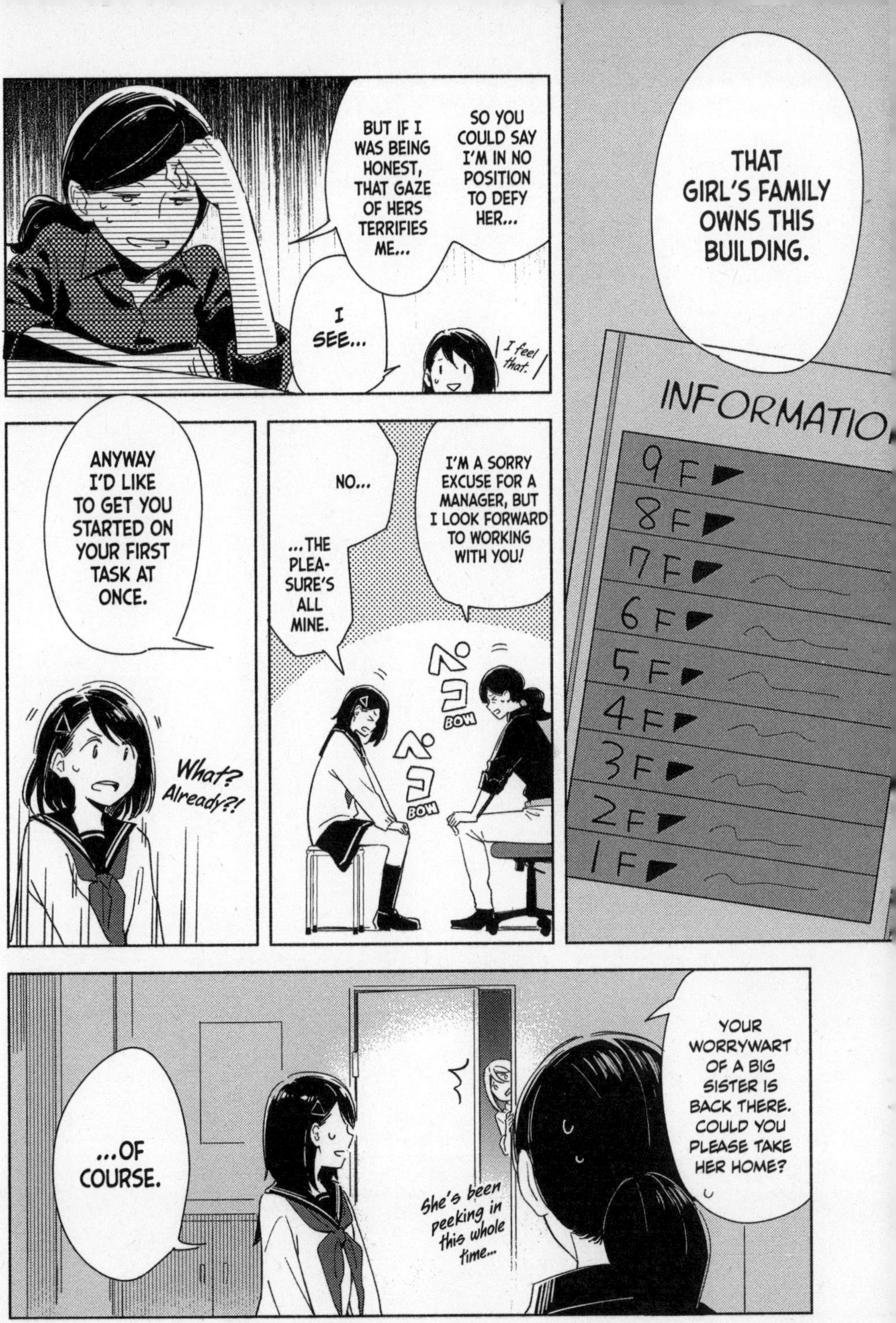

THAT GIRL'S FAMILY OWNS THIS BUILDING.
INFORMATIO
9F
8F
7F
6F
5F
4F
3F
2F
1F
SO YOU COULD SAY I'M IN NO POSITION TO DEFY HER...
BUT IF I WAS BEING HONEST, THAT GAZE OF HERS TERRIFIES ME...
I SEE...
I feel that.
I'M A SORRY EXCUSE FOR A MANAGER, BUT I LOOK FORWARD TO WORKING WITH YOU!
NO...
...THE PLEASURE'S ALL MINE.
ペコ
BOW
ペコ
BOW
ANYWAY I'D LIKE TO GET YOU STARTED ON YOUR FIRST TASK AT ONCE.
What? Already?!
YOUR WORRYWART OF A BIG SISTER IS BACK THERE. COULD YOU PLEASE TAKE HER HOME?
She's been peeking in this whole time...
...OF COURSE.

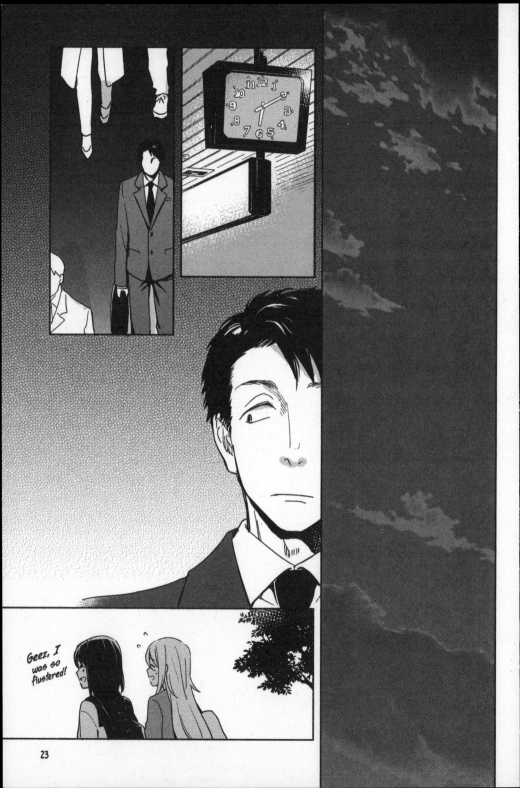

Geez, I was so flustered!

23

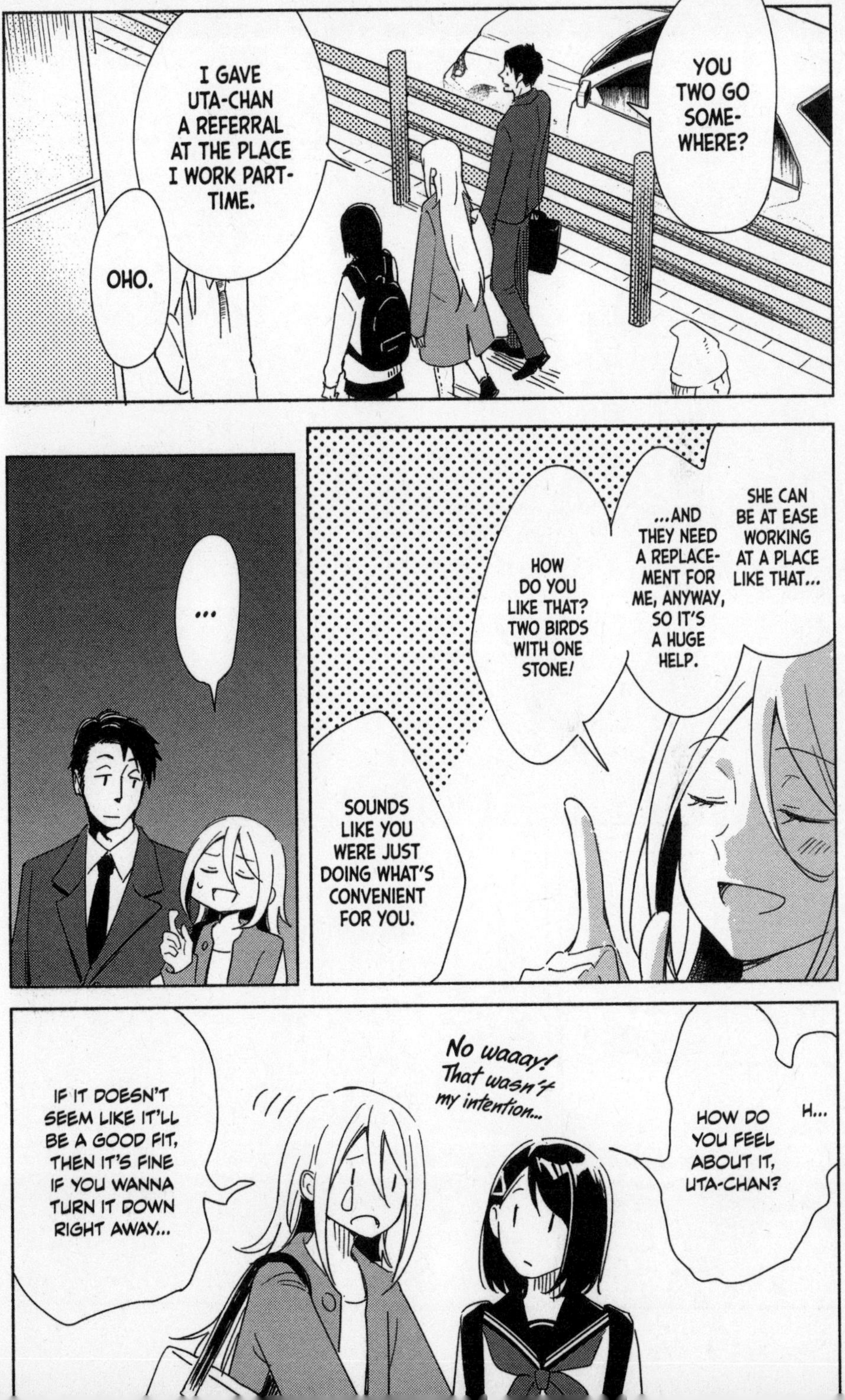
YOU TWO GO SOME-WHERE?
I GAVE UTA-CHAN A REFERRAL AT THE PLACE I WORK PART-TIME.
OHO.
SHE CAN BE AT EASE WORKING AT A PLACE LIKE THAT...
...AND THEY NEED A REPLACE-MENT FOR ME, ANYWAY, SO IT'S A HUGE HELP.
HOW DO YOU LIKE THAT? TWO BIRDS WITH ONE STONE!
SOUNDS LIKE YOU WERE JUST DOING WHAT'S CONVENIENT FOR YOU.
...
H...
HOW DO YOU FEEL ABOUT IT, UTA-CHAN?
No waaay! That wasn't my intention...
IF IT DOESN'T SEEM LIKE IT'LL BE A GOOD FIT, THEN IT'S FINE IF YOU WANNA TURN IT DOWN RIGHT AWAY...

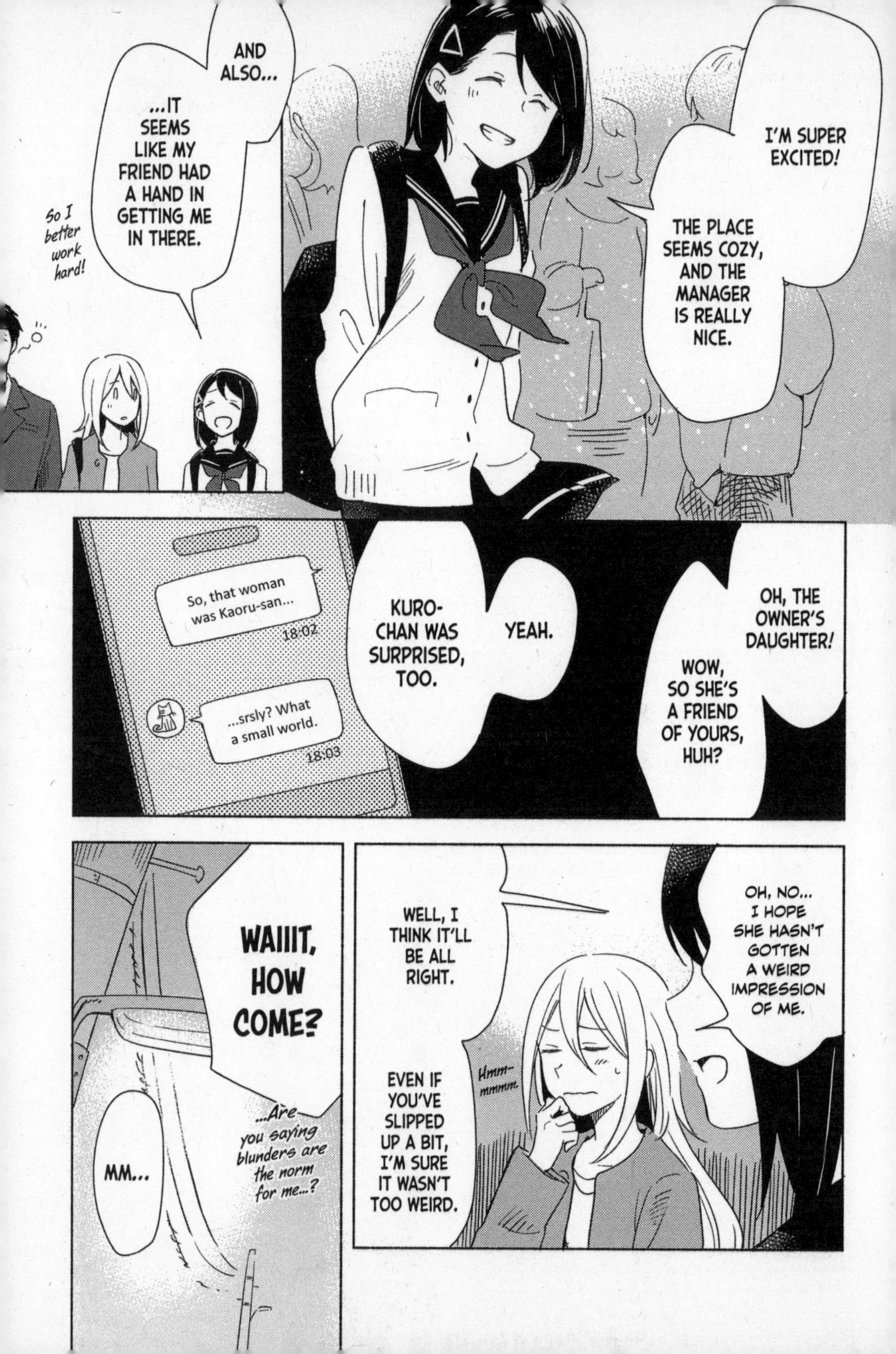
I'M SUPER EXCITED!
THE PLACE SEEMS COZY, AND THE MANAGER IS REALLY NICE.
AND ALSO...
...IT SEEMS LIKE MY FRIEND HAD A HAND IN GETTING ME IN THERE.
So I better work hard!
OH, THE OWNER'S DAUGHTER!
WOW, SO SHE'S A FRIEND OF YOURS, HUH?
YEAH.
KURO-CHAN WAS SURPRISED, TOO.
So, that woman was Kaoru-san...
18:02
...srsly? What a small world.
18:03
OH, NO... I HOPE SHE HASN'T GOTTEN A WEIRD IMPRESSION OF ME.
Hmm-mmmm.
WELL, I THINK IT'LL BE ALL RIGHT.
EVEN IF YOU'VE SLIPPED UP A BIT, I'M SURE IT WASN'T TOO WEIRD.
WAIIIT, HOW COME?
...Are you saying blunders are the norm for me...?
MM...

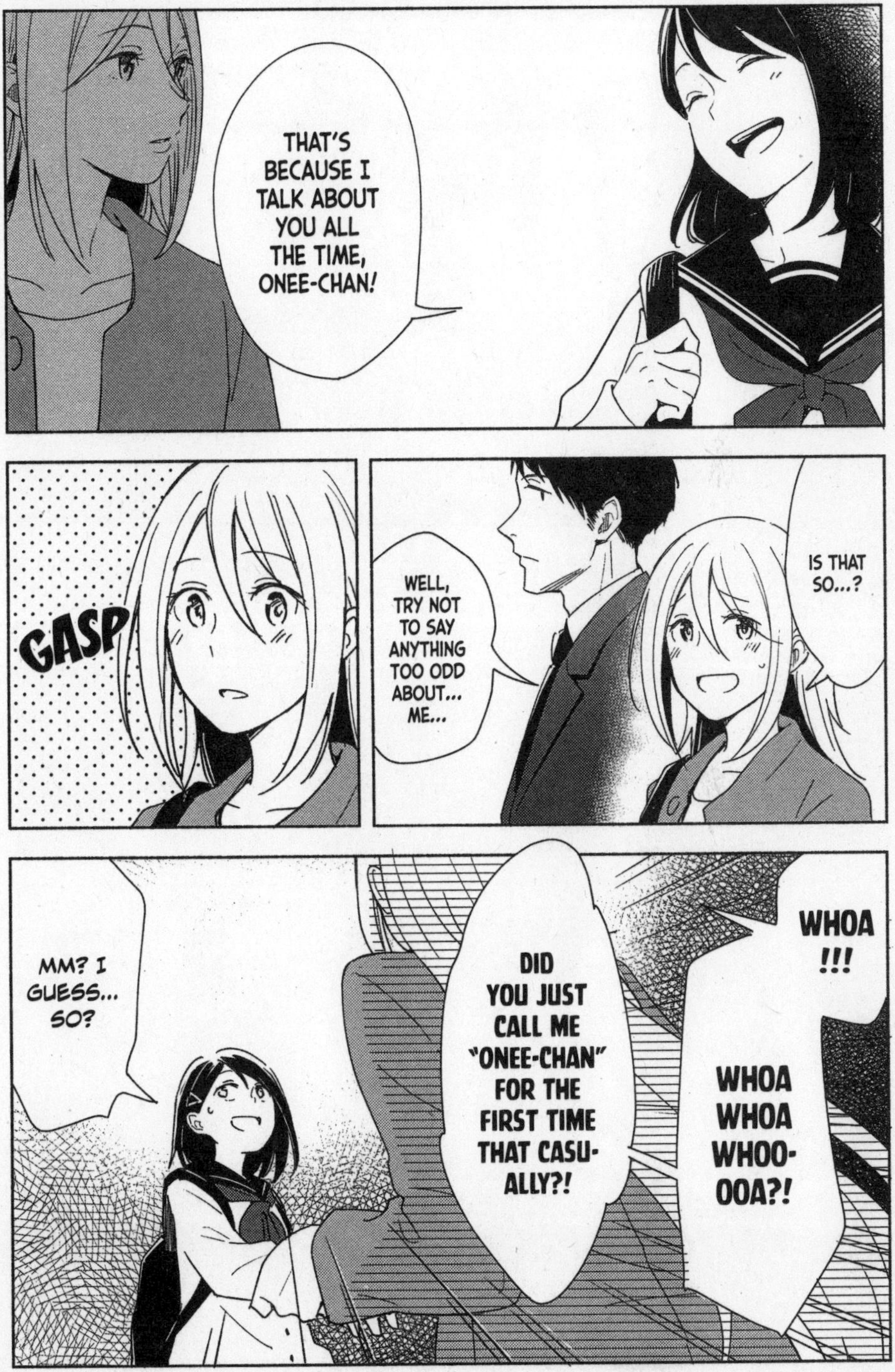
THAT'S BECAUSE I TALK ABOUT YOU ALL THE TIME, ONEE-CHAN!
IS THAT SO...?
WELL, TRY NOT TO SAY ANYTHING TOO ODD ABOUT... ME...
GASP
WHOA !!!
WHOA WHOA WHOO-OOA?!
DID YOU JUST CALL ME "ONEE-CHAN" FOR THE FIRST TIME THAT CASU-ALLY?!
MM? I GUESS... SO?

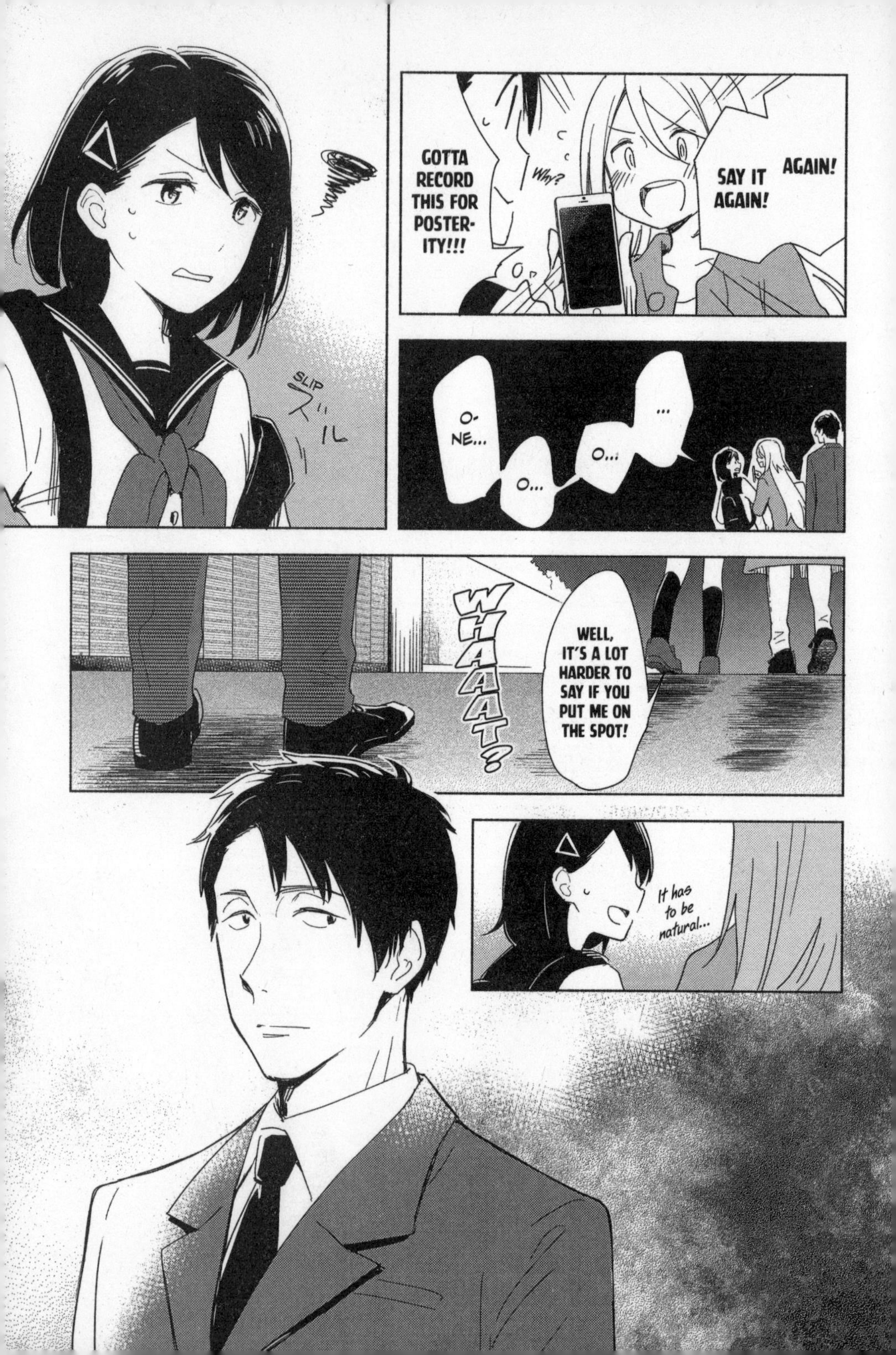
AGAIN!
SAY IT AGAIN!
Why?
GOTTA RECORD THIS FOR POSTERITY!!!
O-NE...
O...
O...
...
SLIP
スルッ
WELL, IT'S A LOT HARDER TO SAY IF YOU PUT ME ON THE SPOT!
WHAAAT?!
It has to be natural...

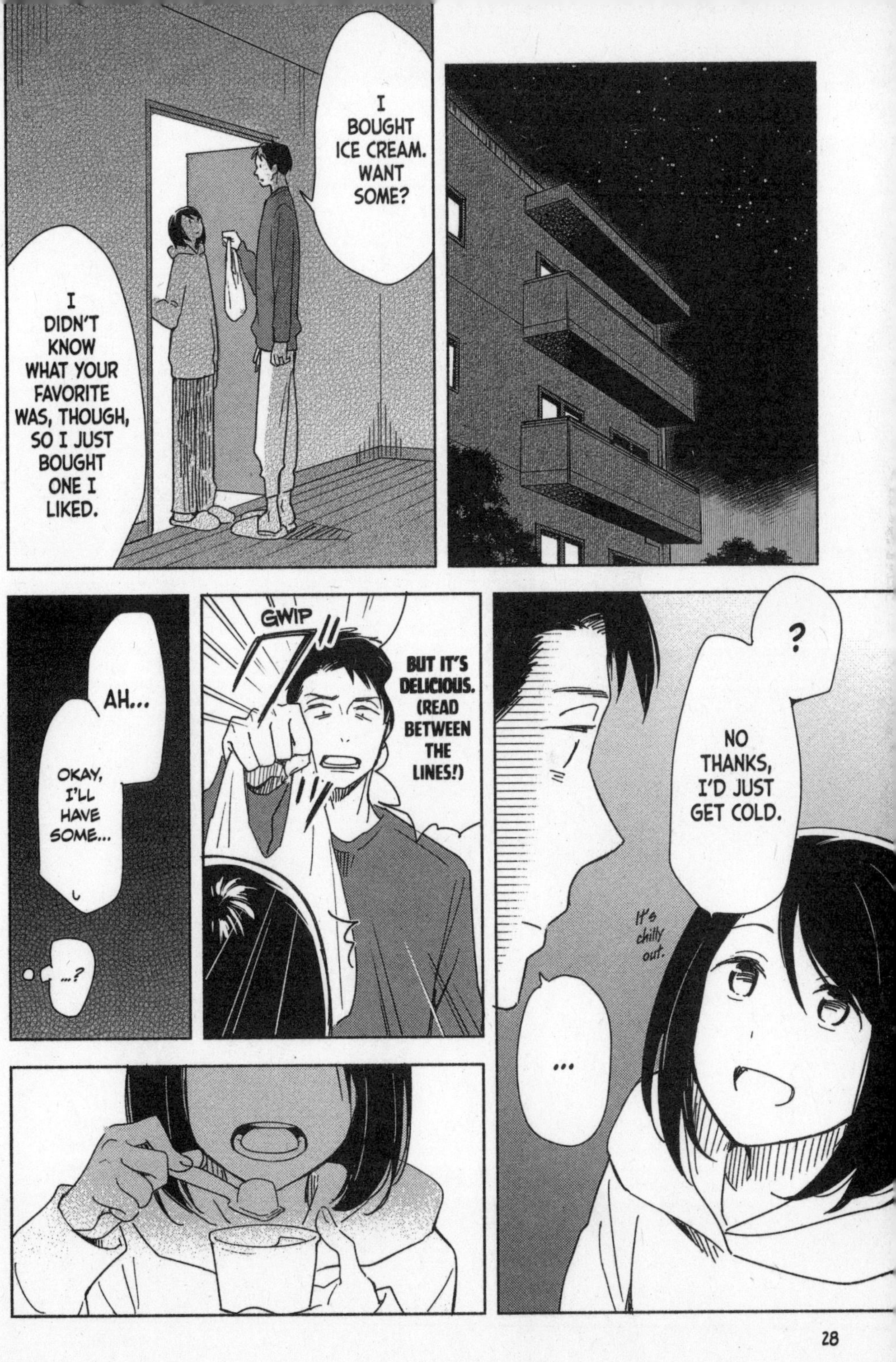
I BOUGHT ICE CREAM. WANT SOME?
I DIDN'T KNOW WHAT YOUR FAVORITE WAS, THOUGH, SO I JUST BOUGHT ONE I LIKED.
?
NO THANKS, I'D JUST GET COLD.
It's chilly out.
...
GWIP
BUT IT'S DELICIOUS. (READ BETWEEN THE LINES!)
AH...
OKAY, I'LL HAVE SOME...
...?

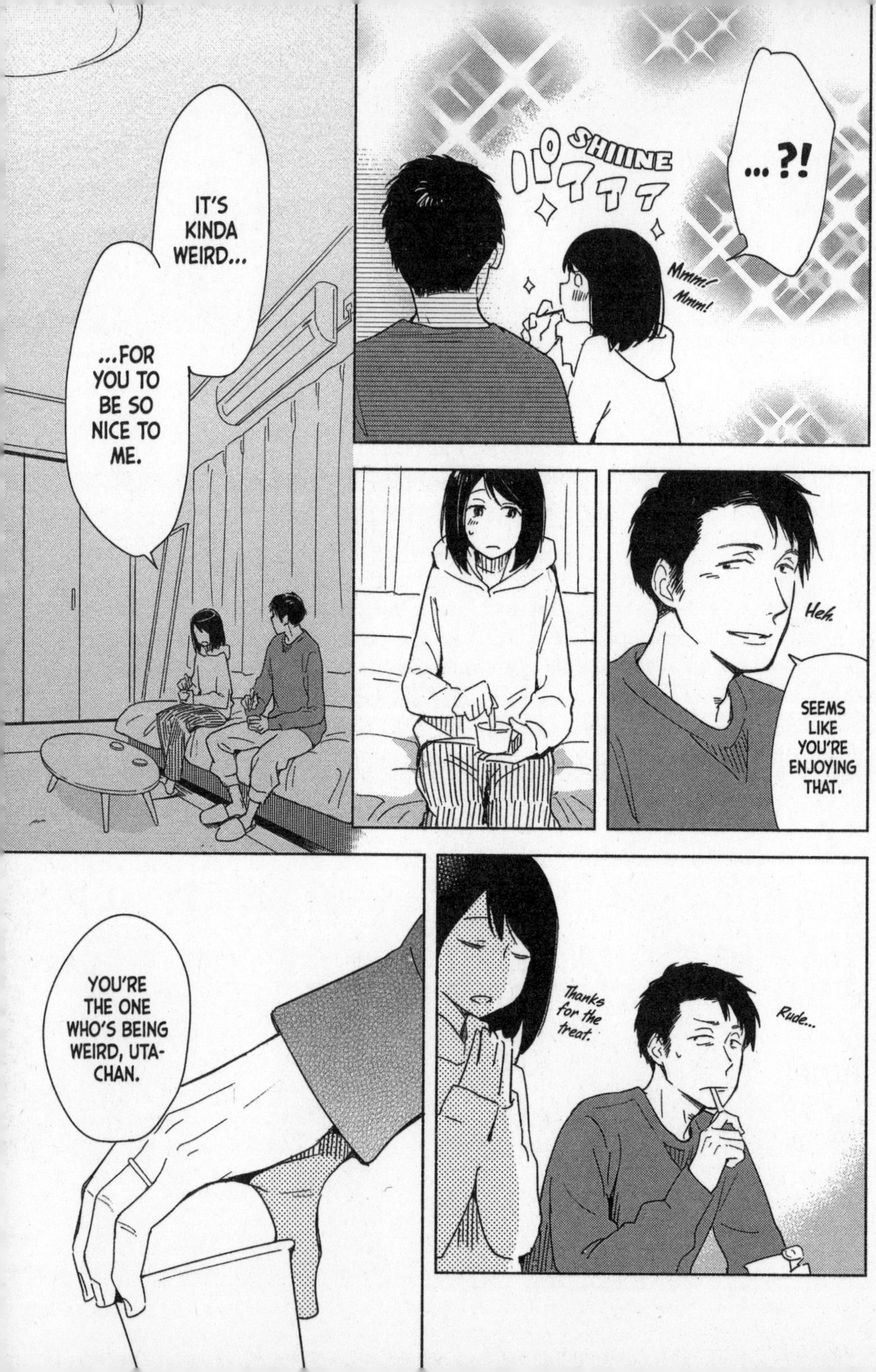
...?!
SHIIINE
Mmm! Mmm!
Heh.
SEEMS LIKE YOU'RE ENJOYING THAT.
IT'S KINDA WEIRD...
...FOR YOU TO BE SO NICE TO ME.
Rude...
Thanks for the treat.
YOU'RE THE ONE WHO'S BEING WEIRD, UTA-CHAN.

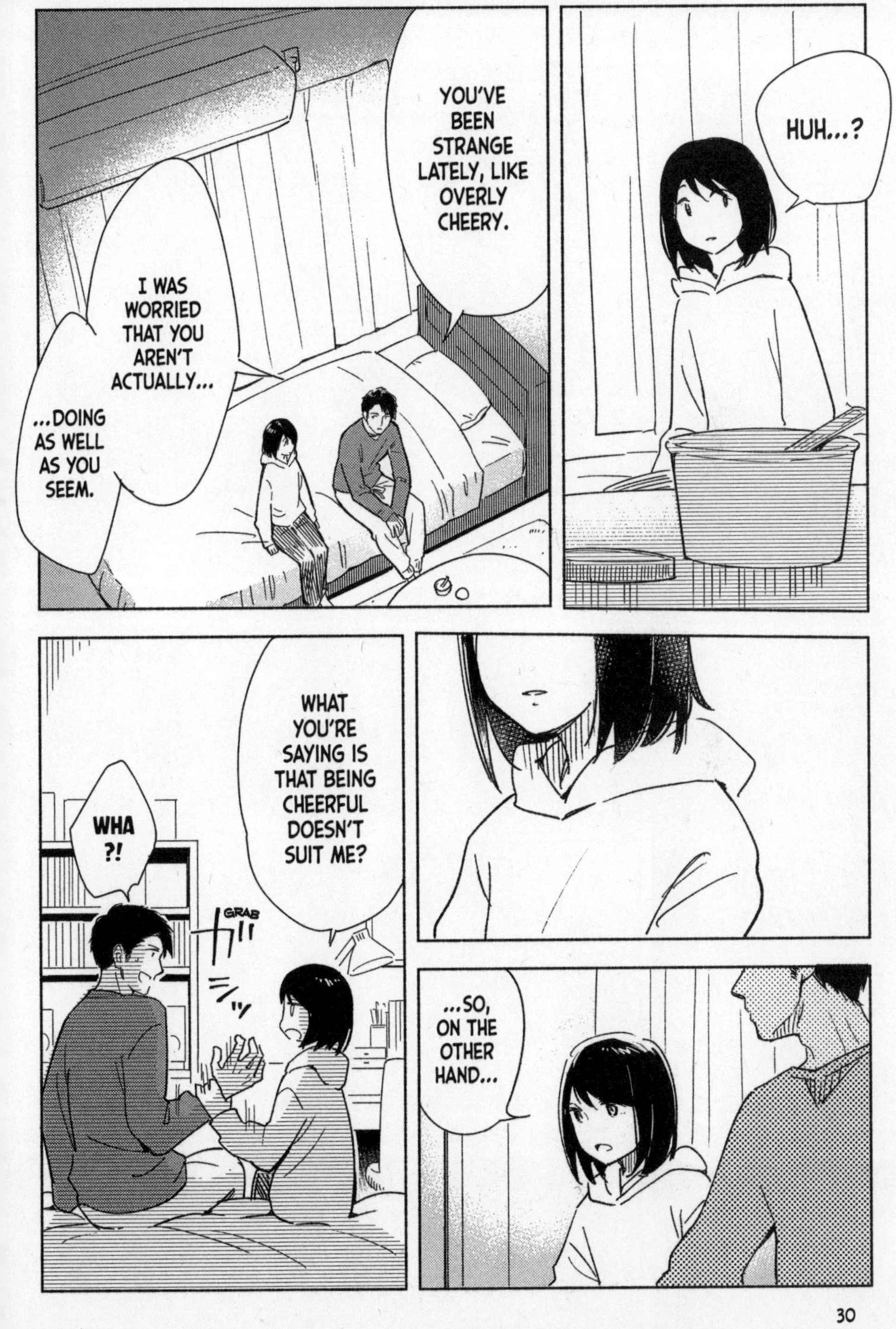
HUH...?
YOU'VE BEEN STRANGE LATELY, LIKE OVERLY CHEERY.
I WAS WORRIED THAT YOU AREN'T ACTUALLY...
...DOING AS WELL AS YOU SEEM.
...SO, ON THE OTHER HAND...
WHAT YOU'RE SAYING IS THAT BEING CHEERFUL DOESN'T SUIT ME?
GRAB
WHA ?!

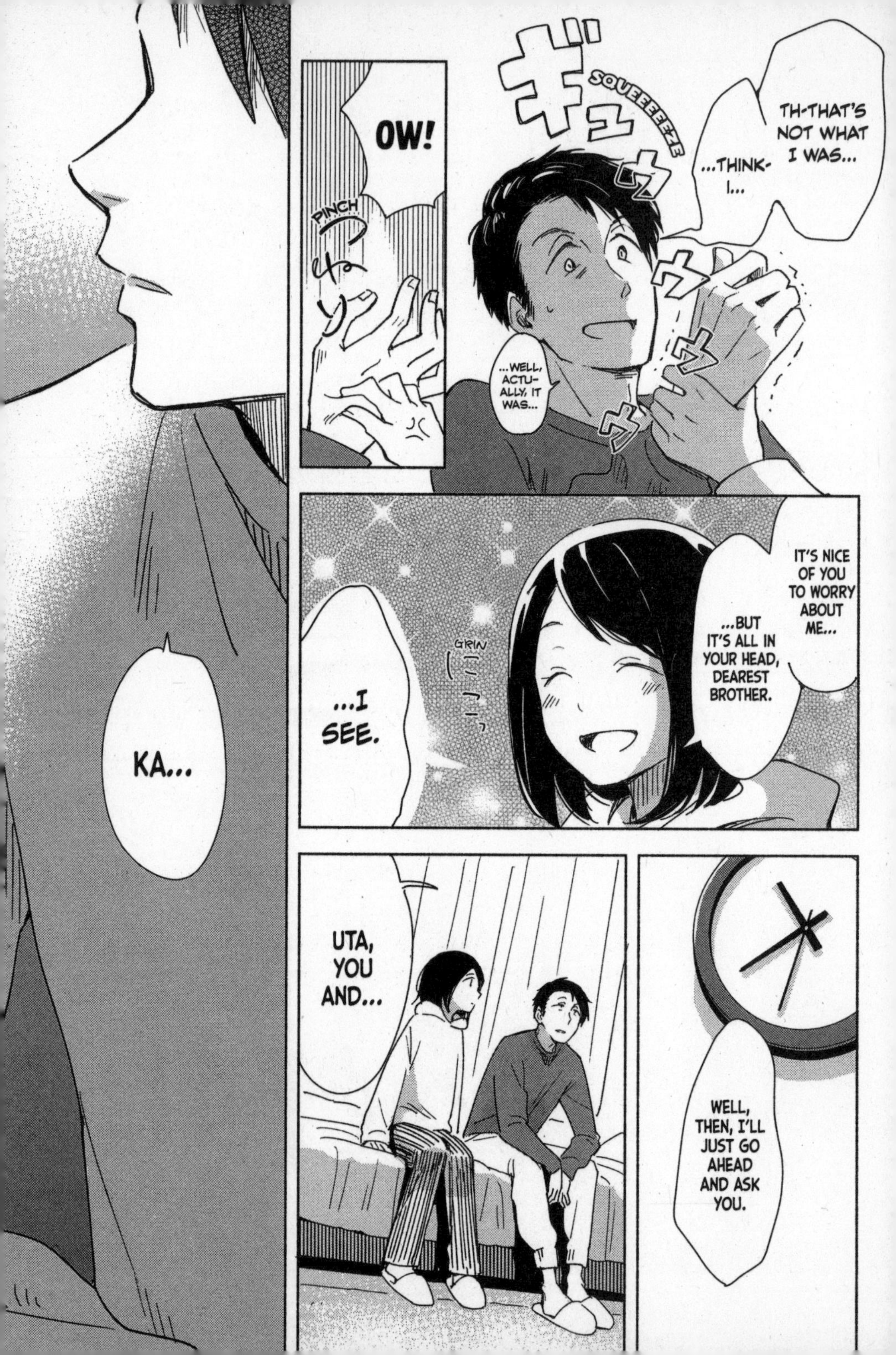
SQUEEEEEEZE
TH-THAT'S NOT WHAT I WAS...
...THINK-I...
...WELL, ACTU-ALLY, IT WAS...
OW!
PINCH
IT'S NICE OF YOU TO WORRY ABOUT ME...
...BUT IT'S ALL IN YOUR HEAD, DEAREST BROTHER.
GRIN
...I SEE.
WELL, THEN, I'LL JUST GO AHEAD AND ASK YOU.
UTA, YOU AND...
KA...

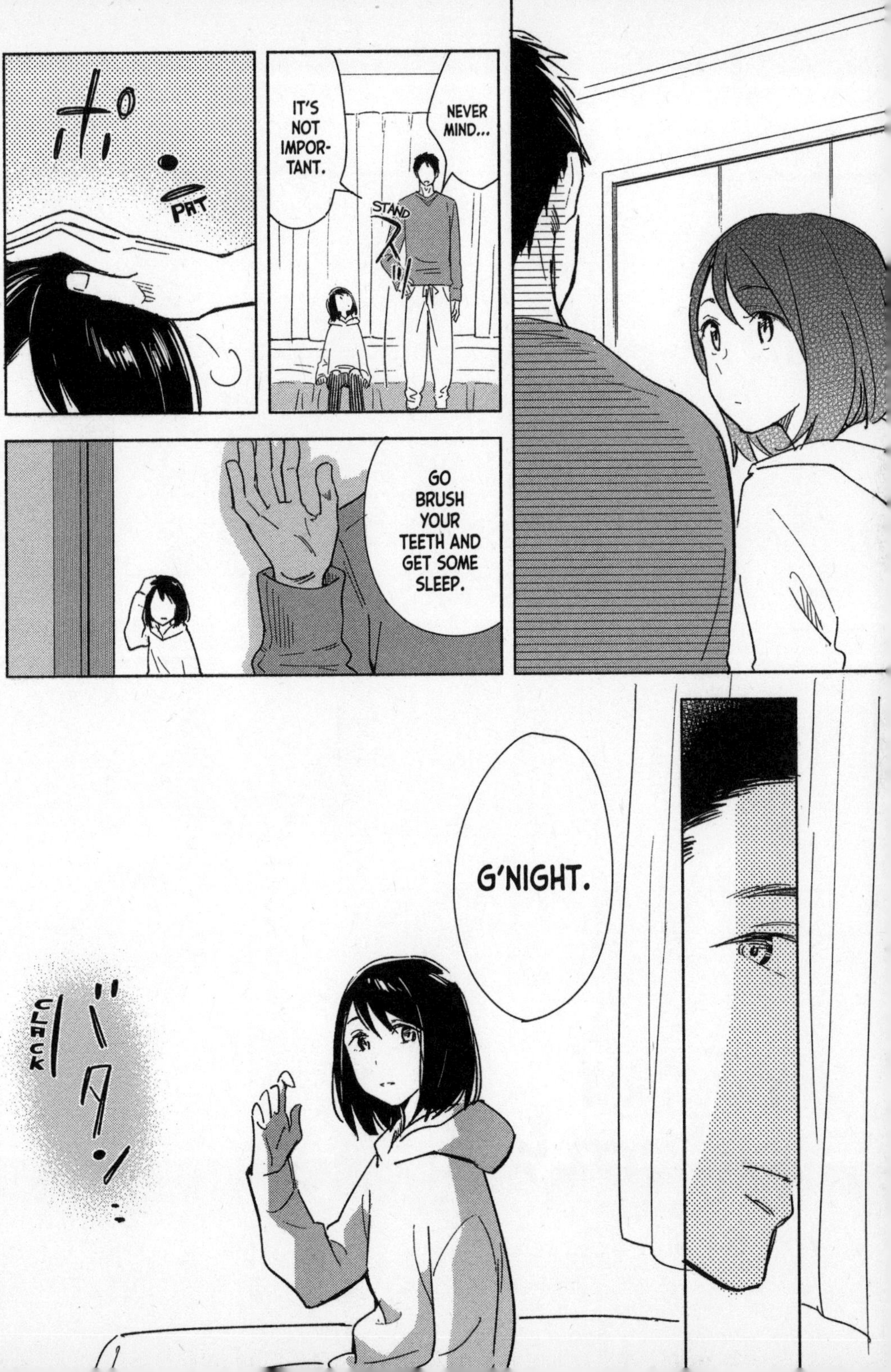

NEVER MIND...
IT'S NOT IMPORTANT.
STAND
PAT
GO BRUSH YOUR TEETH AND GET SOME SLEEP.
G'NIGHT.
CLACK

If I Could
Reach You

If I Could
Reach You

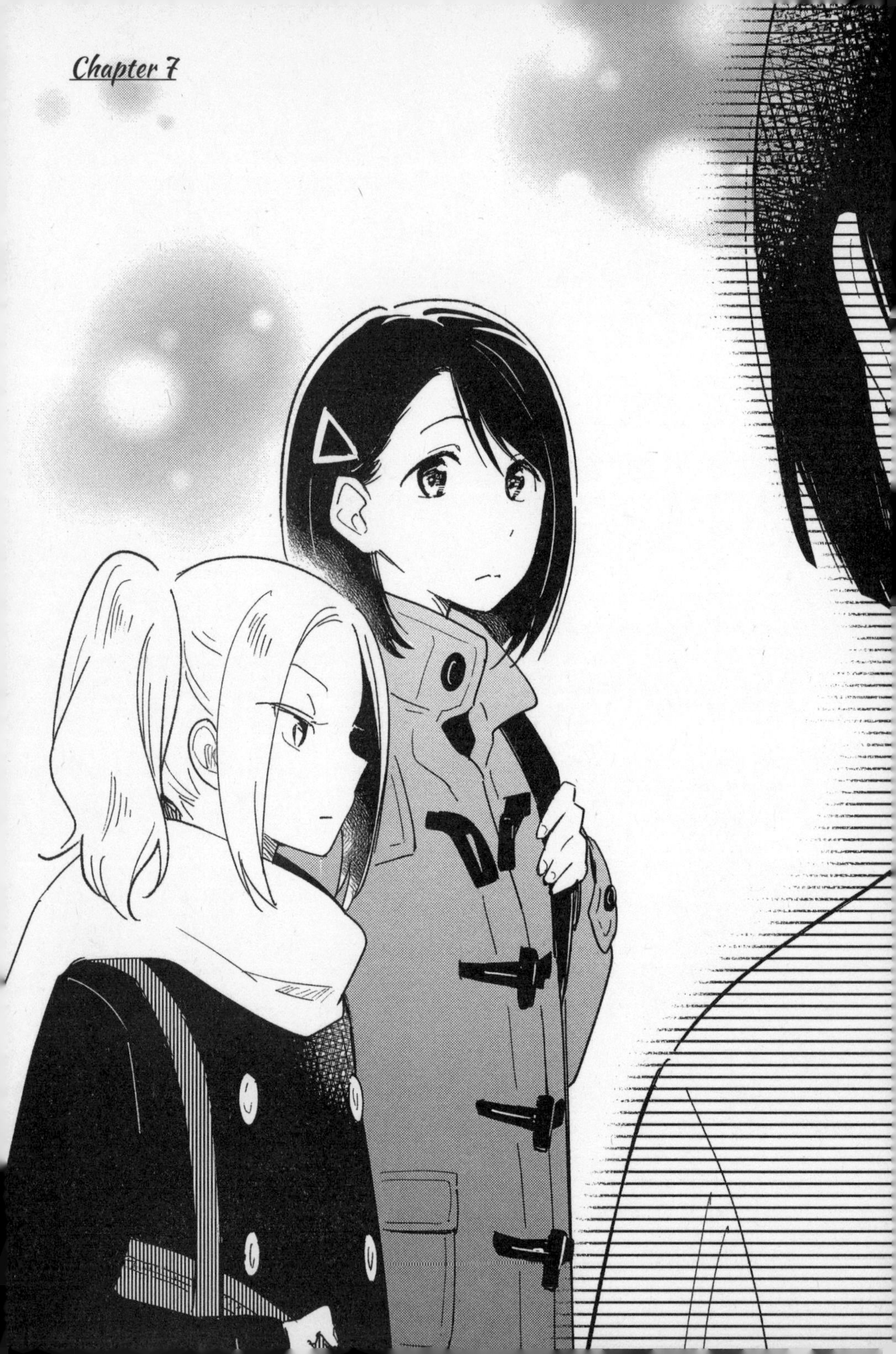
Chapter 7

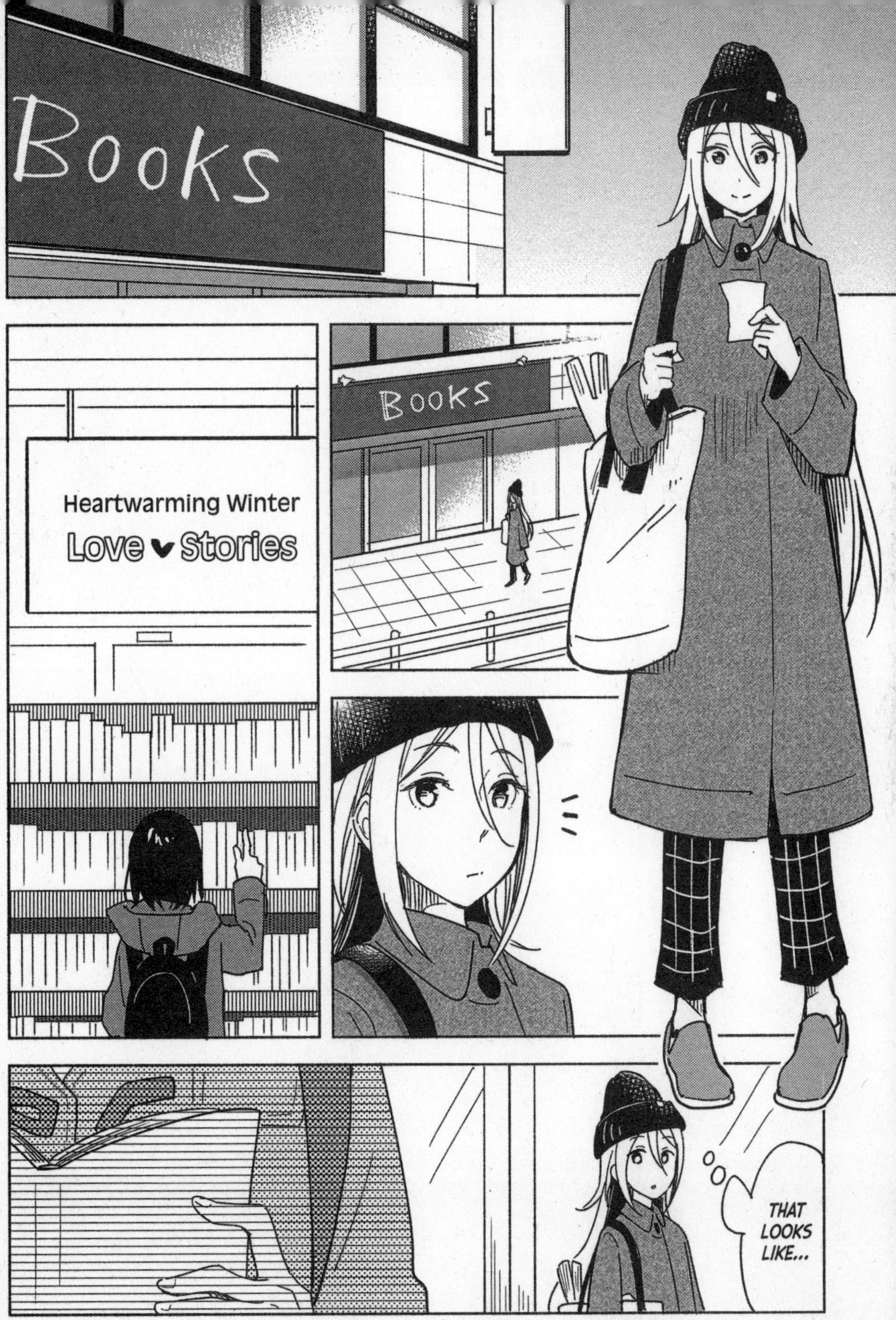
BOOKS
BOOKS
Heartwarming Winter
Love Stories
THAT LOOKS LIKE...

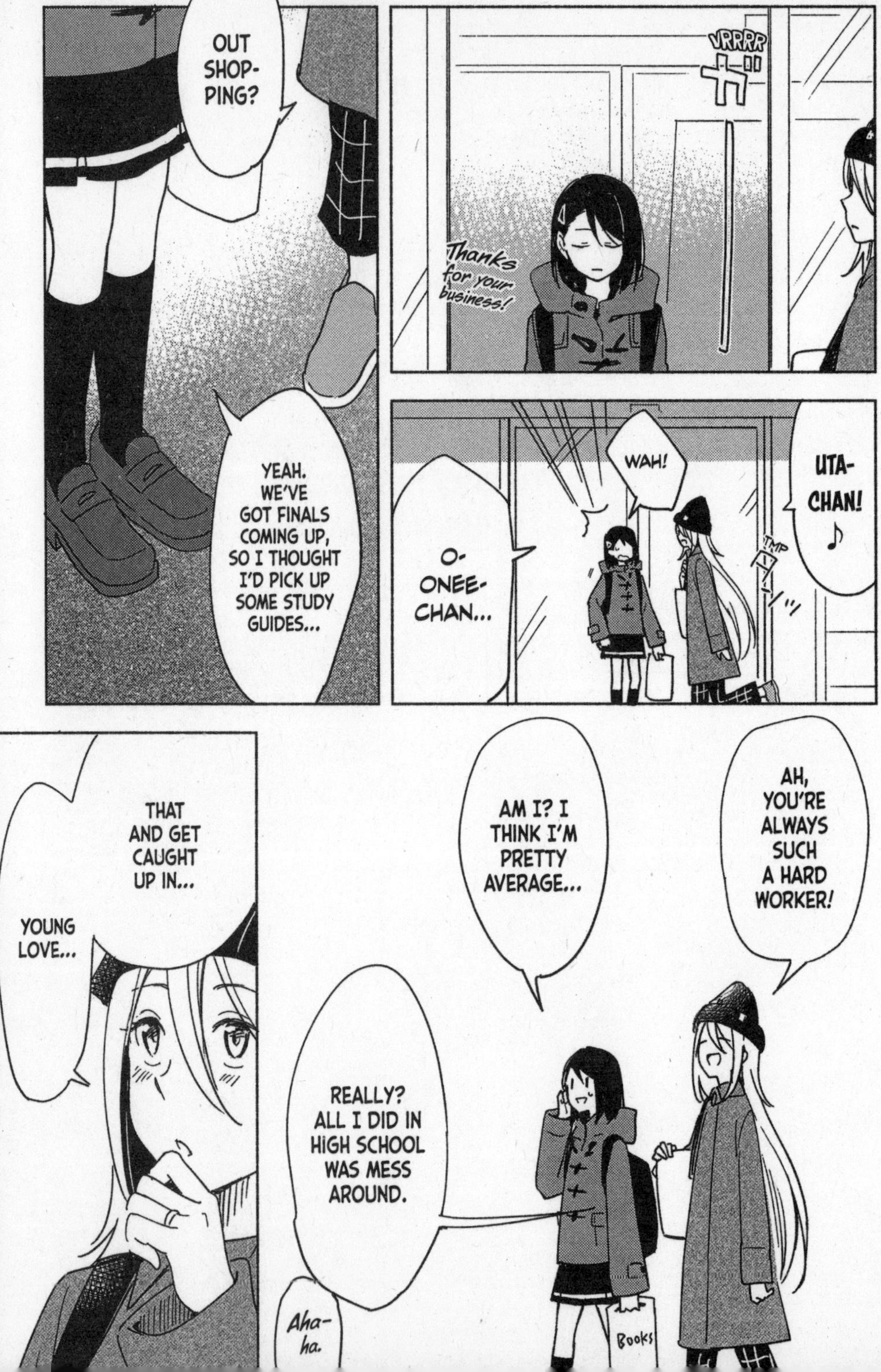
VRRRR
Thanks for your business!
UTA-CHAN! ♪
TMP
WAH!
O-ONEE-CHAN...
OUT SHOP-PING?
YEAH. WE'VE GOT FINALS COMING UP, SO I THOUGHT I'D PICK UP SOME STUDY GUIDES...
AH, YOU'RE ALWAYS SUCH A HARD WORKER!
AM I? I THINK I'M PRETTY AVERAGE...
REALLY? ALL I DID IN HIGH SCHOOL WAS MESS AROUND.
Aha-ha.
Books
THAT AND GET CAUGHT UP IN...
YOUNG LOVE...

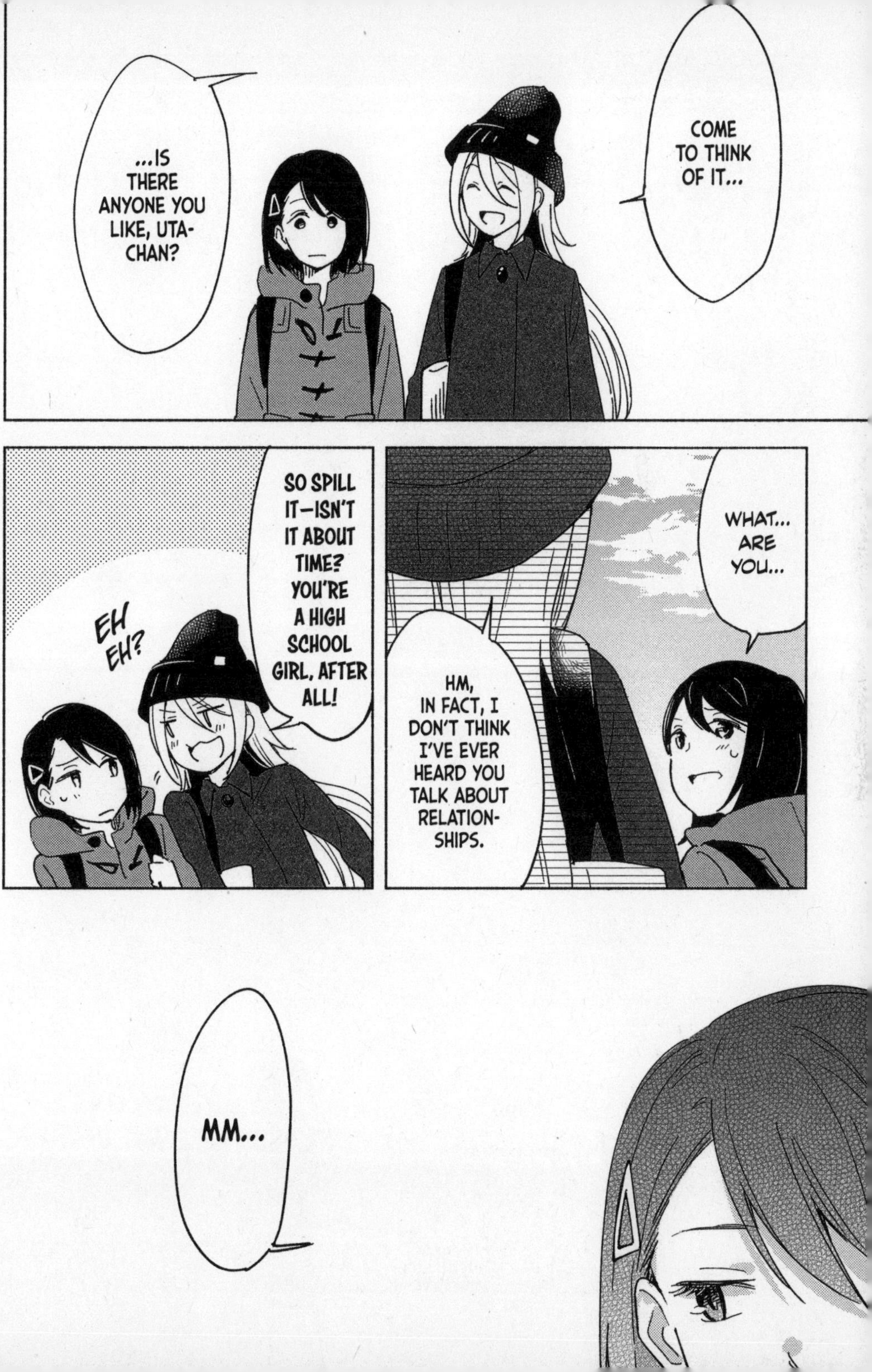
COME TO THINK OF IT...
...IS THERE ANYONE YOU LIKE, UTA-CHAN?
WHAT... ARE YOU...
HM, IN FACT, I DON'T THINK I'VE EVER HEARD YOU TALK ABOUT RELATIONSHIPS.
SO SPILL IT—ISN'T IT ABOUT TIME? YOU'RE A HIGH SCHOOL GIRL, AFTER ALL!
EH EH?
MM...

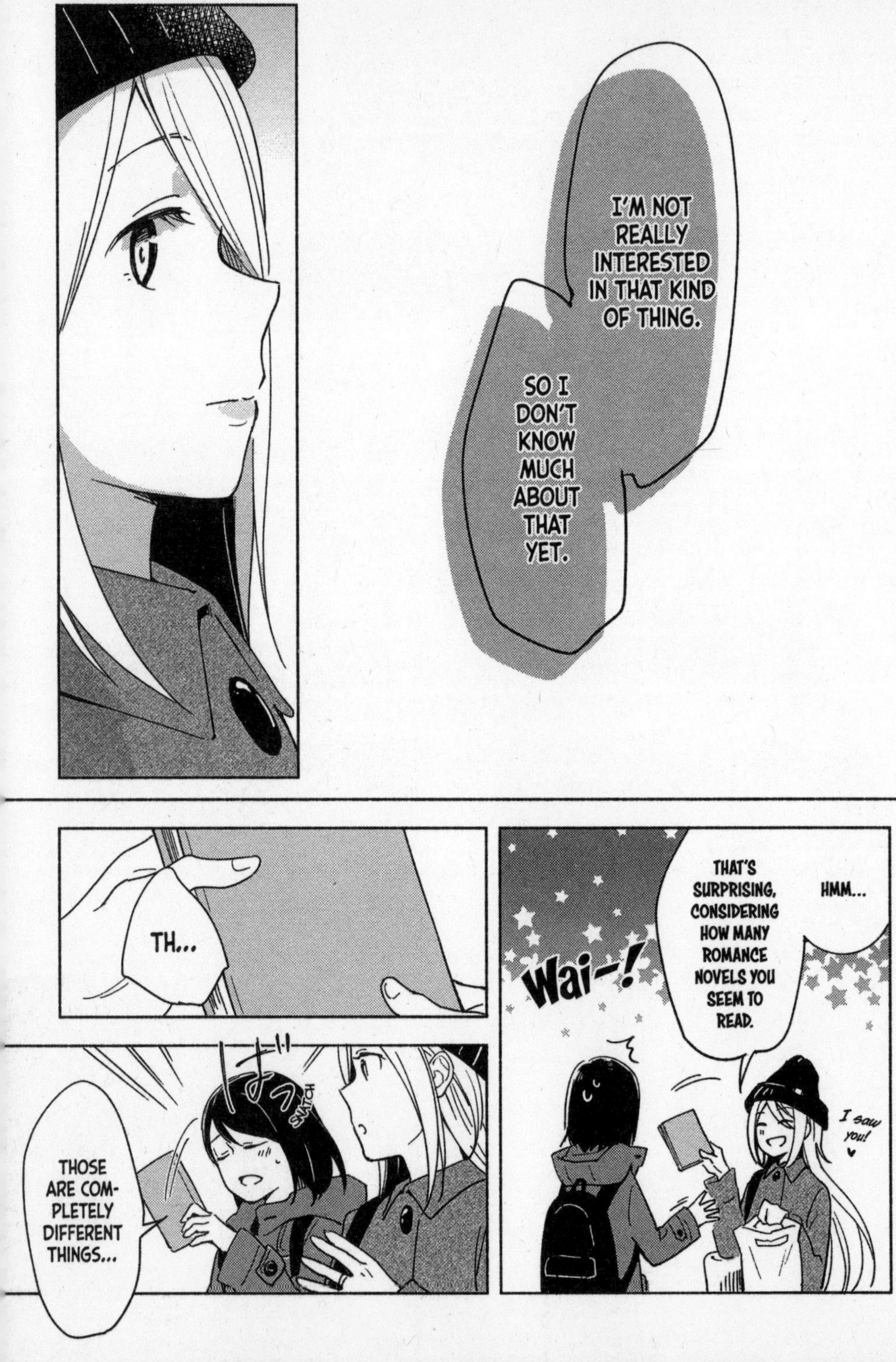
I'M NOT REALLY INTERESTED IN THAT KIND OF THING.
SO I DON'T KNOW MUCH ABOUT THAT YET.
HMM...
THAT'S SURPRISING, CONSIDERING HOW MANY ROMANCE NOVELS YOU SEEM TO READ.
Wai-!
I saw you! ♥
TH...
SNATCH
THOSE ARE COM-PLETELY DIFFERENT THINGS...

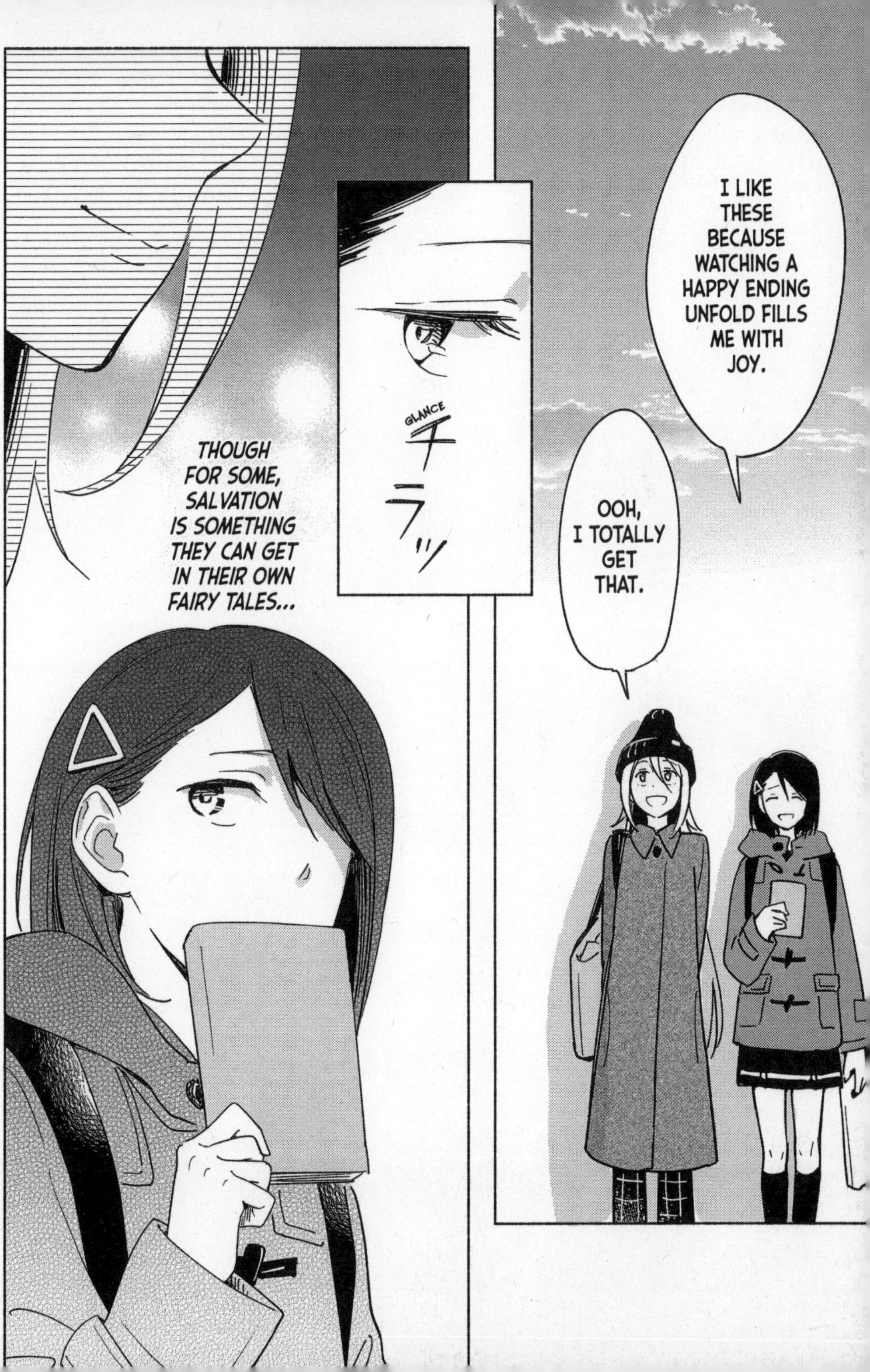
I LIKE THESE BECAUSE WATCHING A HAPPY ENDING UNFOLD FILLS ME WITH JOY.
OOH, I TOTALLY GET THAT.
GLANCE
チラッ
THOUGH FOR SOME, SALVATION IS SOMETHING THEY CAN GET IN THEIR OWN FAIRY TALES...

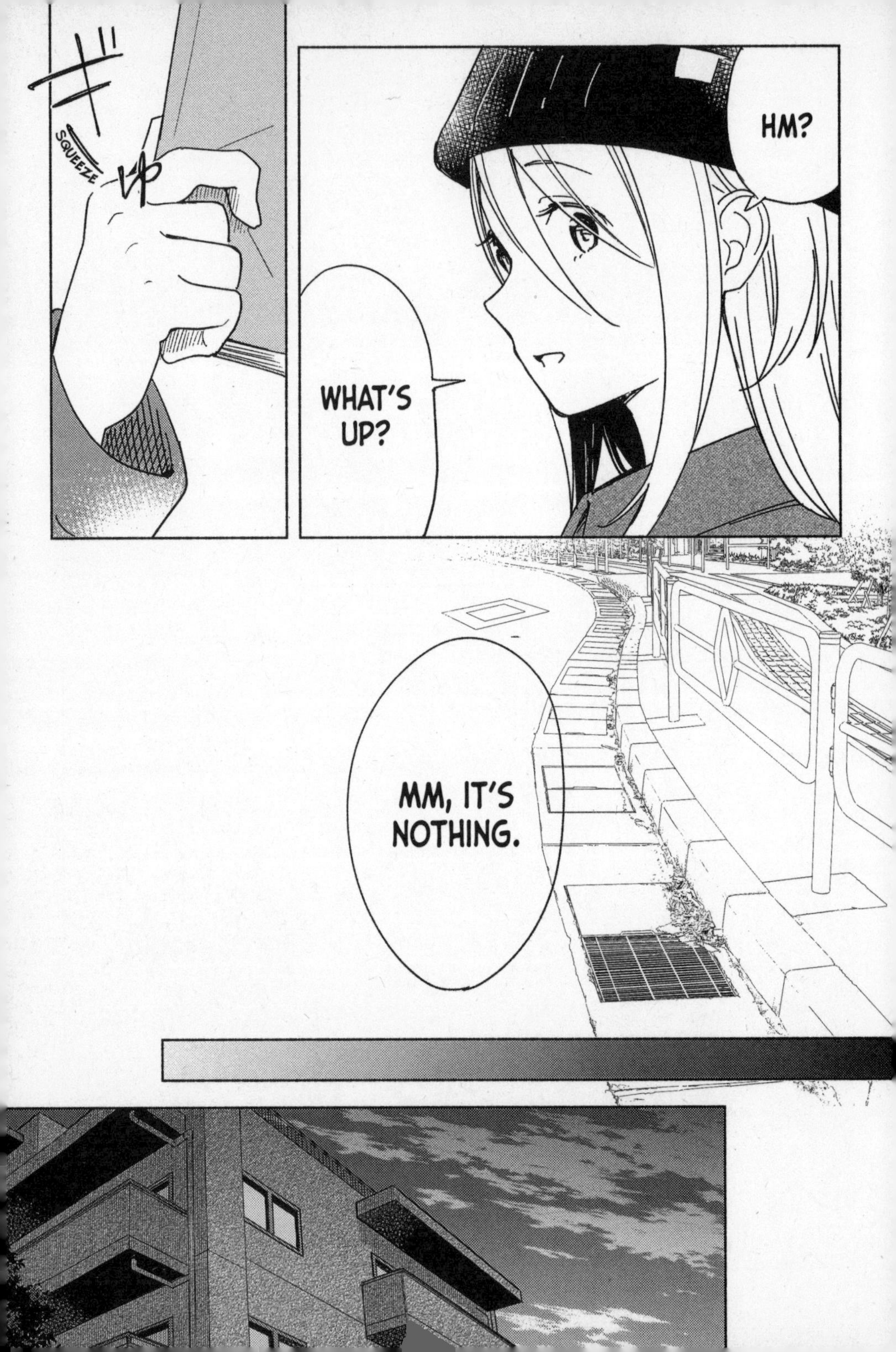
HM?
WHAT'S UP?
ギュ
SQUEEZE
MM, IT'S NOTHING.

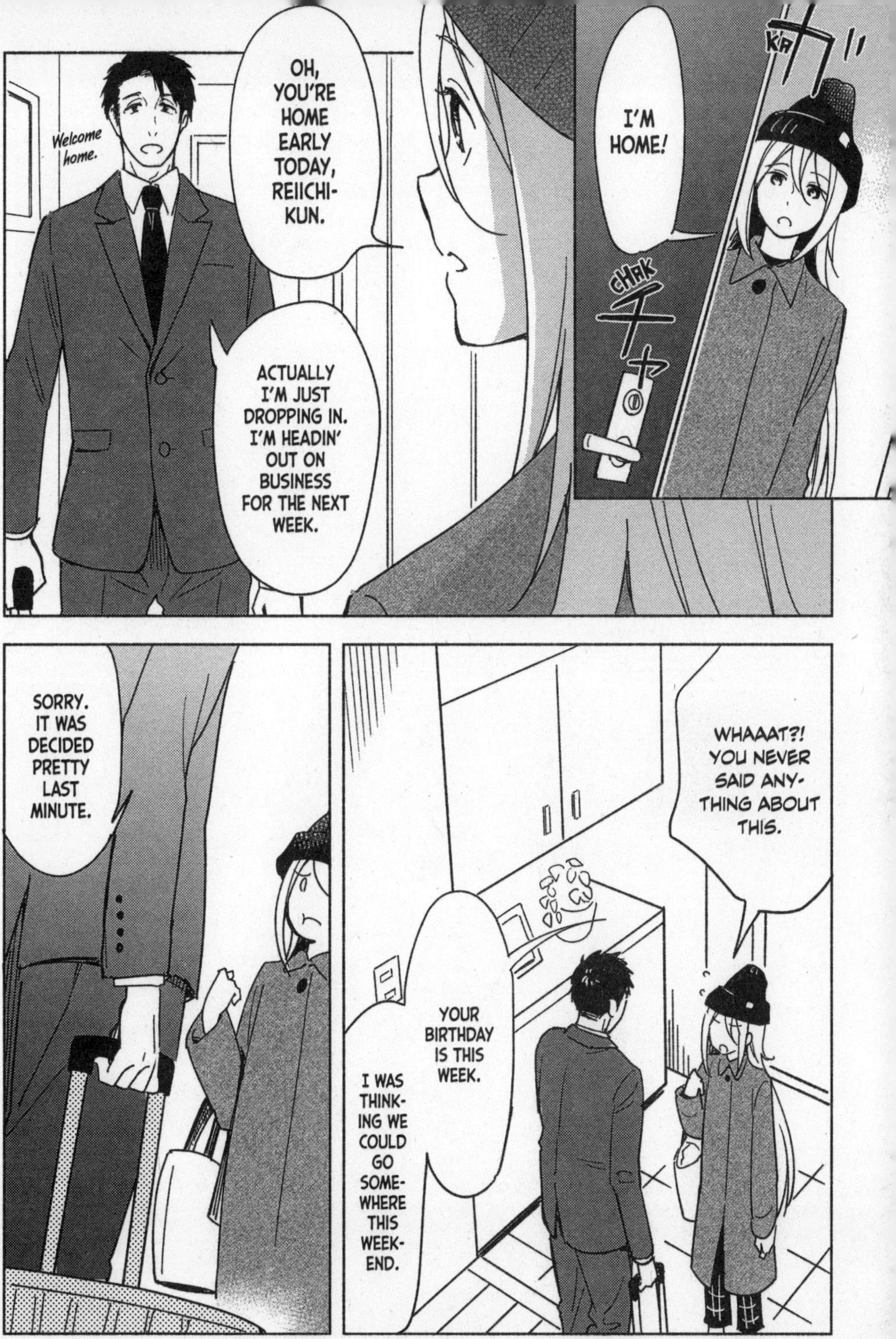
KA
I'M HOME!
CHAK
OH, YOU'RE HOME EARLY TODAY, REIICHI-KUN.
Welcome home.
ACTUALLY I'M JUST DROPPING IN. I'M HEADIN' OUT ON BUSINESS FOR THE NEXT WEEK.
WHAAAT?! YOU NEVER SAID ANY-THING ABOUT THIS.
YOUR BIRTHDAY IS THIS WEEK.
I WAS THINK-ING WE COULD GO SOME-WHERE THIS WEEK-END.
SORRY. IT WAS DECIDED PRETTY LAST MINUTE.

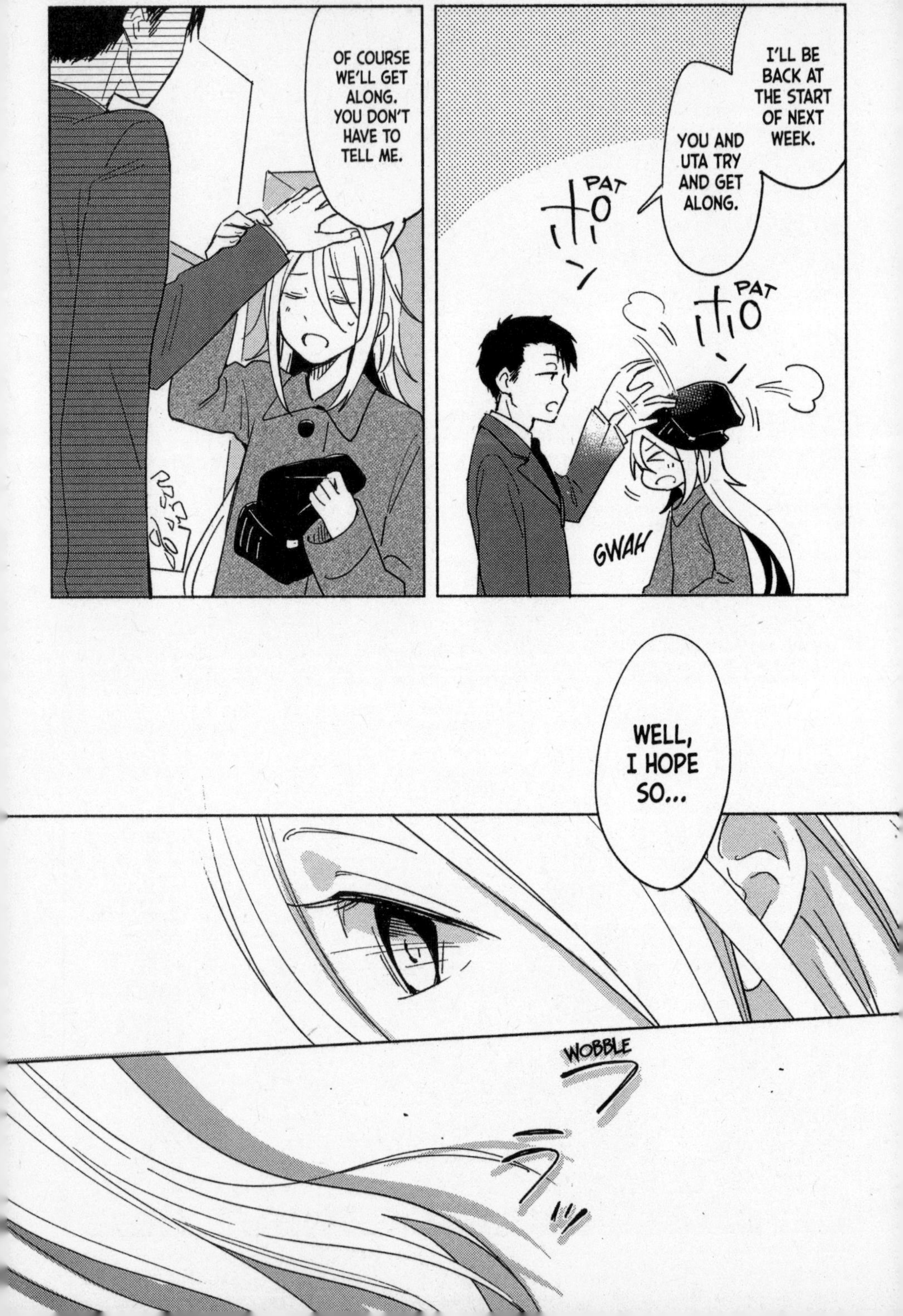
I'LL BE BACK AT THE START OF NEXT WEEK.
YOU AND UTA TRY AND GET ALONG.
PAT
PAT
GWAH
OF COURSE WE'LL GET ALONG. YOU DON'T HAVE TO TELL ME.
WELL, I HOPE SO...
WOBBLE

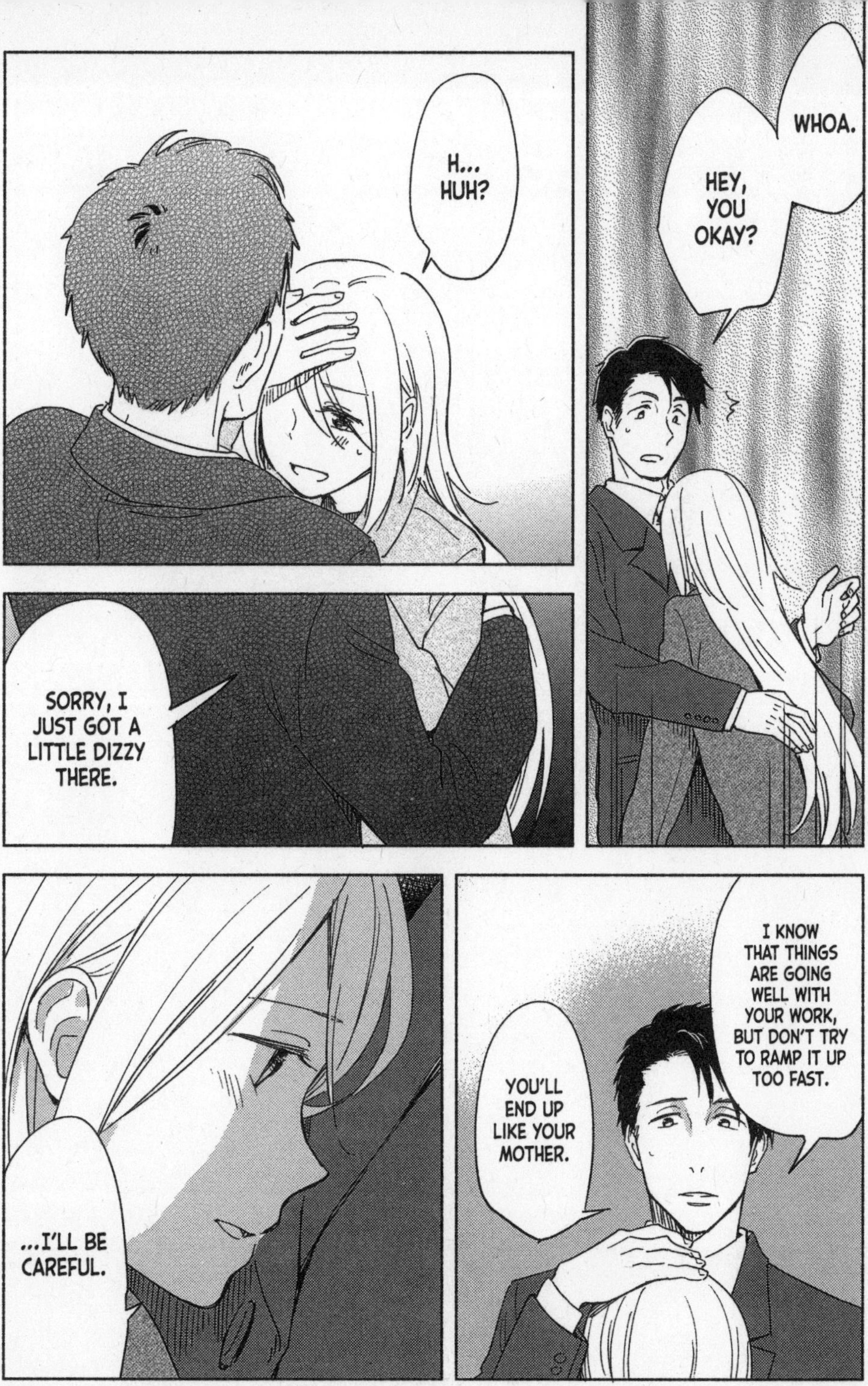
WHOA.
HEY, YOU OKAY?
H... HUH?
SORRY, I JUST GOT A LITTLE DIZZY THERE.
I KNOW THAT THINGS ARE GOING WELL WITH YOUR WORK, BUT DON'T TRY TO RAMP IT UP TOO FAST.
YOU'LL END UP LIKE YOUR MOTHER.
...I'LL BE CAREFUL.

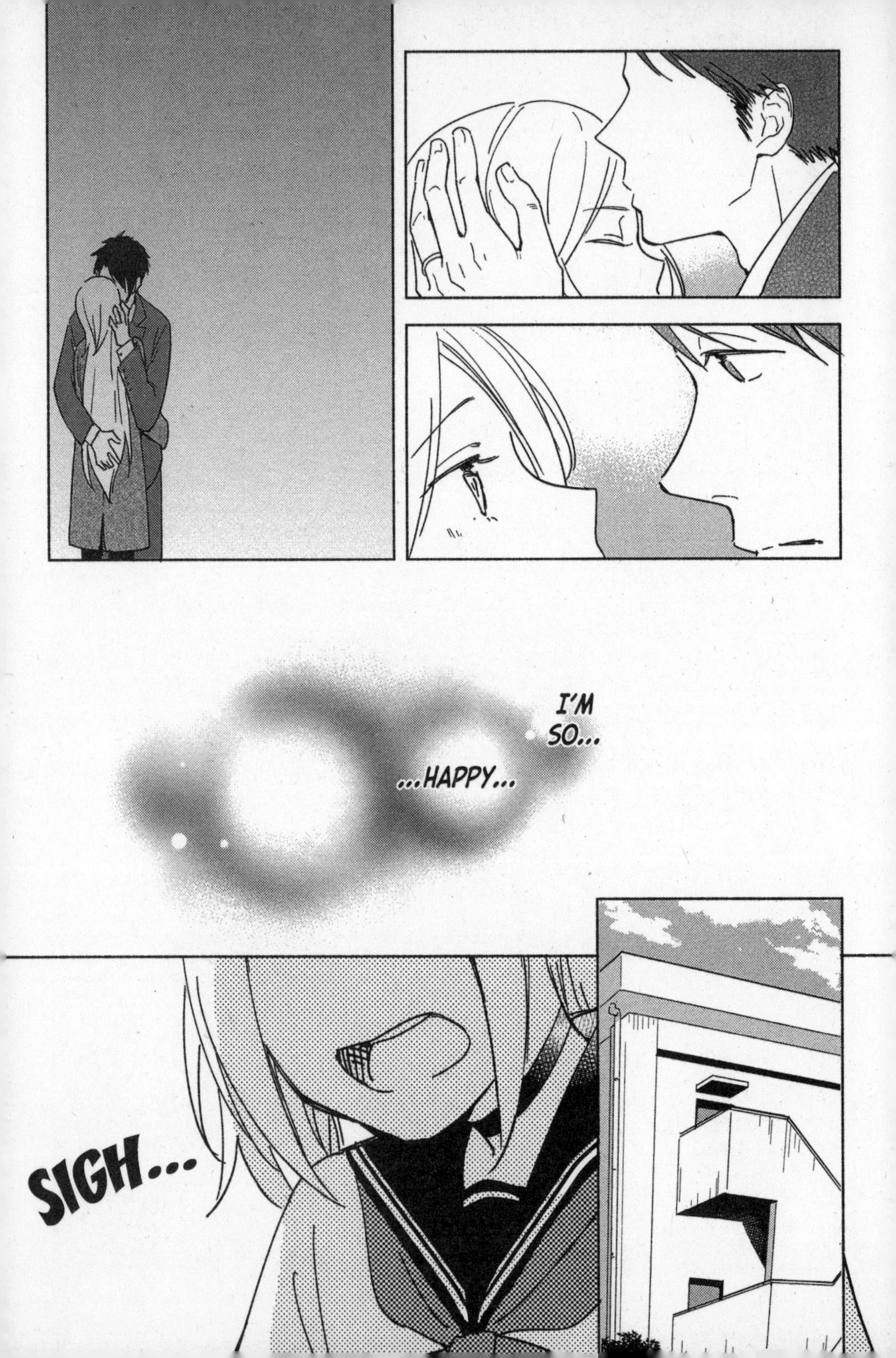
I'M SO...
...HAPPY...
SIGH...

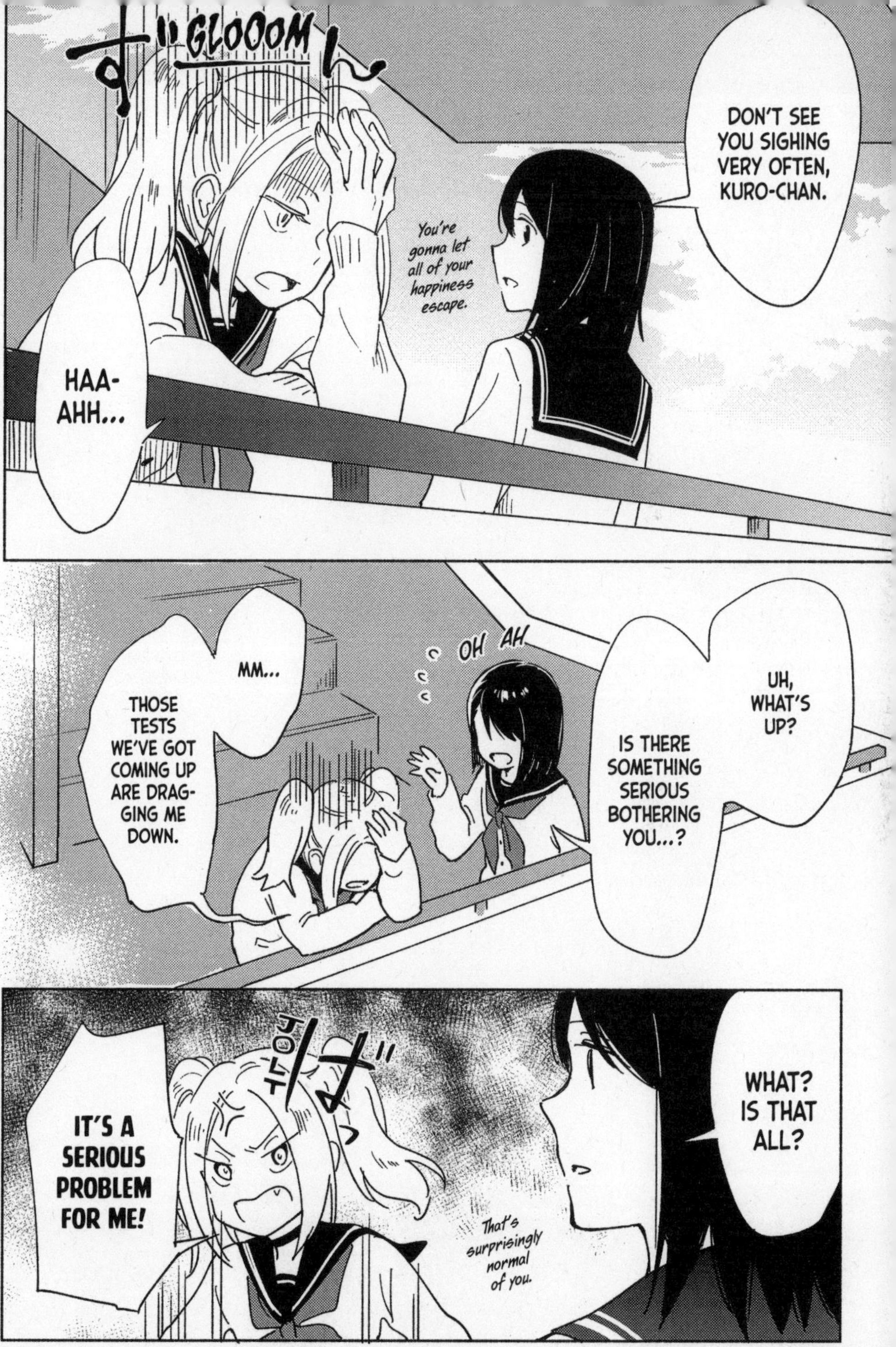
DON'T SEE YOU SIGHING VERY OFTEN, KURO-CHAN.
You're gonna let all of your happiness escape.
GLOOOM
HAA-AHH...
UH, WHAT'S UP?
IS THERE SOMETHING SERIOUS BOTHERING YOU...?
OH AH
MM...
THOSE TESTS WE'VE GOT COMING UP ARE DRAG-GING ME DOWN.
WHAT? IS THAT ALL?
That's surprisingly normal of you.
JOLT
IT'S A SERIOUS PROBLEM FOR ME!

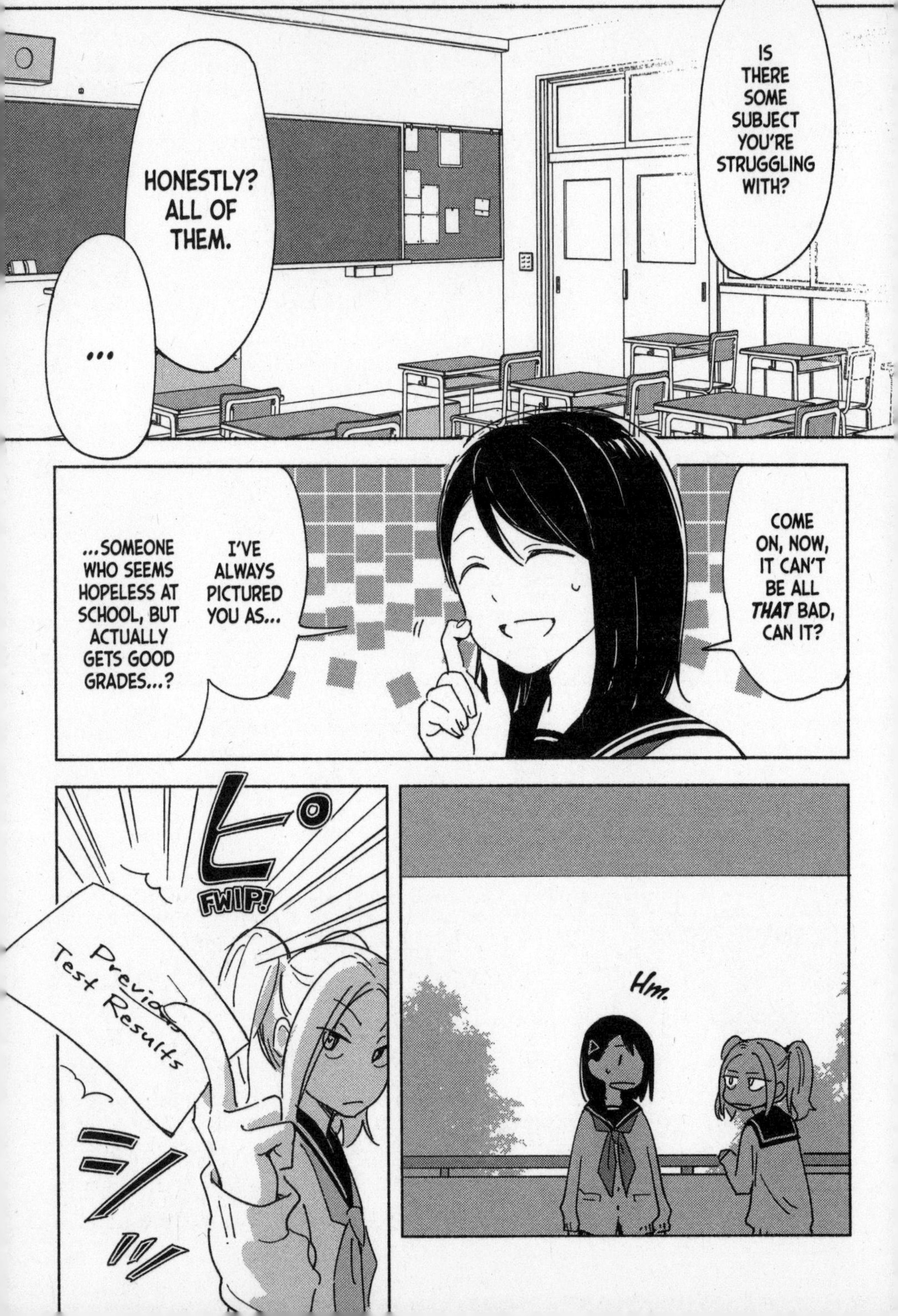
IS THERE SOME SUBJECT YOU'RE STRUGGLING WITH?
HONESTLY? ALL OF THEM.
...
COME ON, NOW, IT CAN'T BE ALL *THAT* BAD, CAN IT?
I'VE ALWAYS PICTURED YOU AS...
...SOMEONE WHO SEEMS HOPELESS AT SCHOOL, BUT ACTUALLY GETS GOOD GRADES...?
Hm.
ピ
FWIP!
Previous Test Results

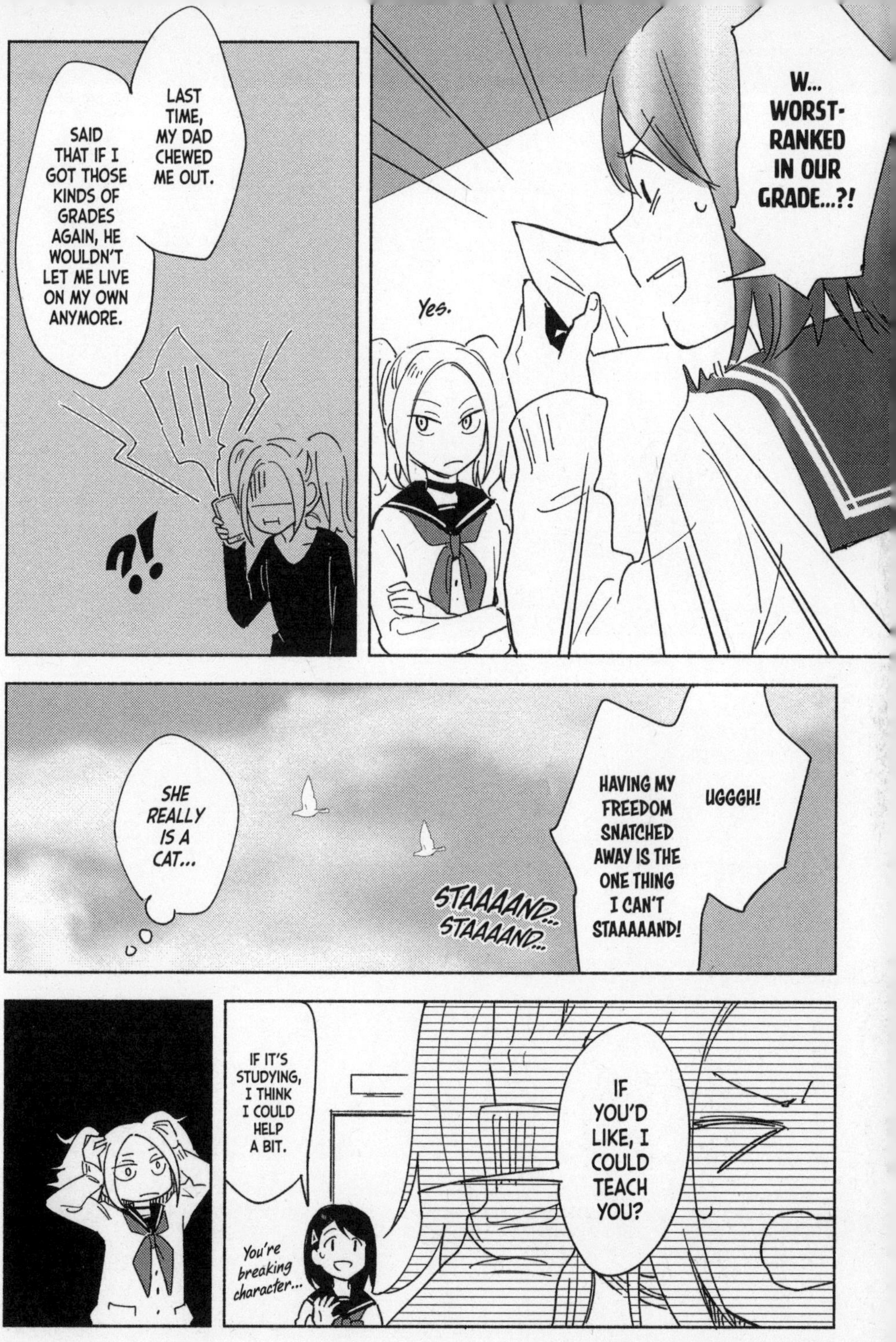
W... WORST-RANKED IN OUR GRADE...?!
Yes.
LAST TIME, MY DAD CHEWED ME OUT.
SAID THAT IF I GOT THOSE KINDS OF GRADES AGAIN, HE WOULDN'T LET ME LIVE ON MY OWN ANYMORE.
?!
UGGGH!
HAVING MY FREEDOM SNATCHED AWAY IS THE ONE THING I CAN'T STAAAAAND!
STAAAAAND... STAAAAND...
SHE REALLY IS A CAT...
IF YOU'D LIKE, I COULD TEACH YOU?
IF IT'S STUDYING, I THINK I COULD HELP A BIT.
You're breaking character...

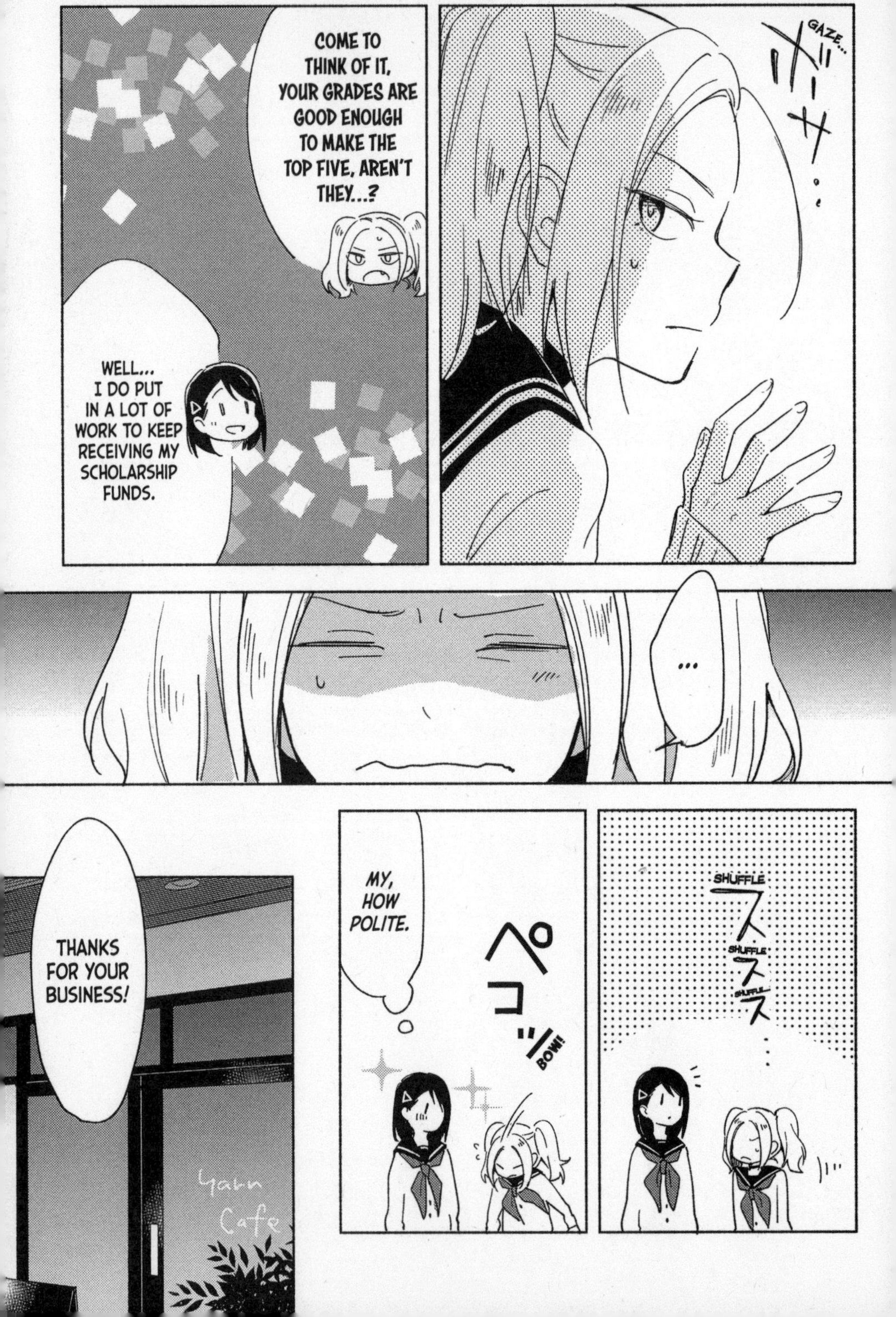
GAZE...
COME TO THINK OF IT, YOUR GRADES ARE GOOD ENOUGH TO MAKE THE TOP FIVE, AREN'T THEY...?
WELL... I DO PUT IN A LOT OF WORK TO KEEP RECEIVING MY SCHOLARSHIP FUNDS.
...
SHUFFLE
SHUFFLE
SHUFFLE
MY, HOW POLITE.
BOW!
THANKS FOR YOUR BUSINESS!
Yarn Cafe

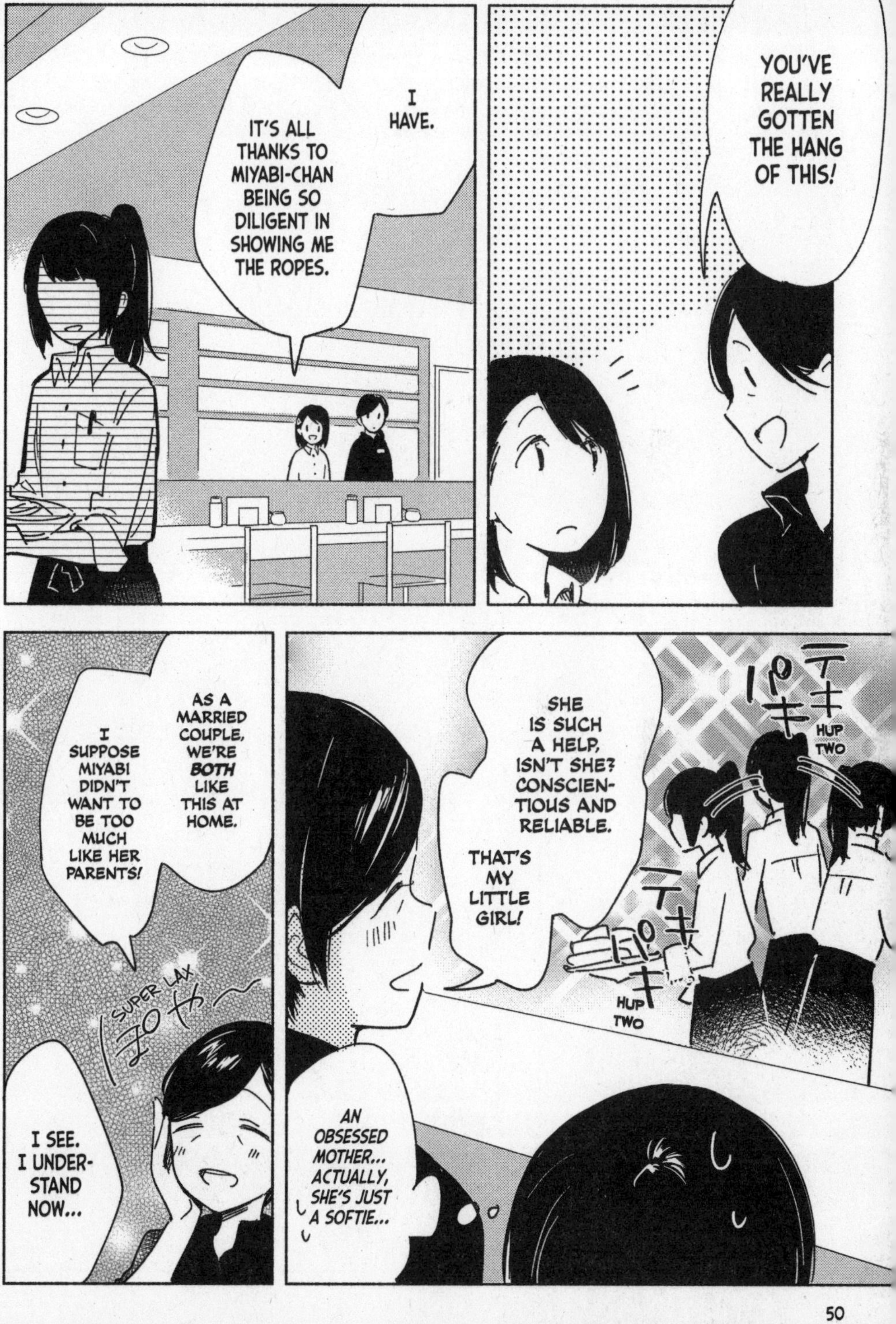
YOU'VE REALLY GOTTEN THE HANG OF THIS!
I HAVE.
IT'S ALL THANKS TO MIYABI-CHAN BEING SO DILIGENT IN SHOWING ME THE ROPES.
HUP TWO
SHE IS SUCH A HELP, ISN'T SHE? CONSCIENTIOUS AND RELIABLE.
THAT'S MY LITTLE GIRL!
HUP TWO
AN OBSESSED MOTHER... ACTUALLY, SHE'S JUST A SOFTIE...
AS A MARRIED COUPLE, WE'RE *BOTH* LIKE THIS AT HOME.
I SUPPOSE MIYABI DIDN'T WANT TO BE TOO MUCH LIKE HER PARENTS!
SUPER LAX
I SEE. I UNDERSTAND NOW...

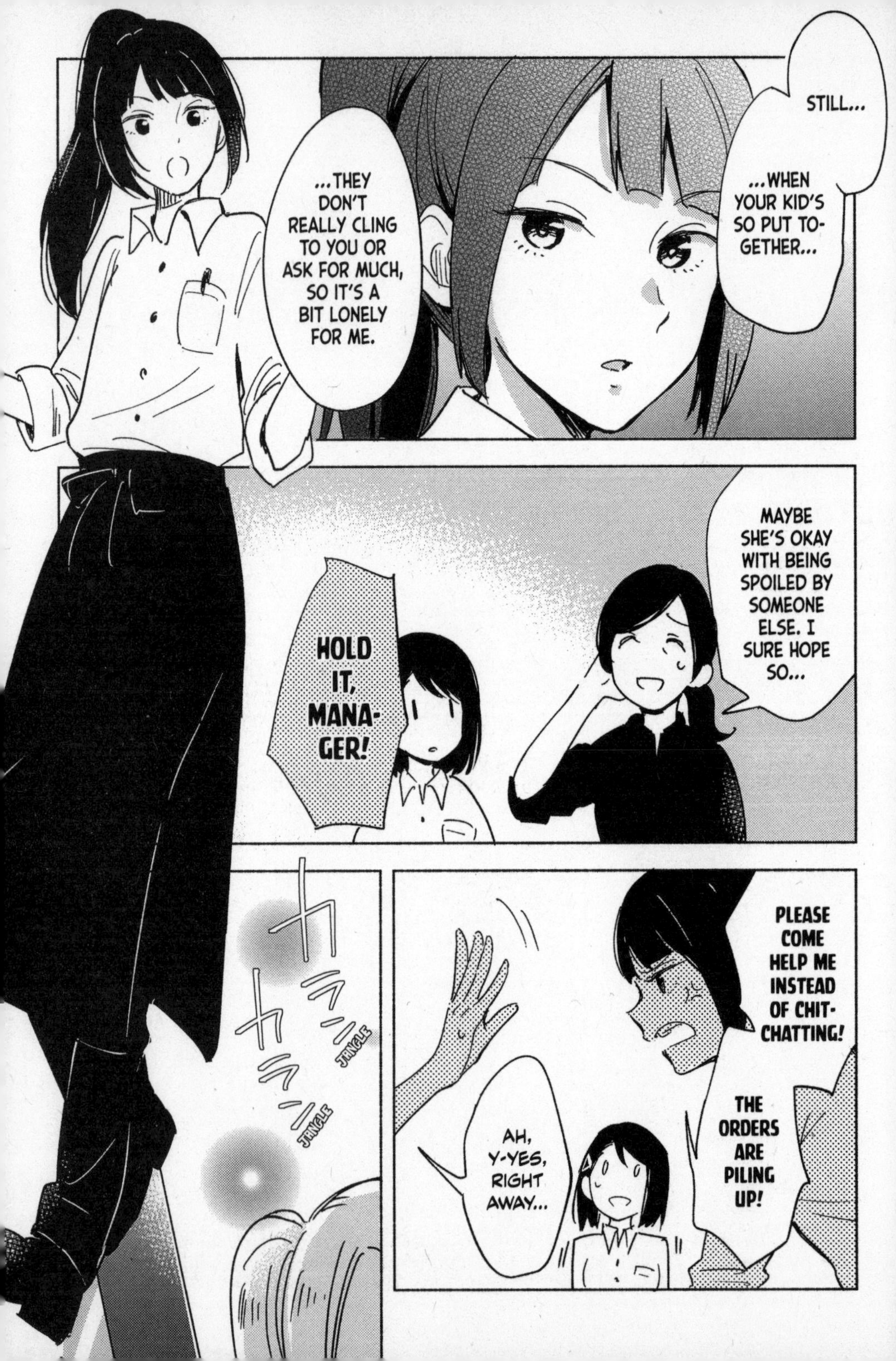
STILL...
...WHEN YOUR KID'S SO PUT TO-GETHER...
...THEY DON'T REALLY CLING TO YOU OR ASK FOR MUCH, SO IT'S A BIT LONELY FOR ME.
MAYBE SHE'S OKAY WITH BEING SPOILED BY SOMEONE ELSE. I SURE HOPE SO...
HOLD IT, MANA-GER!
PLEASE COME HELP ME INSTEAD OF CHIT-CHATTING!
THE ORDERS ARE PILING UP!
AH, Y-YES, RIGHT AWAY...
JINGLE
JINGLE

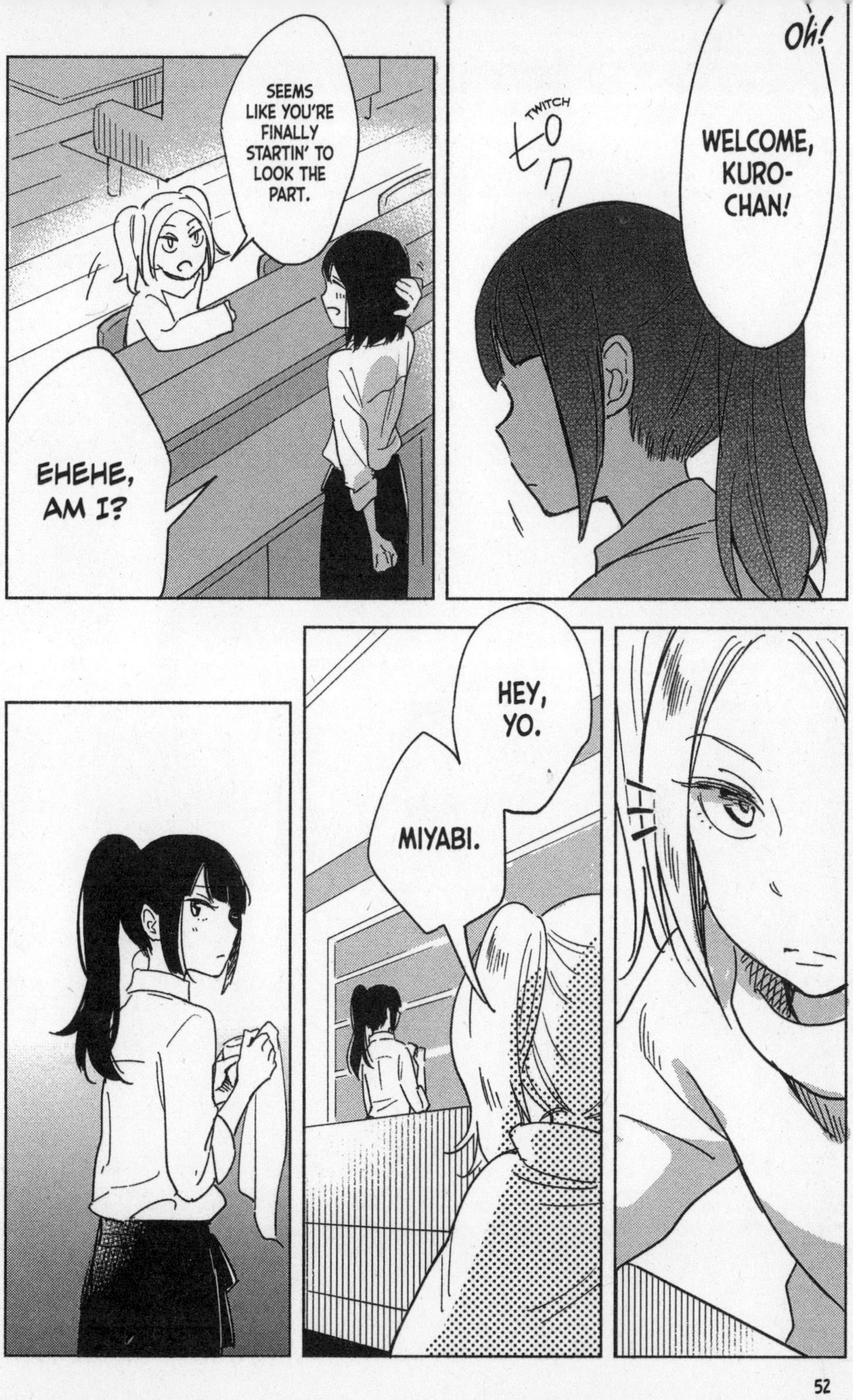
Oh!
WELCOME, KURO-CHAN!
TWITCH
SEEMS LIKE YOU'RE FINALLY STARTIN' TO LOOK THE PART.
EHEHE, AM I?
HEY, YO.
MIYABI.

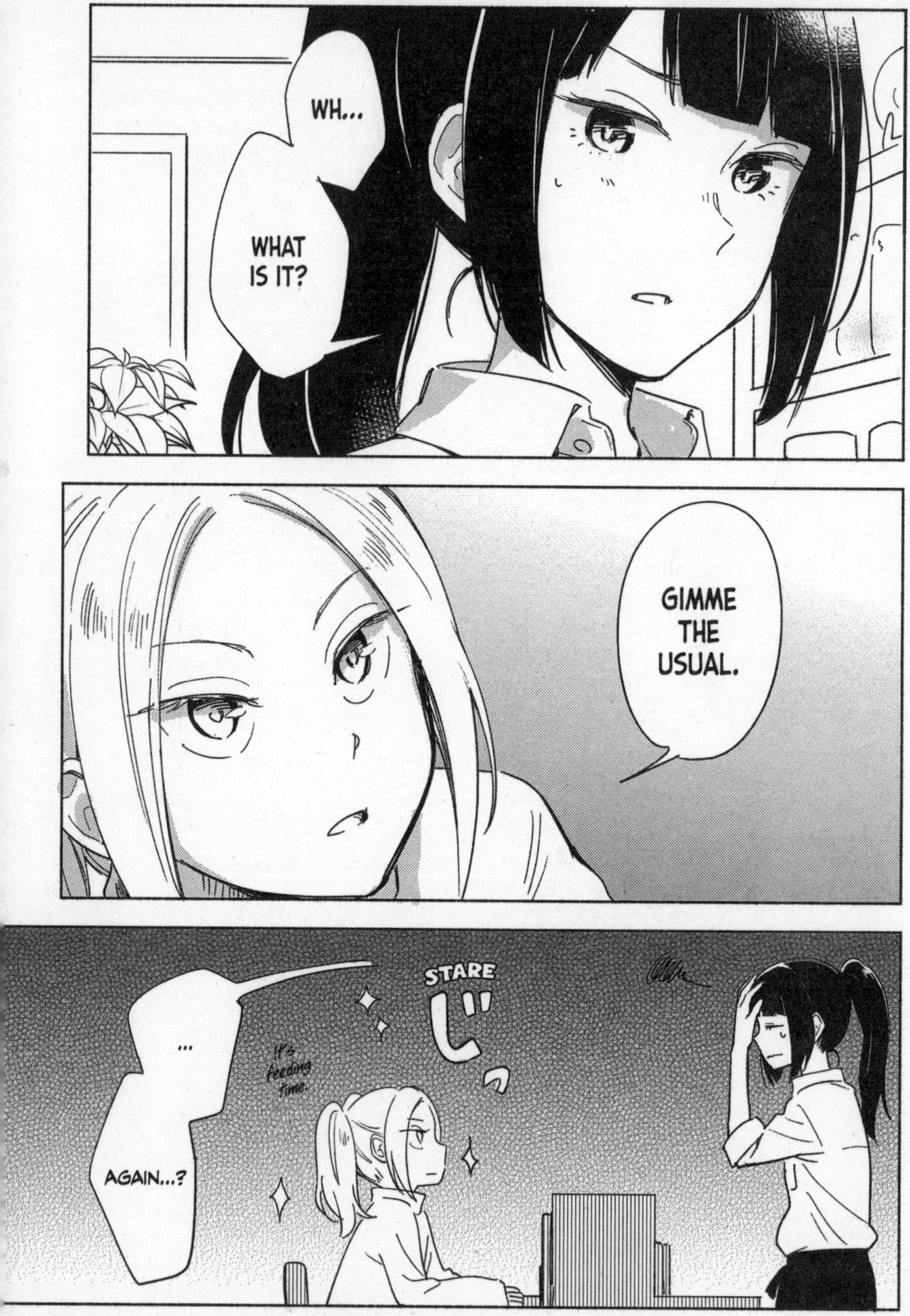
WH... WHAT IS IT?
GIMME THE USUAL.
STARE
じっ
It's feeding time.
... AGAIN...?

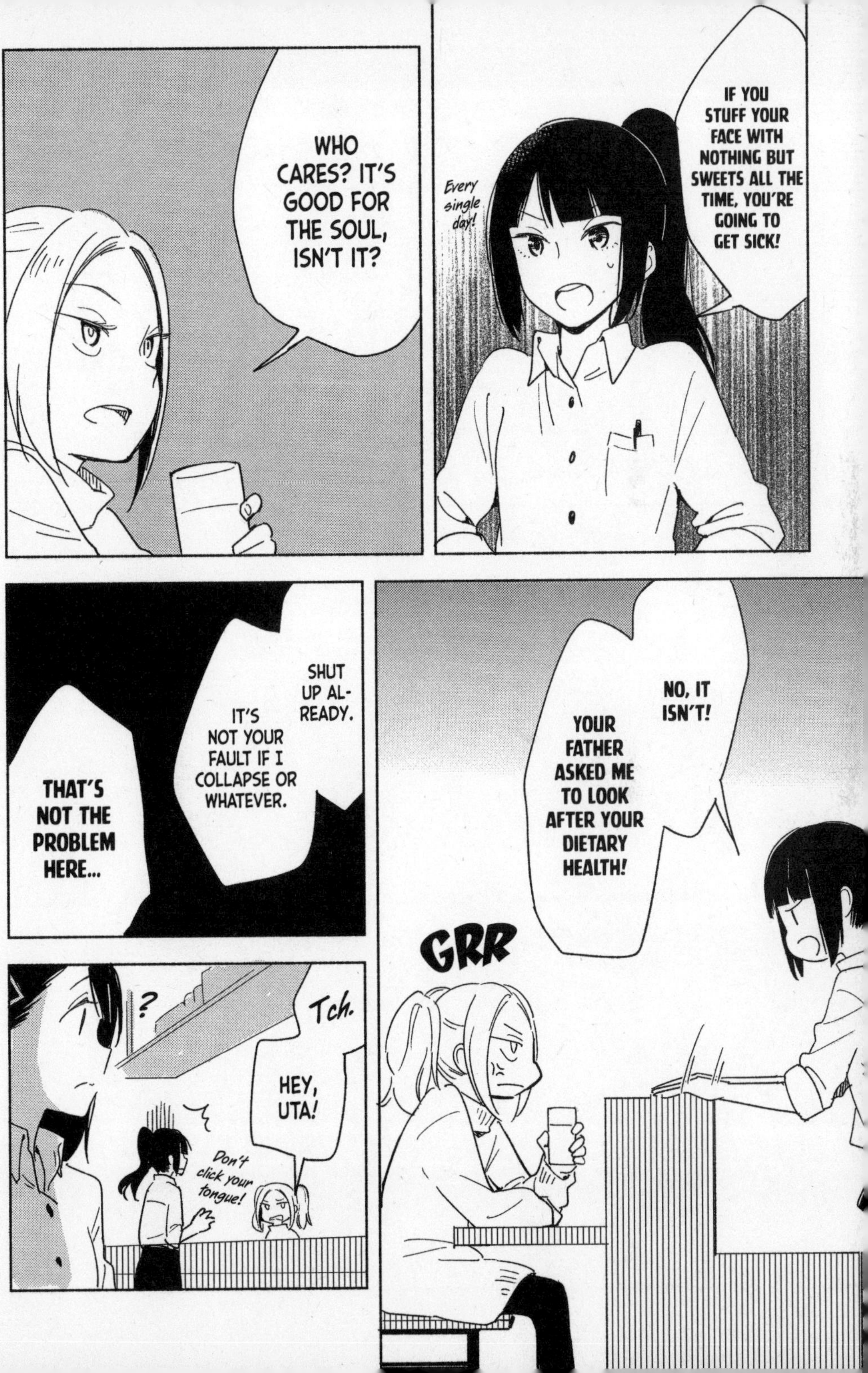
IF YOU STUFF YOUR FACE WITH NOTHING BUT SWEETS ALL THE TIME, YOU'RE GOING TO GET SICK!
Every single day!
WHO CARES? IT'S GOOD FOR THE SOUL, ISN'T IT?
NO, IT ISN'T!
YOUR FATHER ASKED ME TO LOOK AFTER YOUR DIETARY HEALTH!
GRR
SHUT UP AL-READY.
IT'S NOT YOUR FAULT IF I COLLAPSE OR WHATEVER.
THAT'S NOT THE PROBLEM HERE...
Tch.
?
HEY, UTA!
Don't click your tongue!

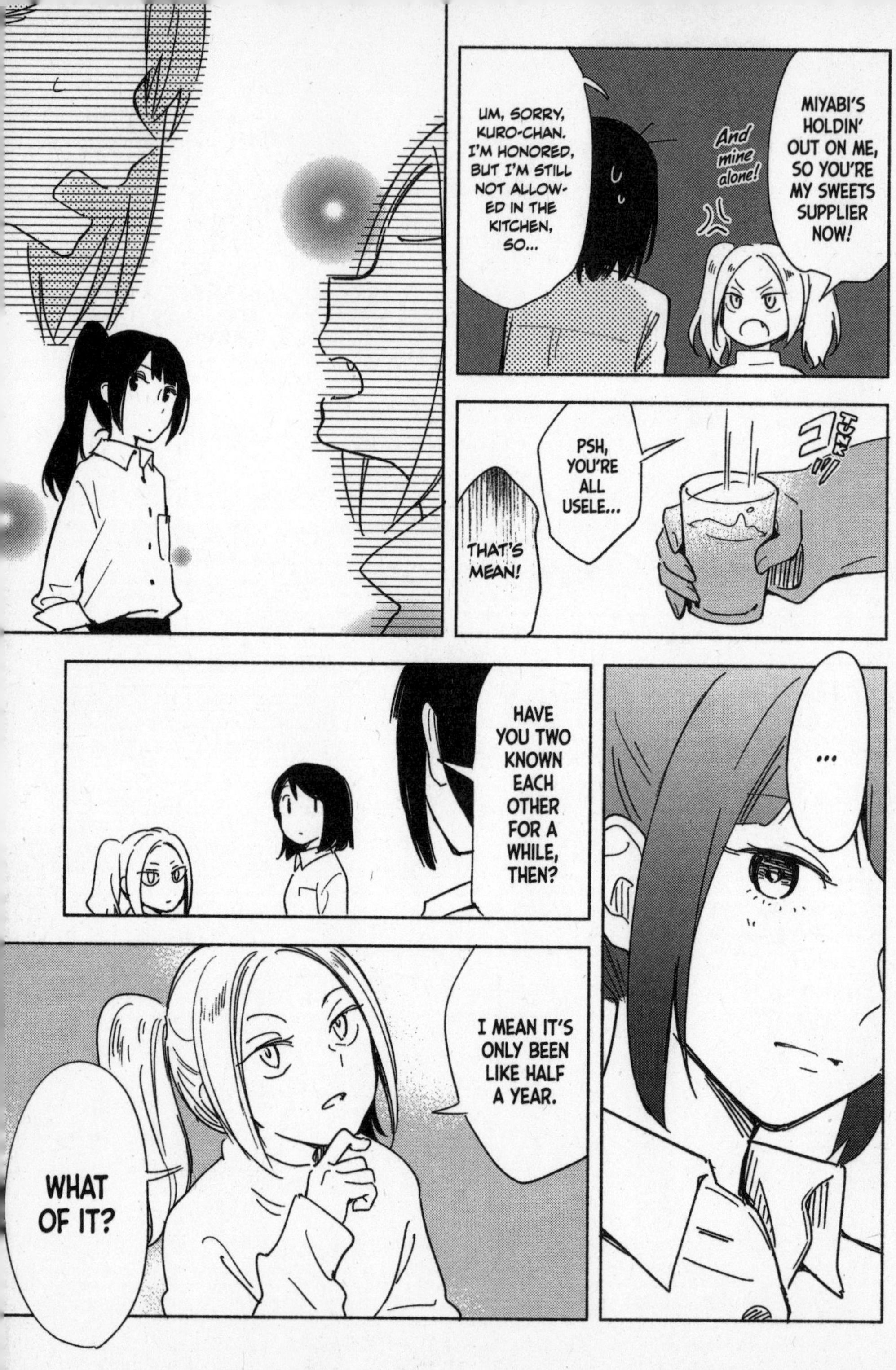
MIYABI'S HOLDIN' OUT ON ME, SO YOU'RE MY SWEETS SUPPLIER NOW!
And mine alone!
UM, SORRY, KURO-CHAN. I'M HONORED, BUT I'M STILL NOT ALLOW-ED IN THE KITCHEN, SO...
PSH, YOU'RE ALL USELE...
THAT'S MEAN!
...
HAVE YOU TWO KNOWN EACH OTHER FOR A WHILE, THEN?
I MEAN IT'S ONLY BEEN LIKE HALF A YEAR.
WHAT OF IT?

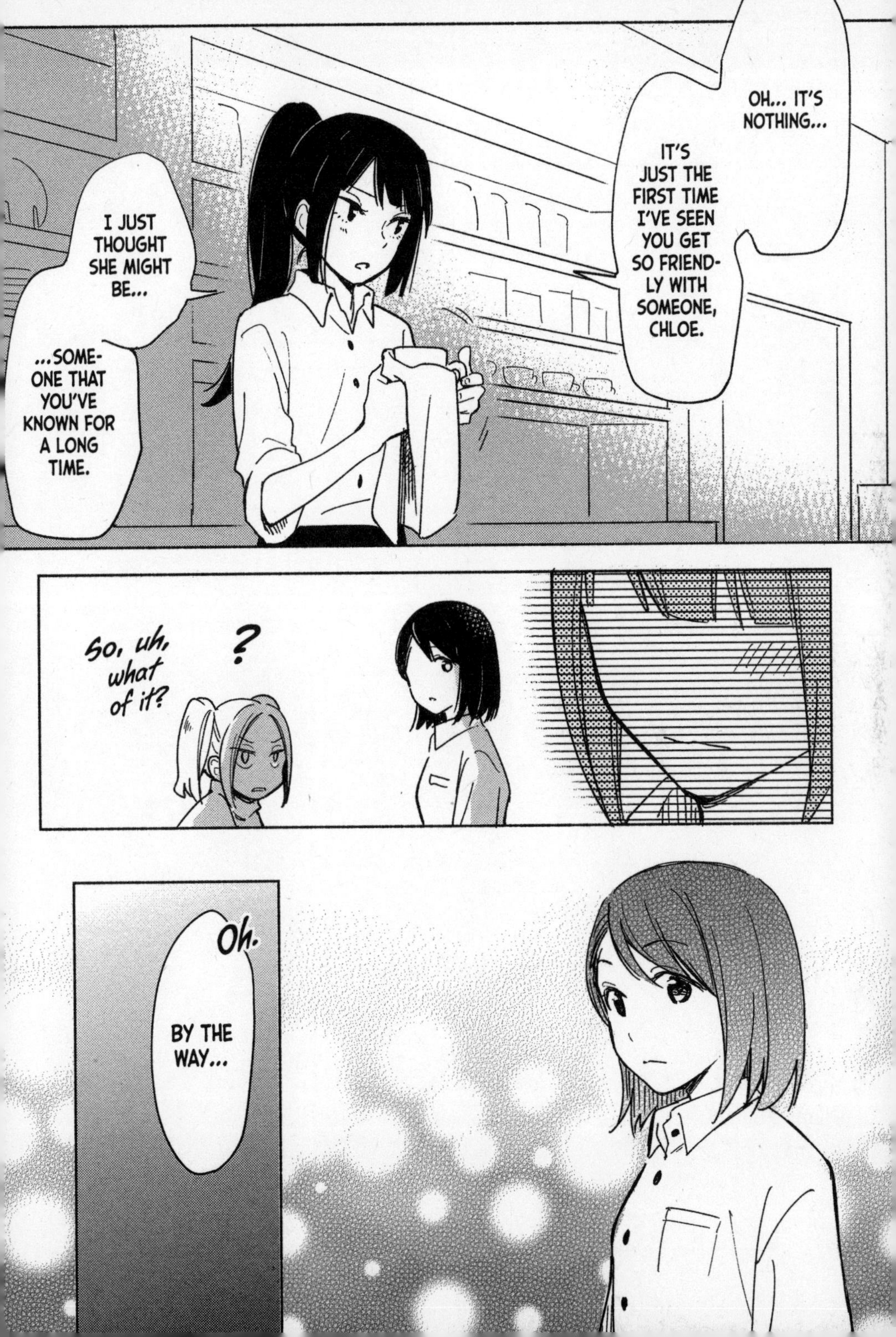
OH... IT'S NOTHING...
IT'S JUST THE FIRST TIME I'VE SEEN YOU GET SO FRIENDLY WITH SOMEONE, CHLOE.
I JUST THOUGHT SHE MIGHT BE...
...SOMEONE THAT YOU'VE KNOWN FOR A LONG TIME.
?
So, uh, what of it?
Oh.
BY THE WAY...

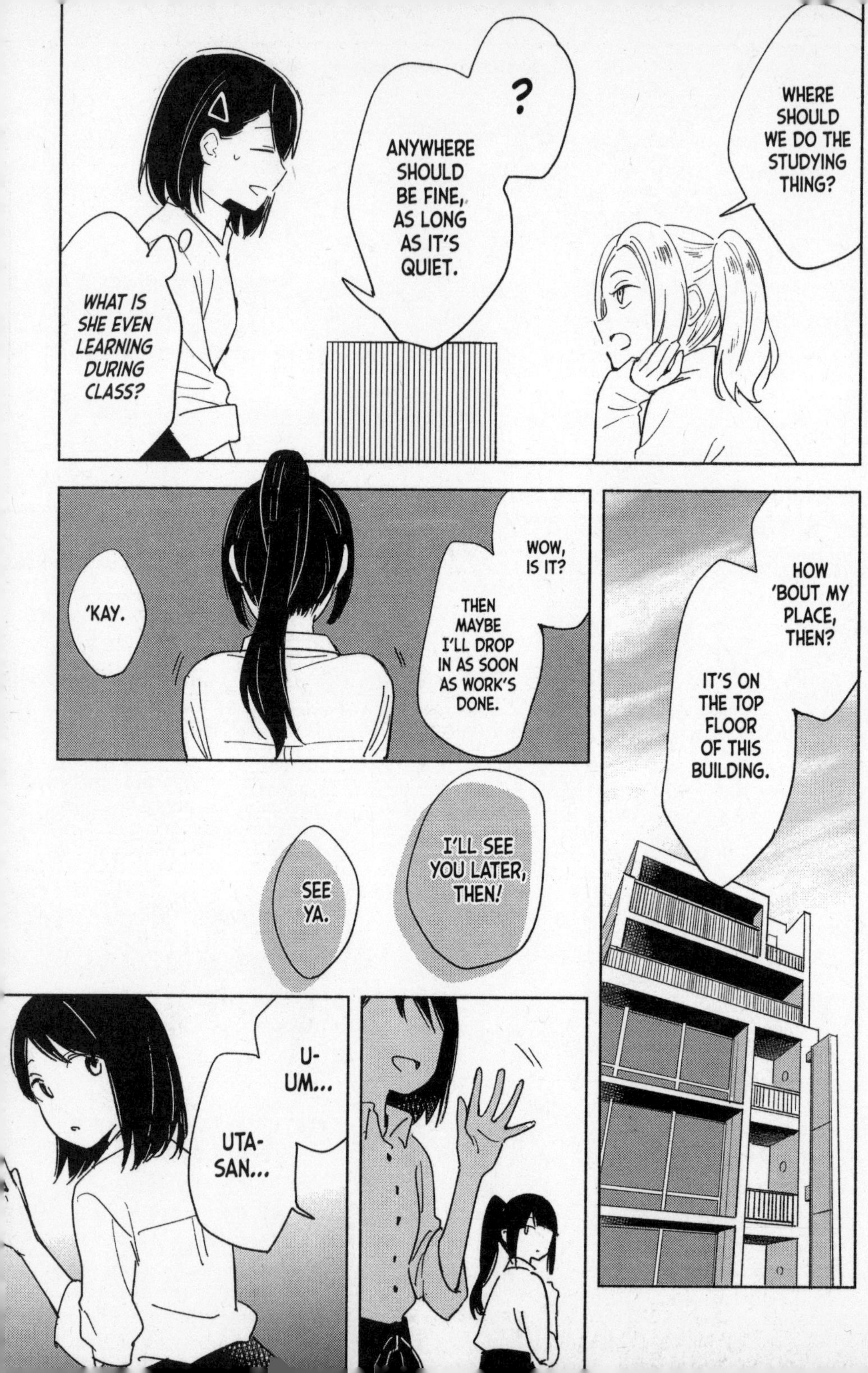
WHERE SHOULD WE DO THE STUDYING THING?
?
ANYWHERE SHOULD BE FINE, AS LONG AS IT'S QUIET.
WHAT IS SHE EVEN LEARNING DURING CLASS?
HOW 'BOUT MY PLACE, THEN?
IT'S ON THE TOP FLOOR OF THIS BUILDING.
WOW, IS IT?
THEN MAYBE I'LL DROP IN AS SOON AS WORK'S DONE.
'KAY.
I'LL SEE YOU LATER, THEN!
SEE YA.
U- UM...
UTA-SAN...

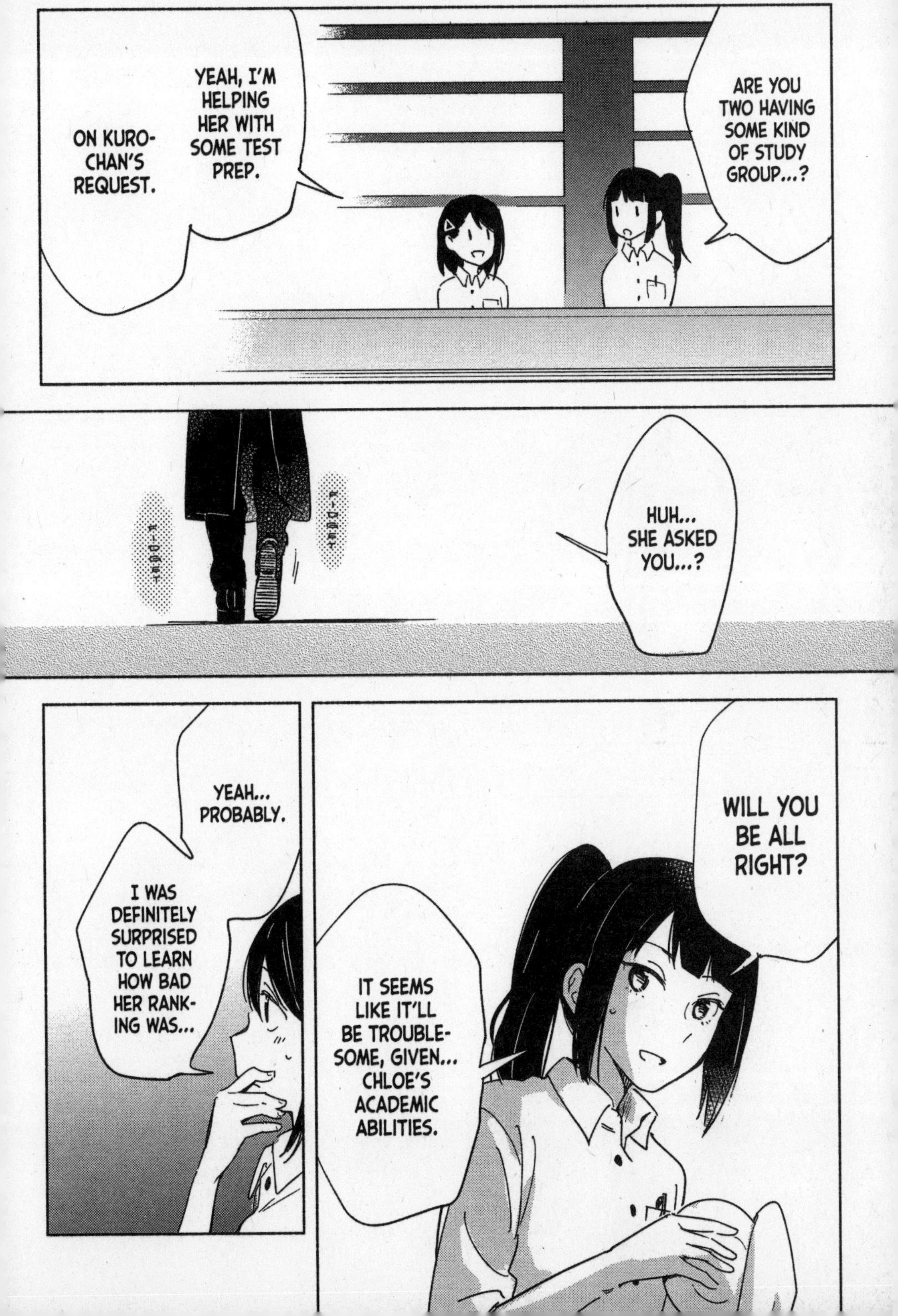
ARE YOU TWO HAVING SOME KIND OF STUDY GROUP...?
YEAH, I'M HELPING HER WITH SOME TEST PREP.
ON KURO-CHAN'S REQUEST.
HUH... SHE ASKED YOU...?
FIDGET
FIDGET
WILL YOU BE ALL RIGHT?
IT SEEMS LIKE IT'LL BE TROUBLE-SOME, GIVEN... CHLOE'S ACADEMIC ABILITIES.
YEAH... PROBABLY.
I WAS DEFINITELY SURPRISED TO LEARN HOW BAD HER RANK-ING WAS...

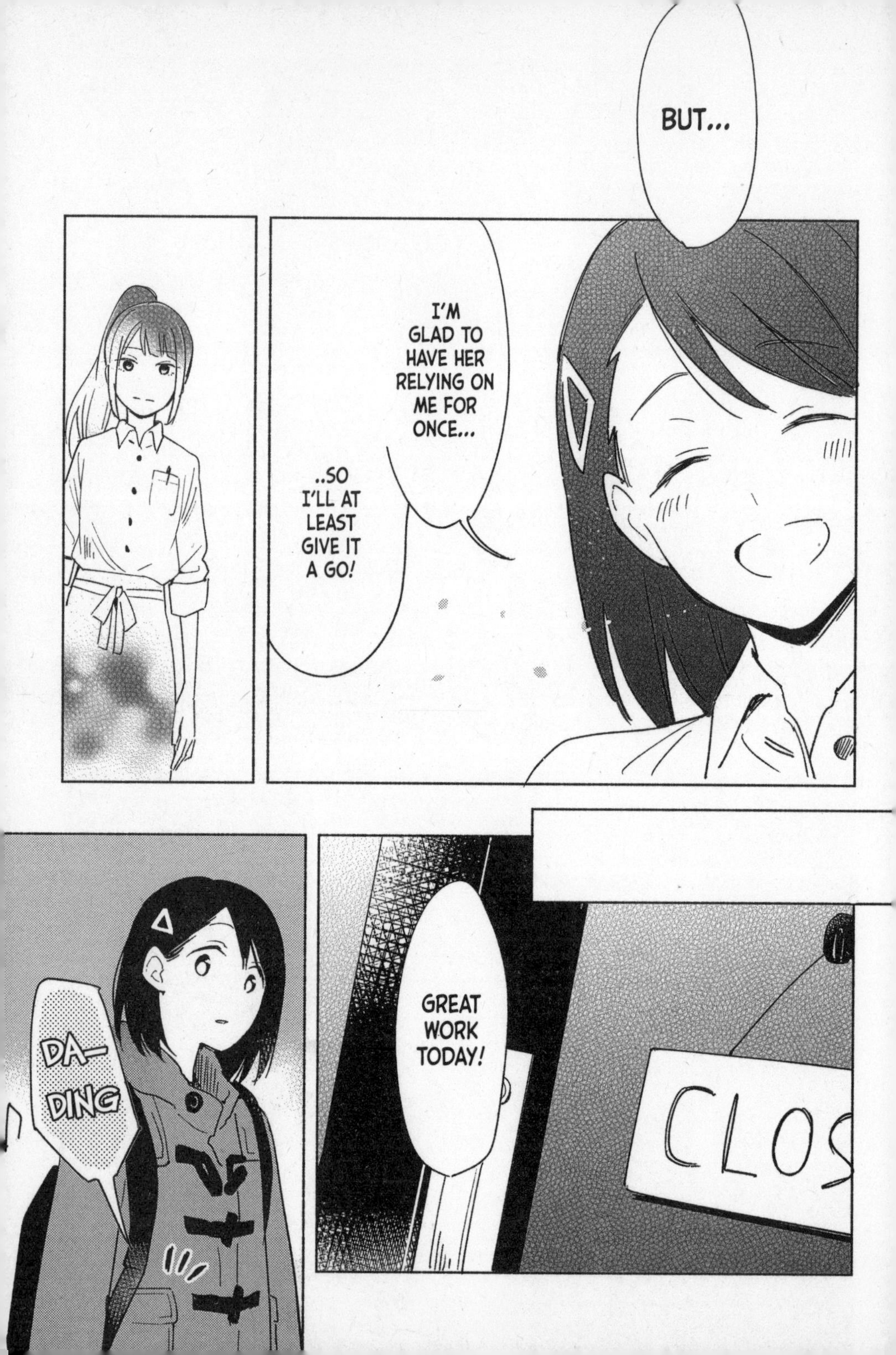
BUT...
I'M GLAD TO HAVE HER RELYING ON ME FOR ONCE...
..SO I'LL AT LEAST GIVE IT A GO!
GREAT WORK TODAY!
CLOS
DA-DING

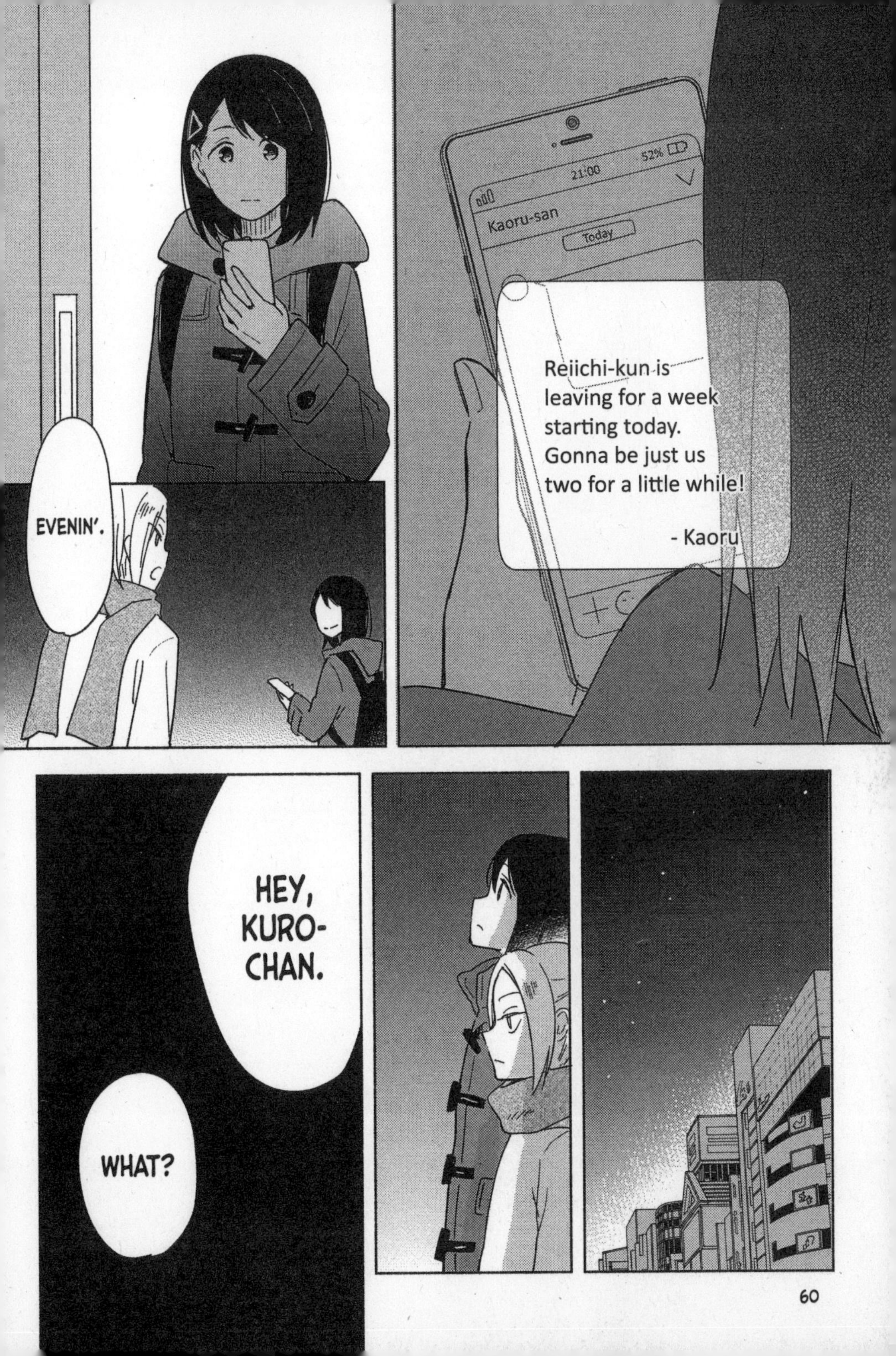
52%
21:00
Kaoru-san
Today
Reiichi-kun is leaving for a week starting today. Gonna be just us two for a little while!
- Kaoru
EVENIN'.
HEY, KURO-CHAN.
WHAT?

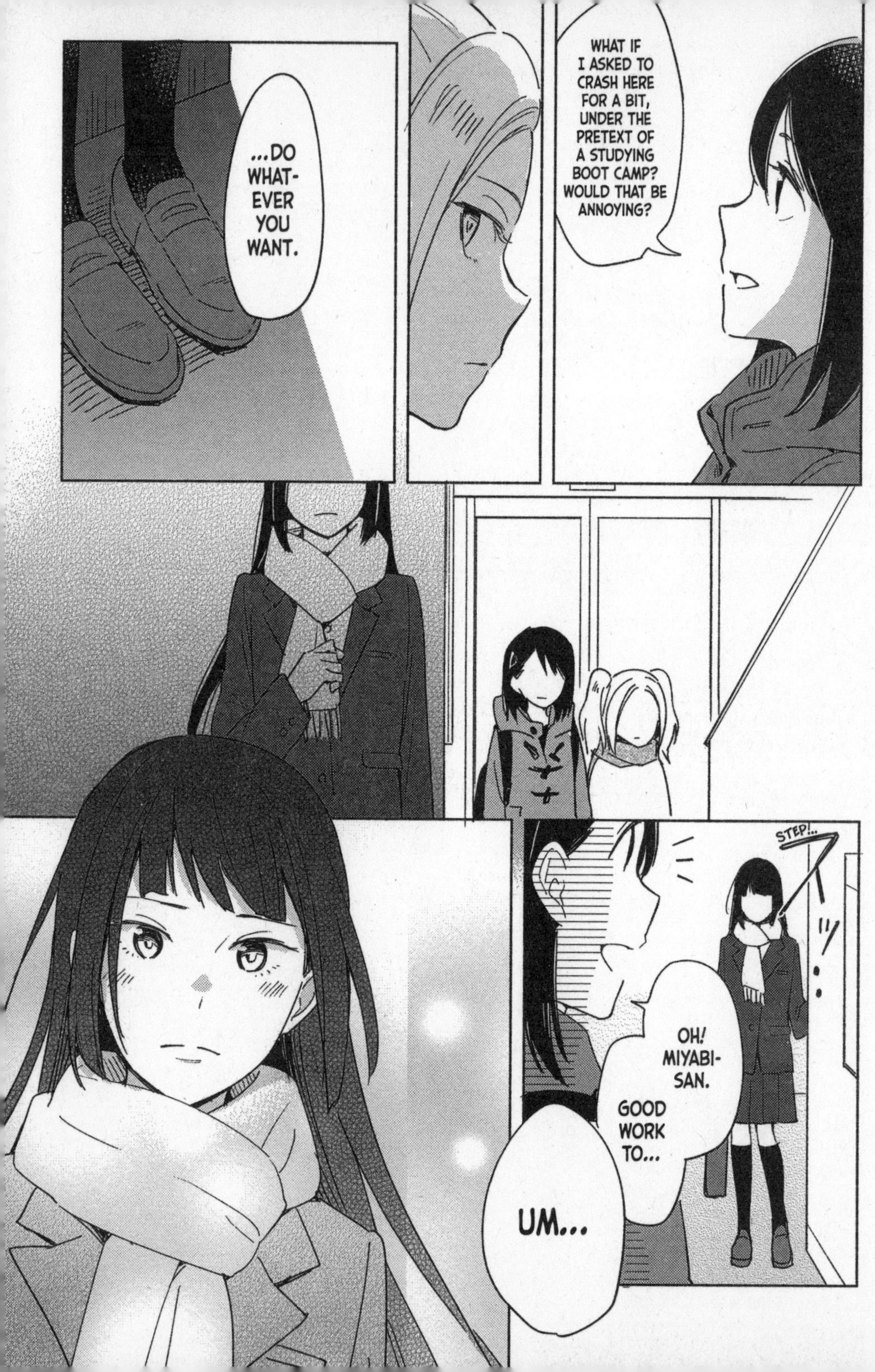
WHAT IF I ASKED TO CRASH HERE FOR A BIT, UNDER THE PRETEXT OF A STUDYING BOOT CAMP? WOULD THAT BE ANNOYING?
...DO WHAT-EVER YOU WANT.
STEP...
OH! MIYABI-SAN.
GOOD WORK TO...
UM...

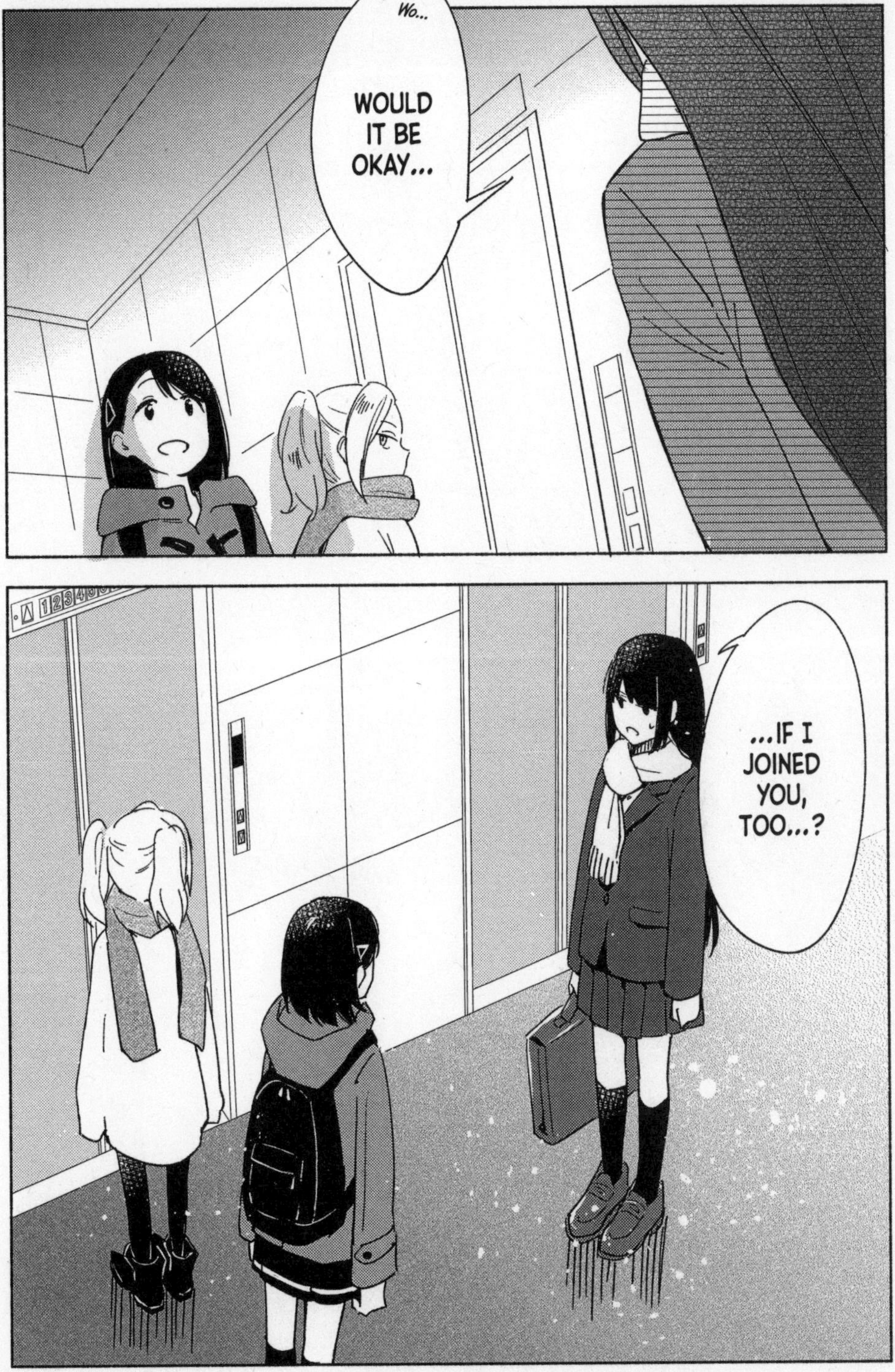
Wo...
WOULD IT BE OKAY...
...IF I JOINED YOU, TOO...?

If I Could
Reach You

If I Could
Reach You

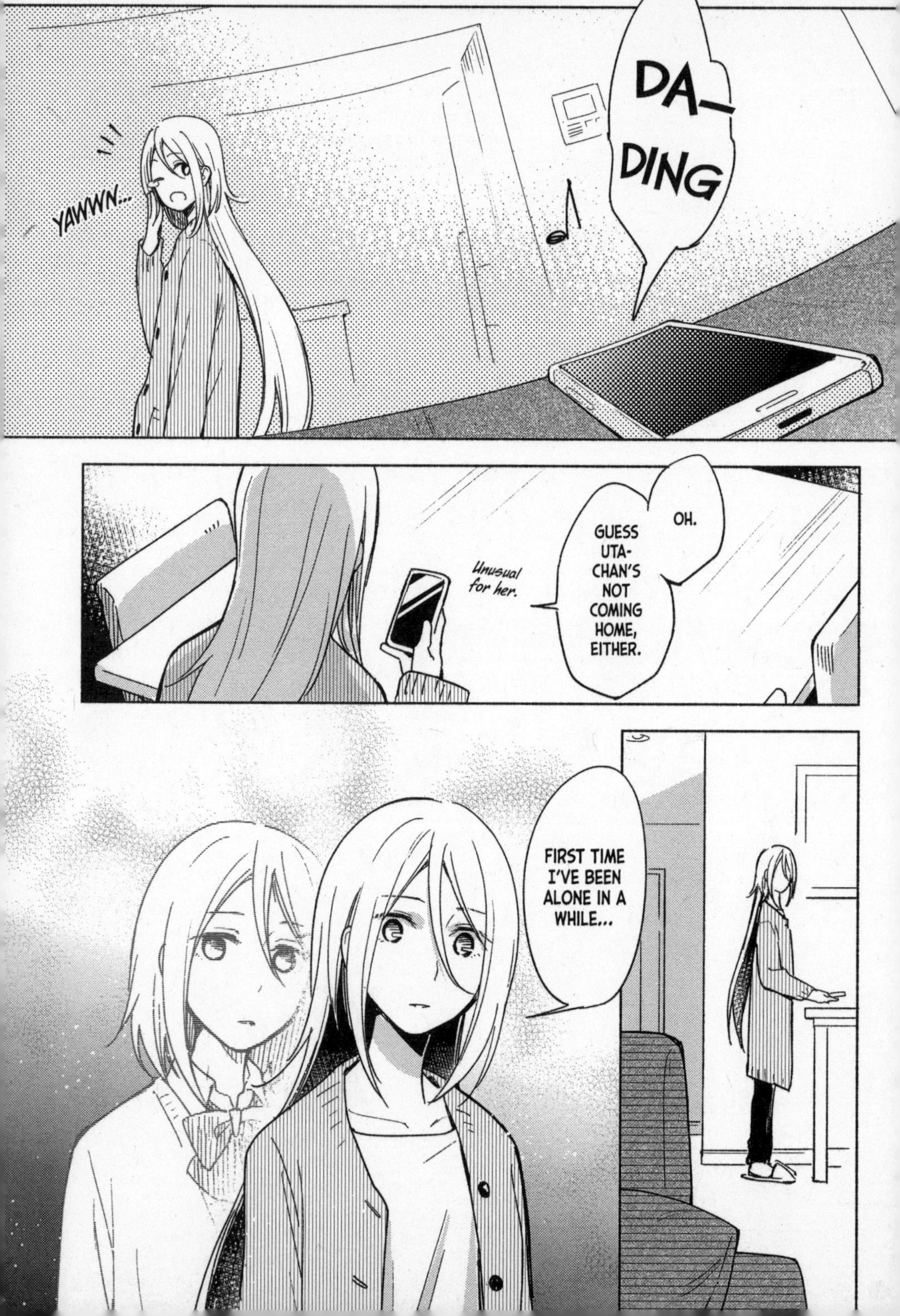
DA-DING
YAWWN...
OH.
GUESS UTA-CHAN'S NOT COMING HOME, EITHER.
Unusual for her.
FIRST TIME I'VE BEEN ALONE IN A WHILE...

Chapter 8

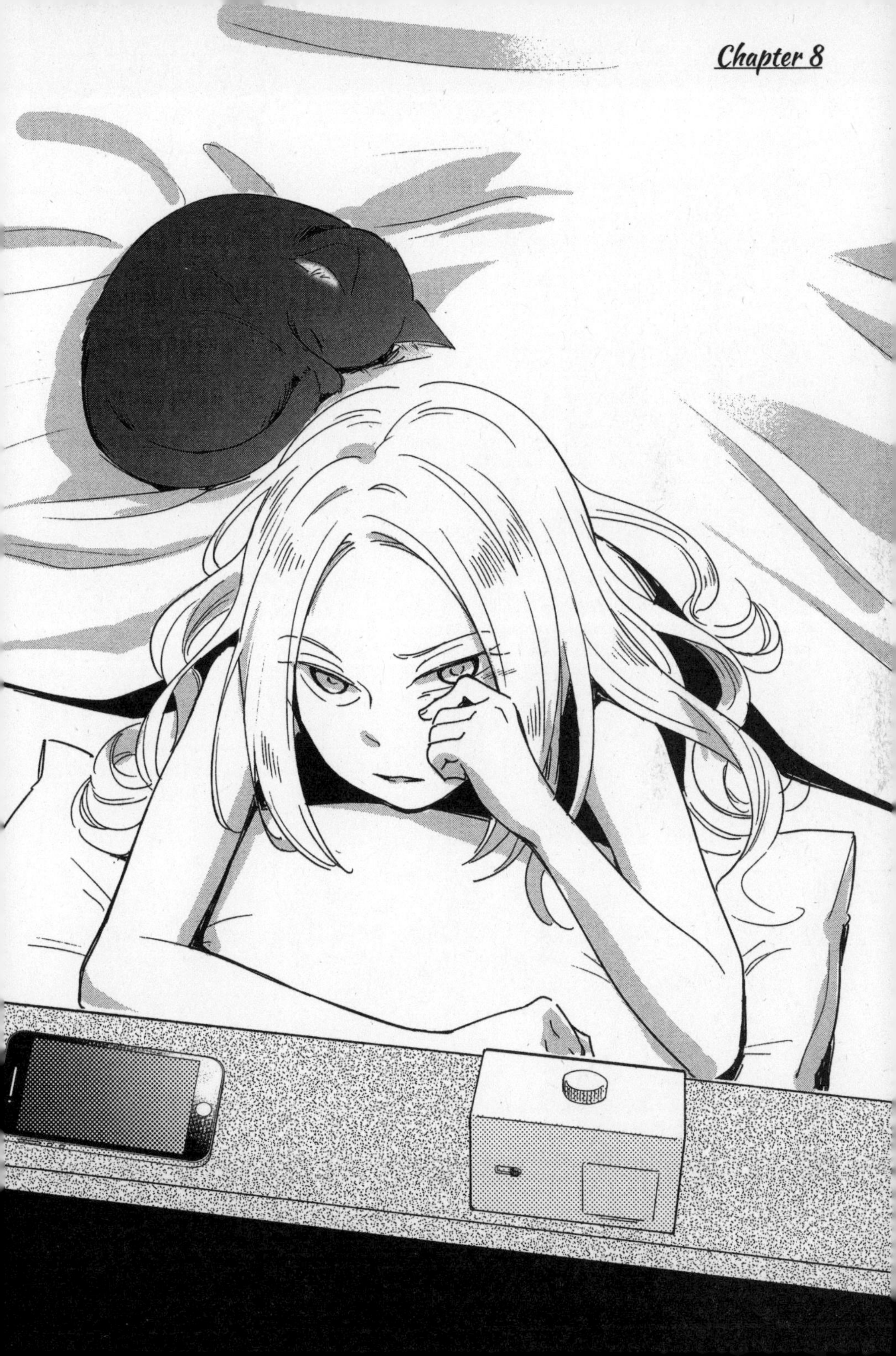

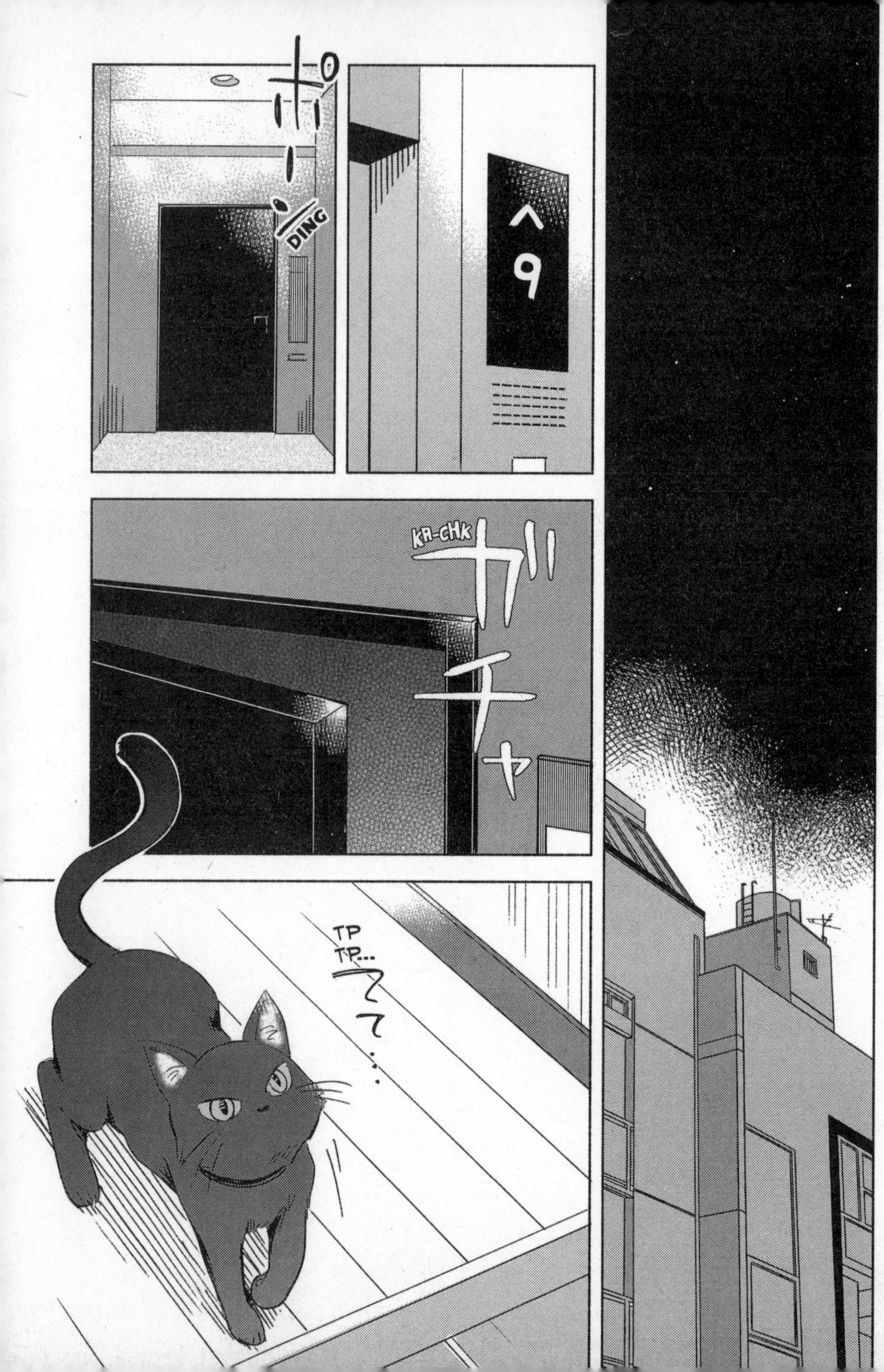
9
ポーン
DING
ガチャ
KA-CHK
てて…
TP TP...

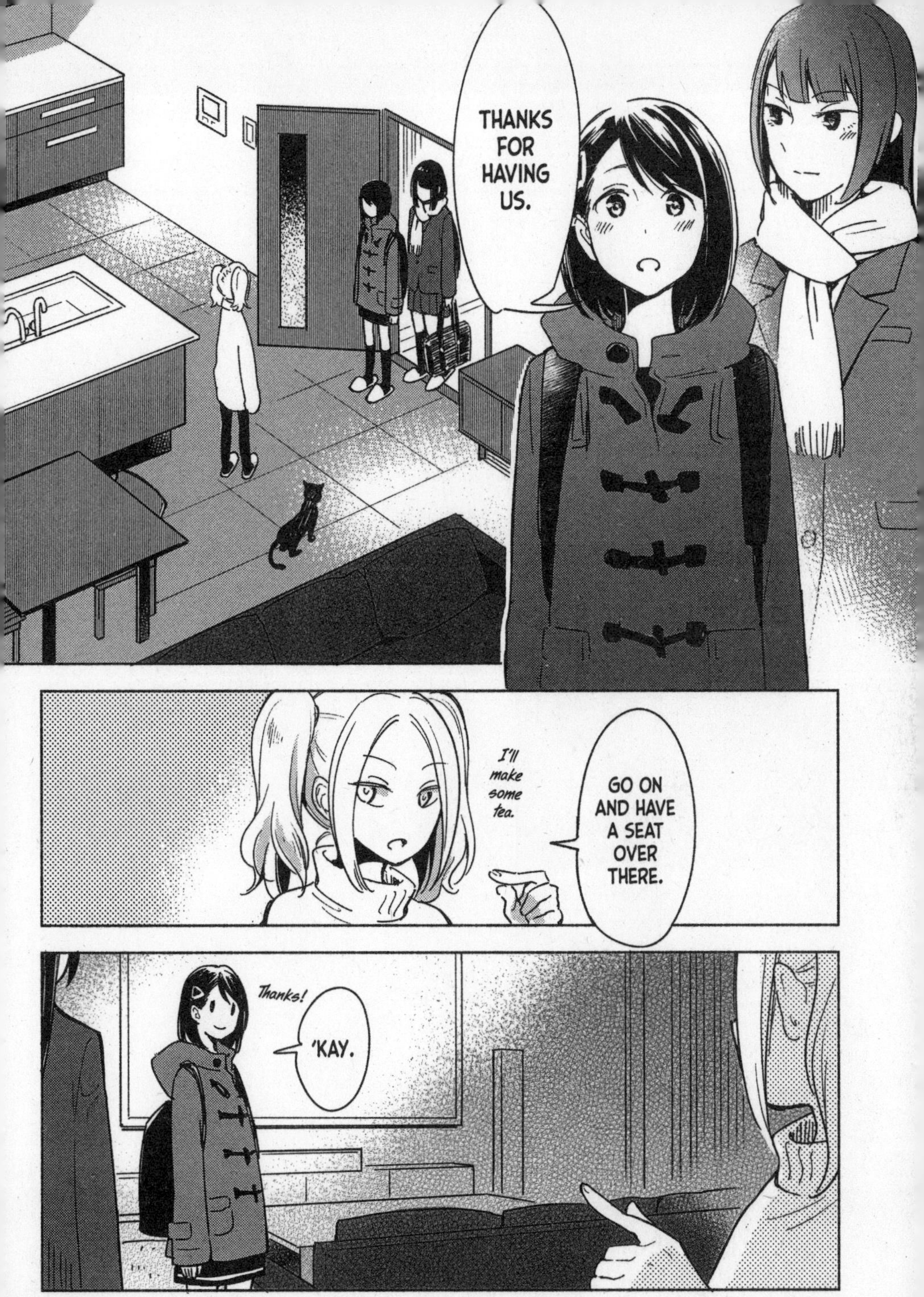
THANKS FOR HAVING US.
GO ON AND HAVE A SEAT OVER THERE.
I'll make some tea.
'KAY.
Thanks!

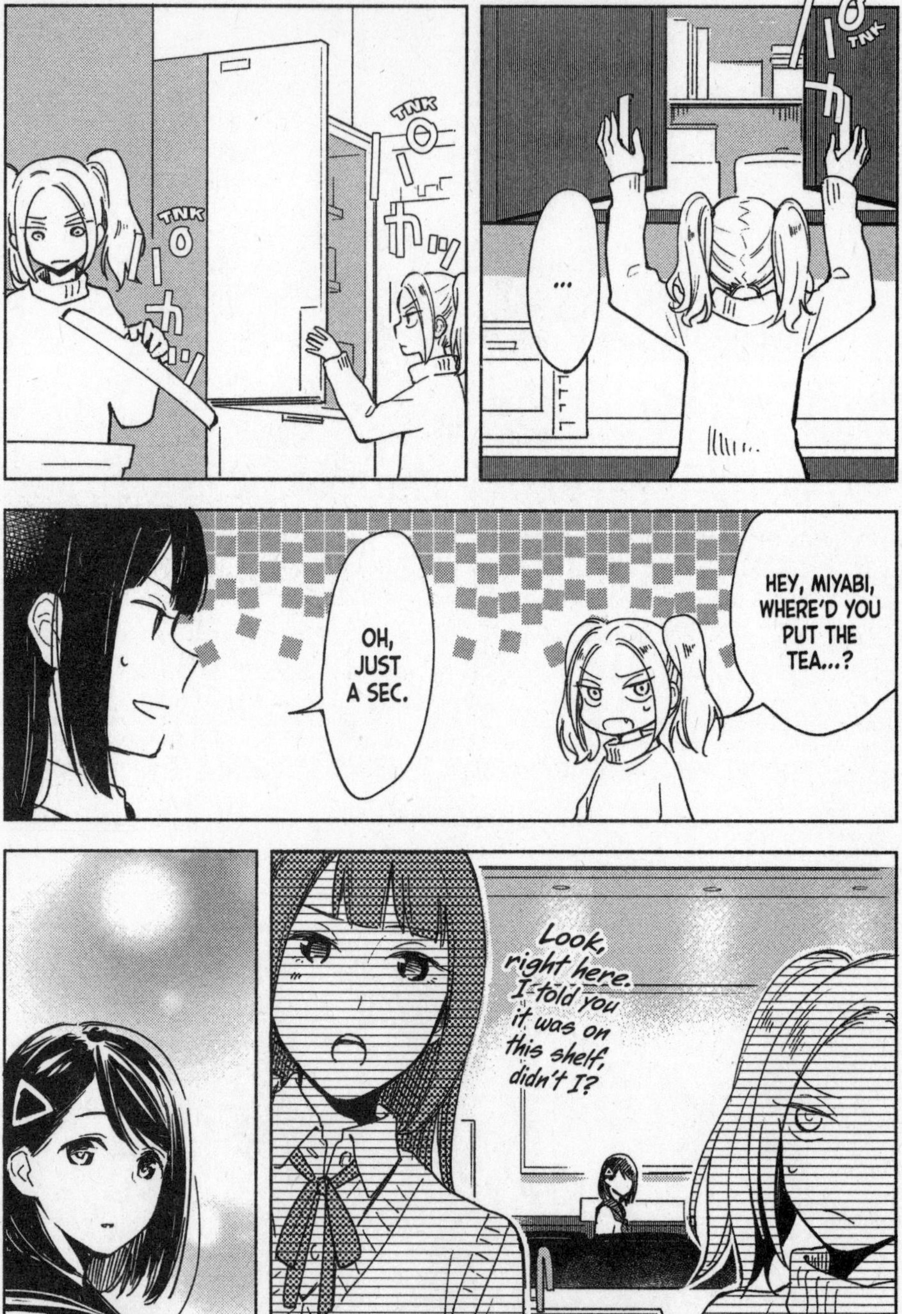
TNK
...
TNK
TNK
HEY, MIYABI, WHERE'D YOU PUT THE TEA...?
OH, JUST A SEC.
Look, right here. I told you it was on this shelf, didn't I?

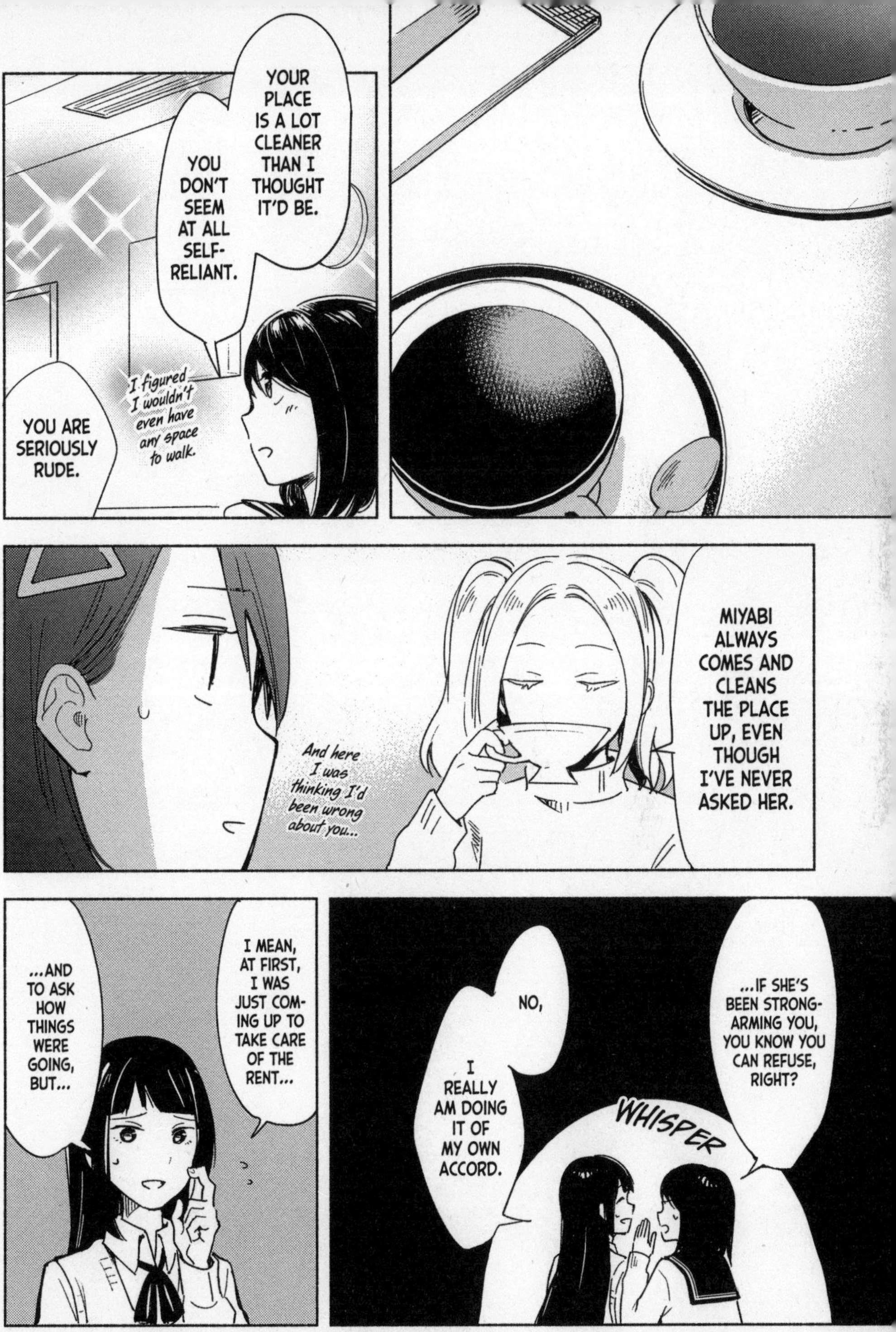
YOUR PLACE IS A LOT CLEANER THAN I THOUGHT IT'D BE.
YOU DON'T SEEM AT ALL SELF-RELIANT.
I figured I wouldn't even have any space to walk.
YOU ARE SERIOUSLY RUDE.
MIYABI ALWAYS COMES AND CLEANS THE PLACE UP, EVEN THOUGH I'VE NEVER ASKED HER.
And here I was thinking I'd been wrong about you...
...IF SHE'S BEEN STRONG-ARMING YOU, YOU KNOW YOU CAN REFUSE, RIGHT?
WHISPER
NO,
I REALLY AM DOING IT OF MY OWN ACCORD.
I MEAN, AT FIRST, I WAS JUST COMING UP TO TAKE CARE OF THE RENT...
...AND TO ASK HOW THINGS WERE GOING, BUT...

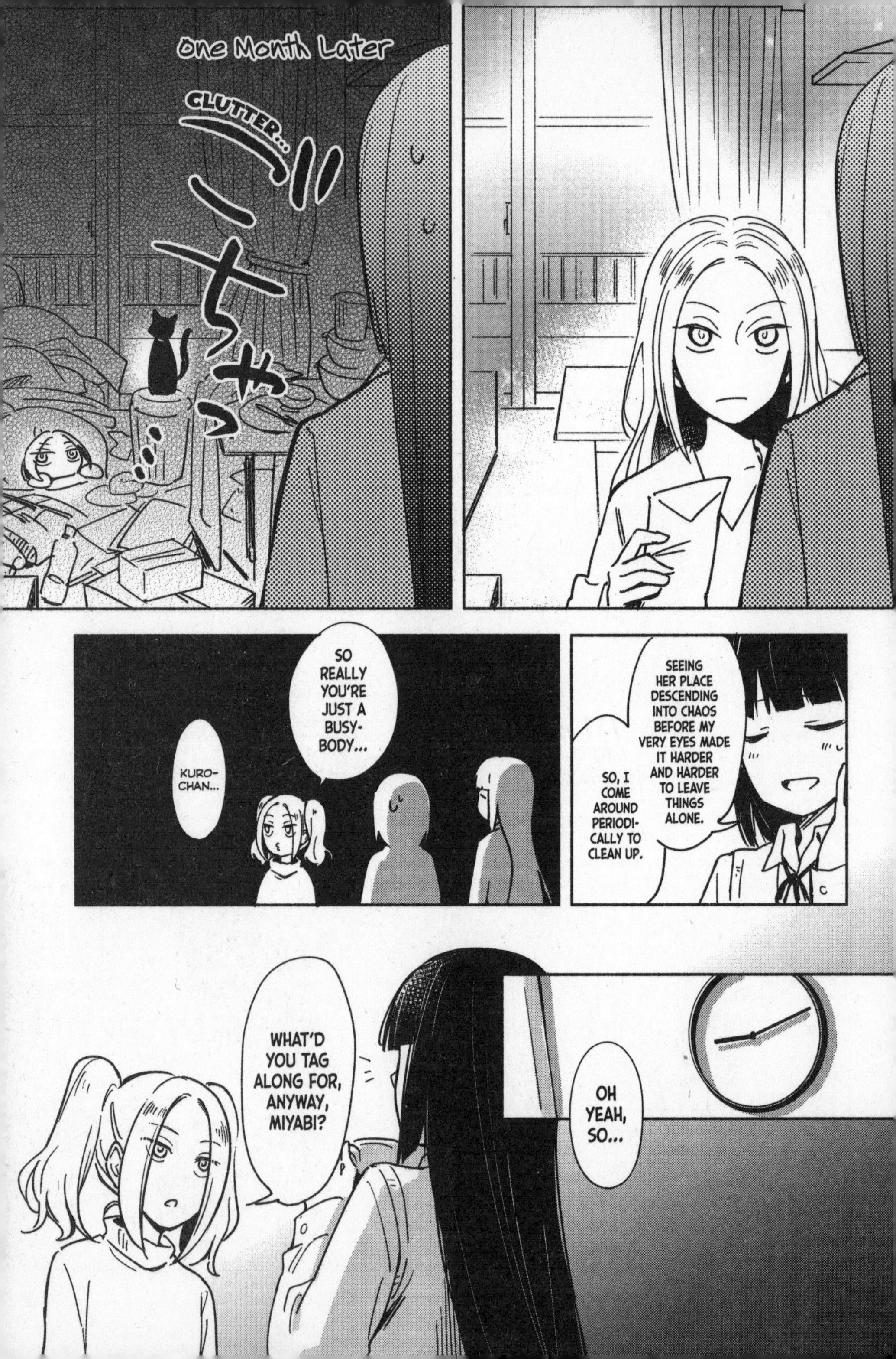
One Month Later
CLUTTER...
ごちゃっ…
SEEING HER PLACE DESCENDING INTO CHAOS BEFORE MY VERY EYES MADE IT HARDER AND HARDER TO LEAVE THINGS ALONE.
SO, I COME AROUND PERIODI-CALLY TO CLEAN UP.
SO REALLY YOU'RE JUST A BUSY-BODY...
KURO-CHAN...
WHAT'D YOU TAG ALONG FOR, ANYWAY, MIYABI?
OH YEAH, SO...

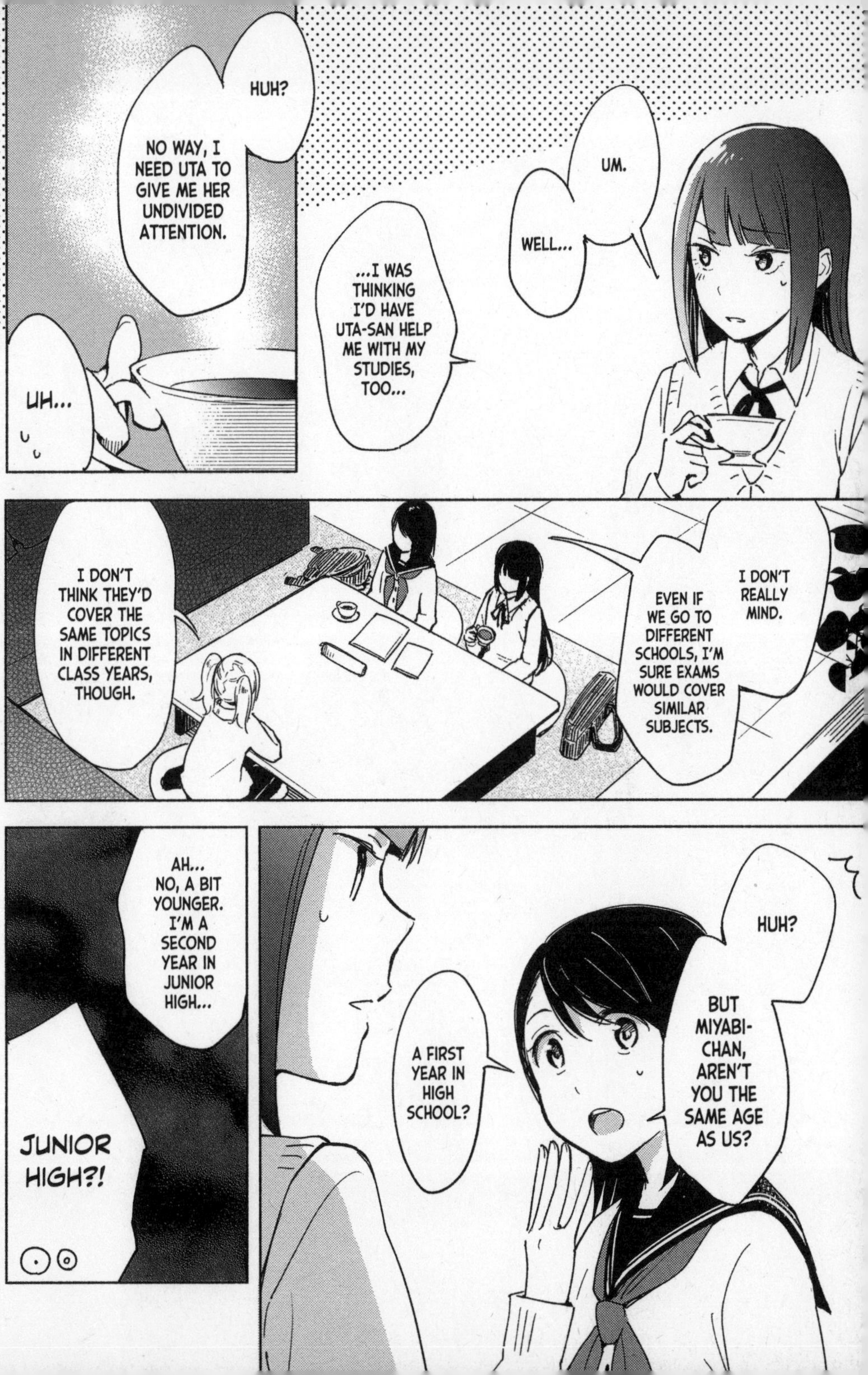
UM.
WELL...
...I WAS THINKING I'D HAVE UTA-SAN HELP ME WITH MY STUDIES, TOO...
HUH?
NO WAY, I NEED UTA TO GIVE ME HER UNDIVIDED ATTENTION.
UH...
I DON'T REALLY MIND.
EVEN IF WE GO TO DIFFERENT SCHOOLS, I'M SURE EXAMS WOULD COVER SIMILAR SUBJECTS.
I DON'T THINK THEY'D COVER THE SAME TOPICS IN DIFFERENT CLASS YEARS, THOUGH.
HUH?
BUT MIYABI-CHAN, AREN'T YOU THE SAME AGE AS US?
A FIRST YEAR IN HIGH SCHOOL?
AH... NO, A BIT YOUNGER. I'M A SECOND YEAR IN JUNIOR HIGH...
JUNIOR HIGH?!

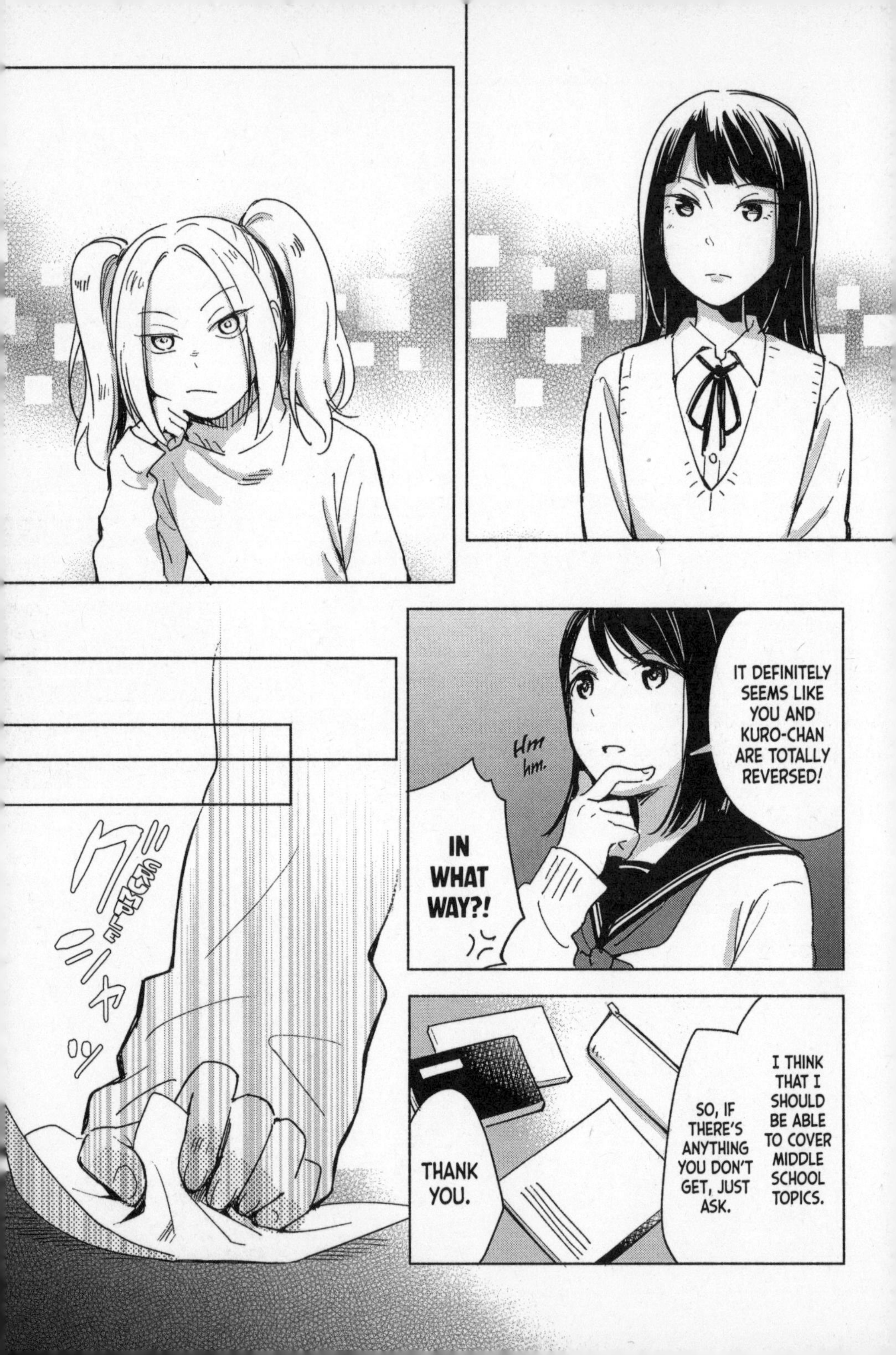
IT DEFINITELY SEEMS LIKE YOU AND KURO-CHAN ARE TOTALLY REVERSED!
Hm hm.
IN WHAT WAY?!
I THINK THAT I SHOULD BE ABLE TO COVER MIDDLE SCHOOL TOPICS.
SO, IF THERE'S ANYTHING YOU DON'T GET, JUST ASK.
THANK YOU.
グシャッ

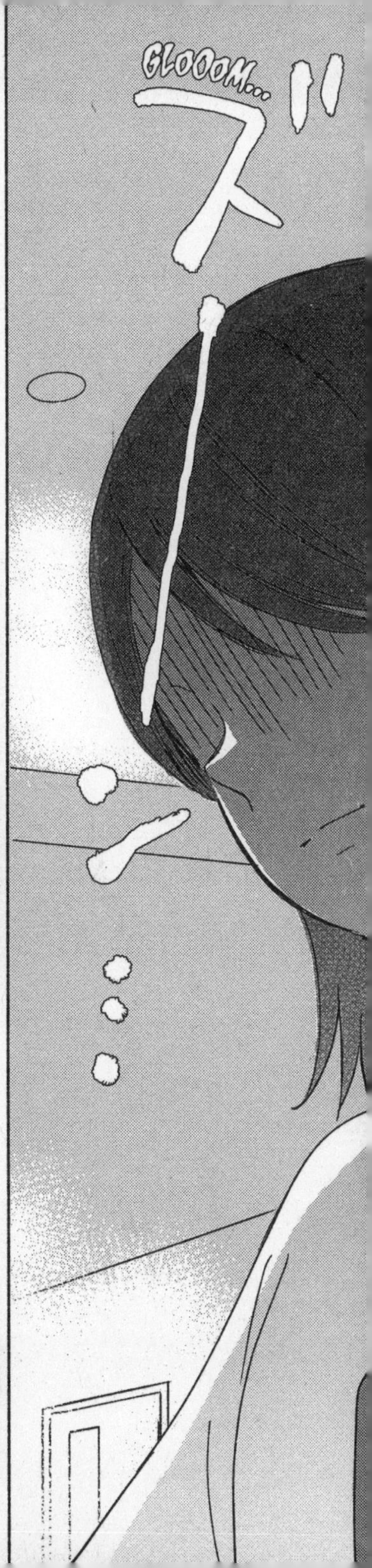
GLOOOM...

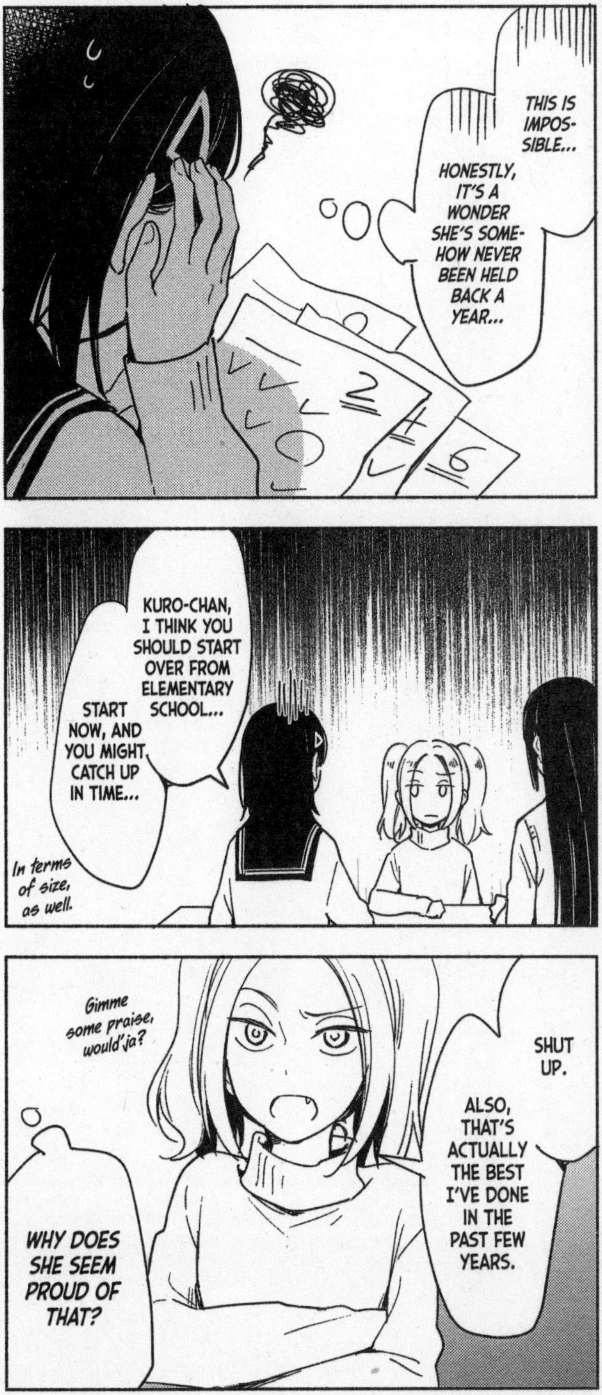
THIS IS IMPOSSIBLE...
HONESTLY, IT'S A WONDER SHE'S SOMEHOW NEVER BEEN HELD BACK A YEAR...
KURO-CHAN, I THINK YOU SHOULD START OVER FROM ELEMENTARY SCHOOL...
START NOW, AND YOU MIGHT CATCH UP IN TIME...
In terms of size, as well.
SHUT UP.
ALSO, THAT'S ACTUALLY THE BEST I'VE DONE IN THE PAST FEW YEARS.
Gimme some praise, would'ja?
WHY DOES SHE SEEM PROUD OF THAT?

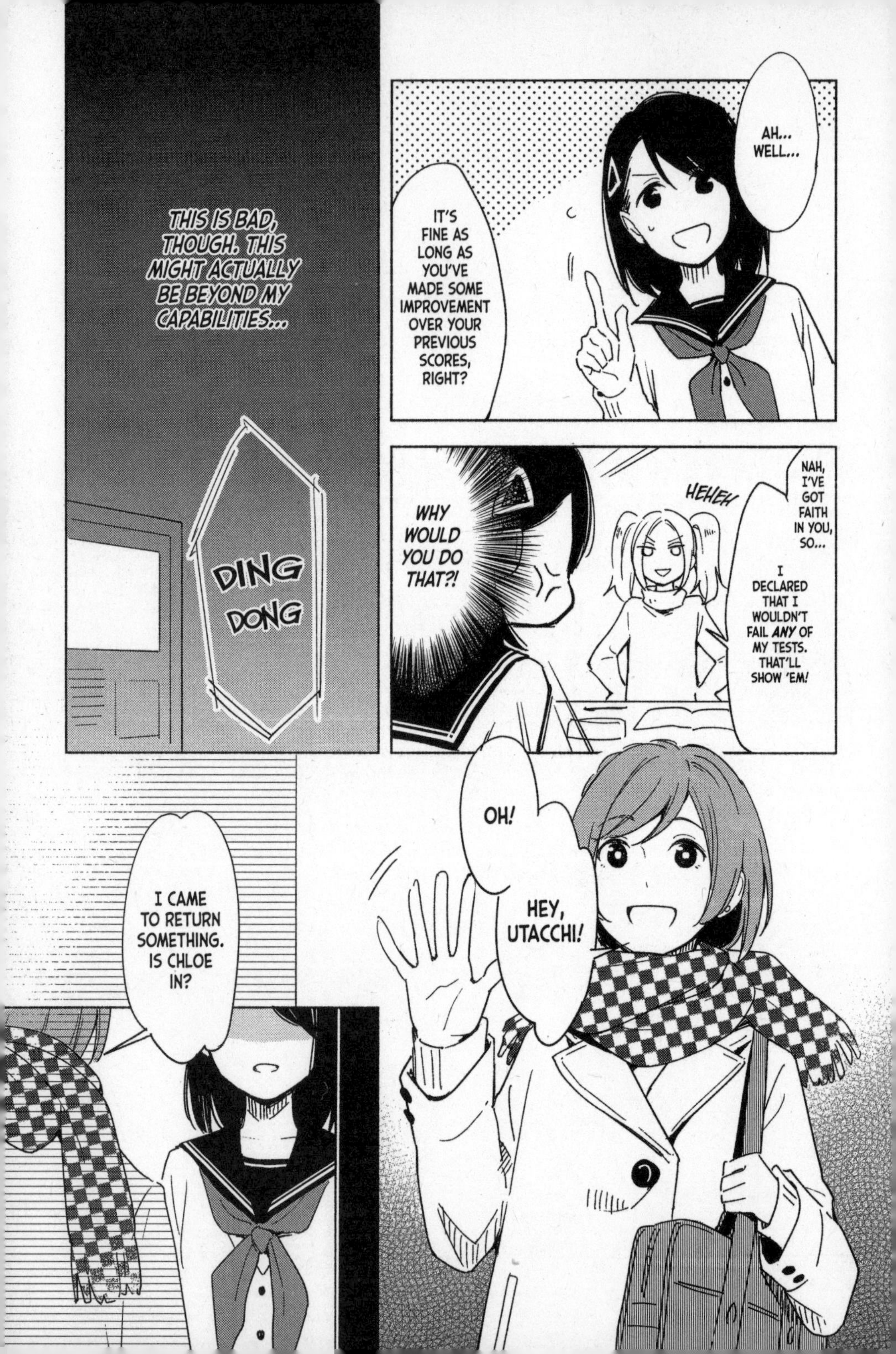
AH... WELL...
IT'S FINE AS LONG AS YOU'VE MADE SOME IMPROVEMENT OVER YOUR PREVIOUS SCORES, RIGHT?
NAH, I'VE GOT FAITH IN YOU, SO...
HEHEH
I DECLARED THAT I WOULDN'T FAIL *ANY* OF MY TESTS. THAT'LL SHOW 'EM!
WHY WOULD YOU DO THAT?!
THIS IS BAD, THOUGH. THIS MIGHT ACTUALLY BE BEYOND MY CAPABILITIES...
DING DONG
OH!
HEY, UTACCHI!
I CAME TO RETURN SOMETHING. IS CHLOE IN?

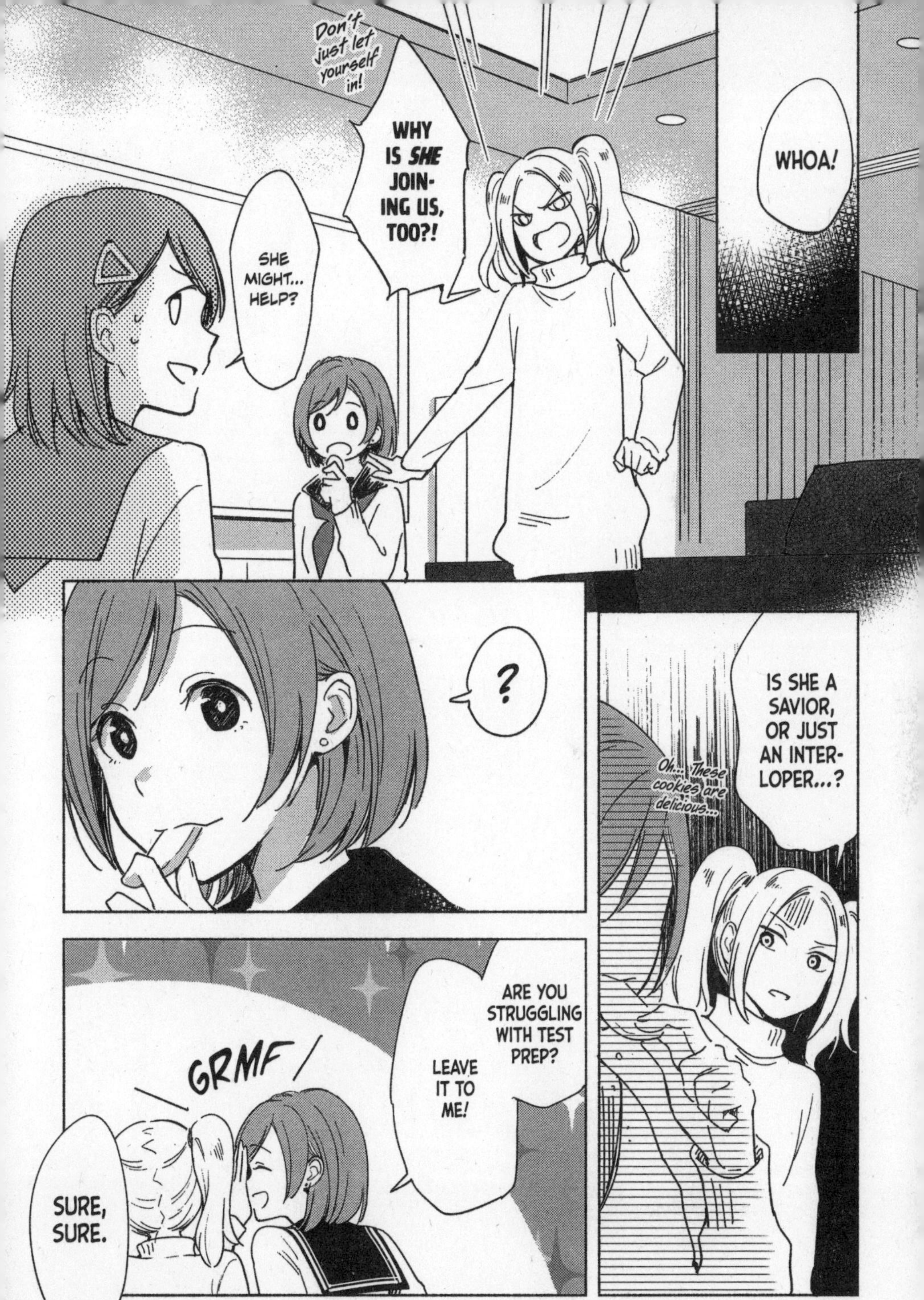
WHOA!
WHY IS SHE JOIN-ING US, TOO?!
Don't just let yourself in!
SHE MIGHT... HELP?
IS SHE A SAVIOR, OR JUST AN INTER-LOPER...?
Oh... These cookies are delicious...
?
ARE YOU STRUGGLING WITH TEST PREP?
LEAVE IT TO ME!
GRMF
SURE, SURE.

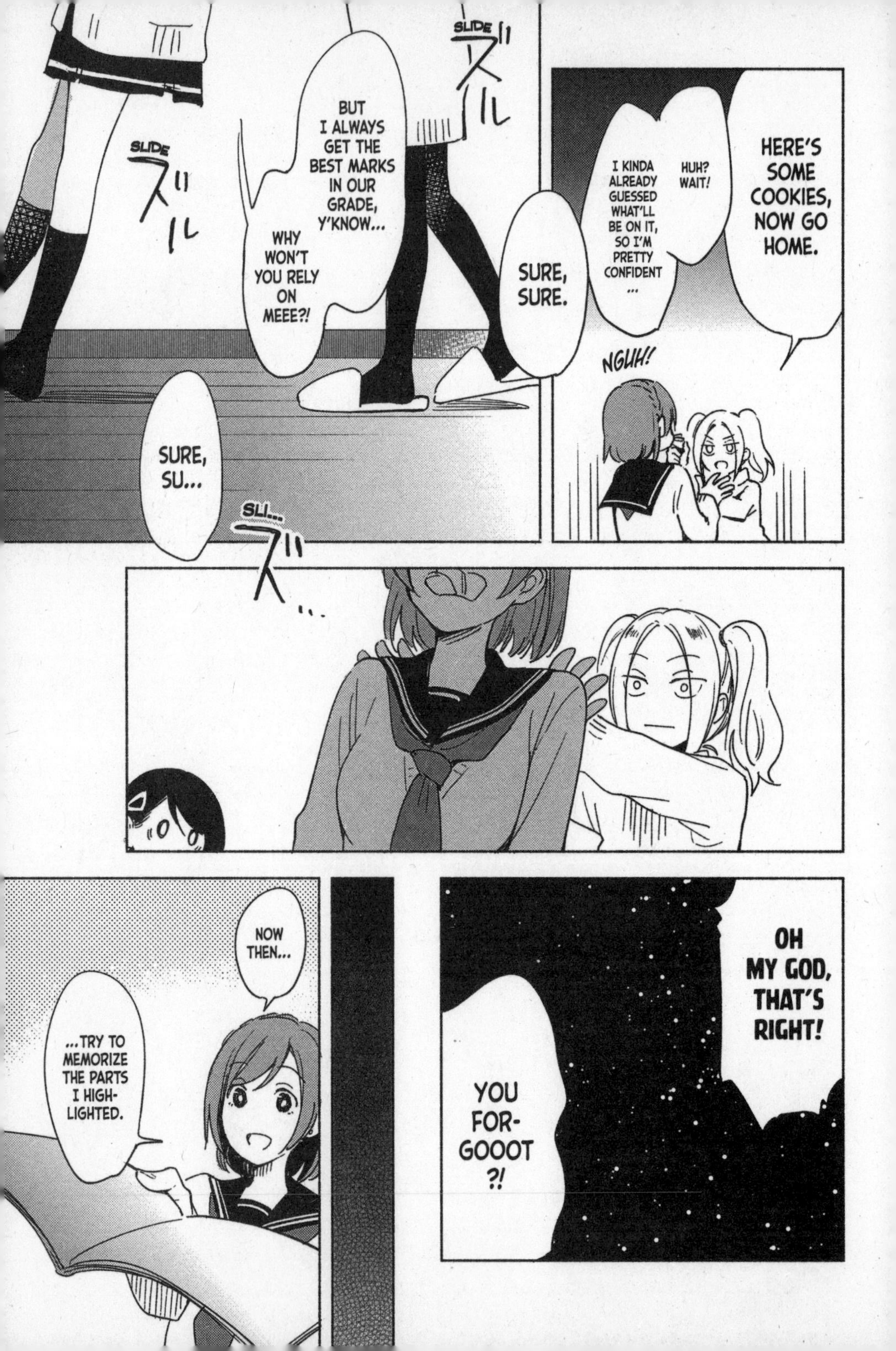
HERE'S SOME COOKIES, NOW GO HOME.
HUH? WAIT!
I KINDA ALREADY GUESSED WHAT'LL BE ON IT, SO I'M PRETTY CONFIDENT...
NGUH!
SURE, SURE.
SLIDE
BUT I ALWAYS GET THE BEST MARKS IN OUR GRADE, Y'KNOW...
WHY WON'T YOU RELY ON MEEE?!
SLIDE
SURE, SU...
SLI...
OH MY GOD, THAT'S RIGHT!
YOU FOR-GOOOT?!
NOW THEN...
...TRY TO MEMORIZE THE PARTS I HIGH-LIGHTED.

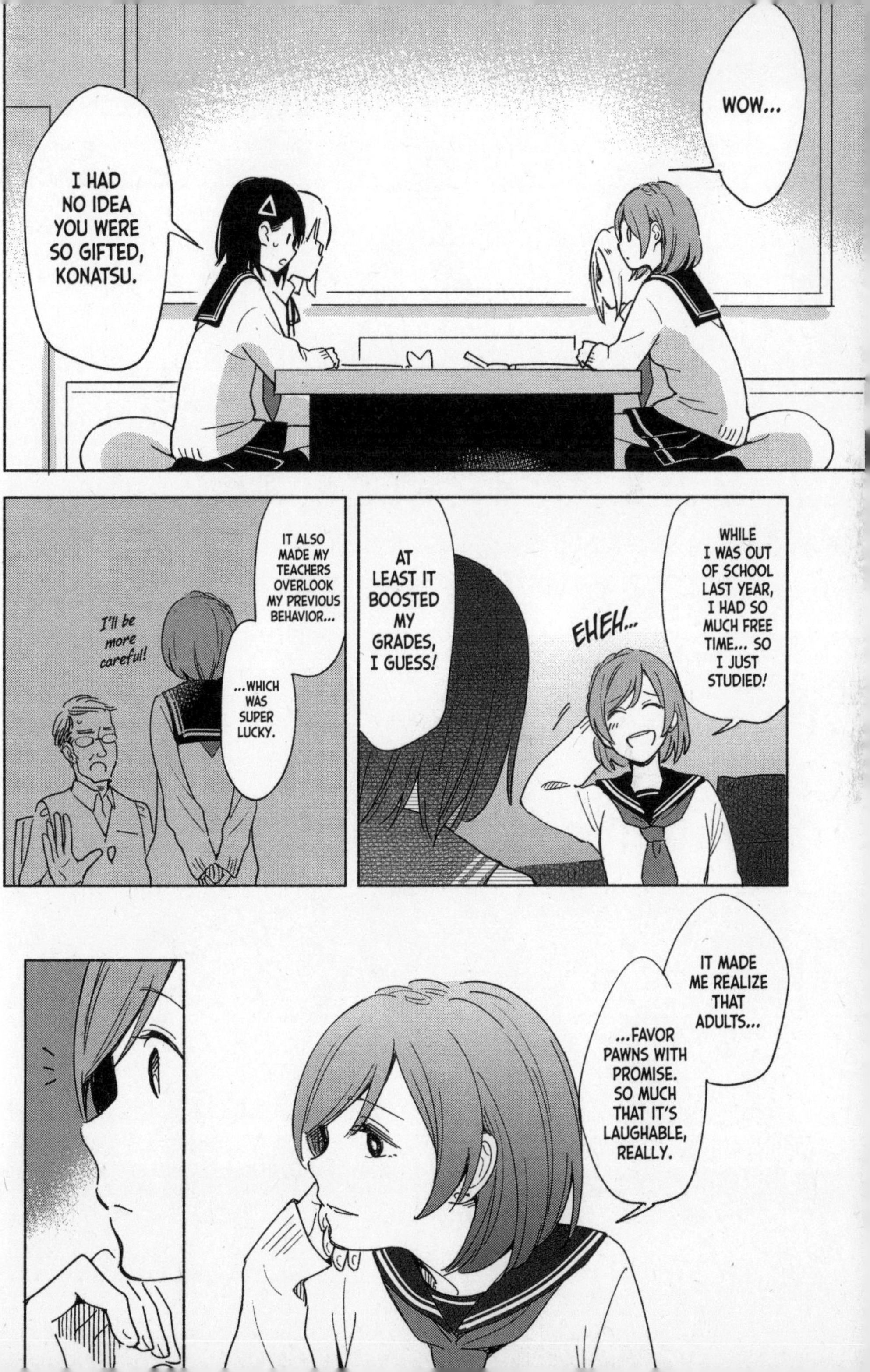
WOW...
I HAD NO IDEA YOU WERE SO GIFTED, KONATSU.
WHILE I WAS OUT OF SCHOOL LAST YEAR, I HAD SO MUCH FREE TIME... SO I JUST STUDIED!
EHEH...
AT LEAST IT BOOSTED MY GRADES, I GUESS!
IT ALSO MADE MY TEACHERS OVERLOOK MY PREVIOUS BEHAVIOR...
I'll be more careful!
...WHICH WAS SUPER LUCKY.
IT MADE ME REALIZE THAT ADULTS...
...FAVOR PAWNS WITH PROMISE. SO MUCH THAT IT'S LAUGHABLE, REALLY.

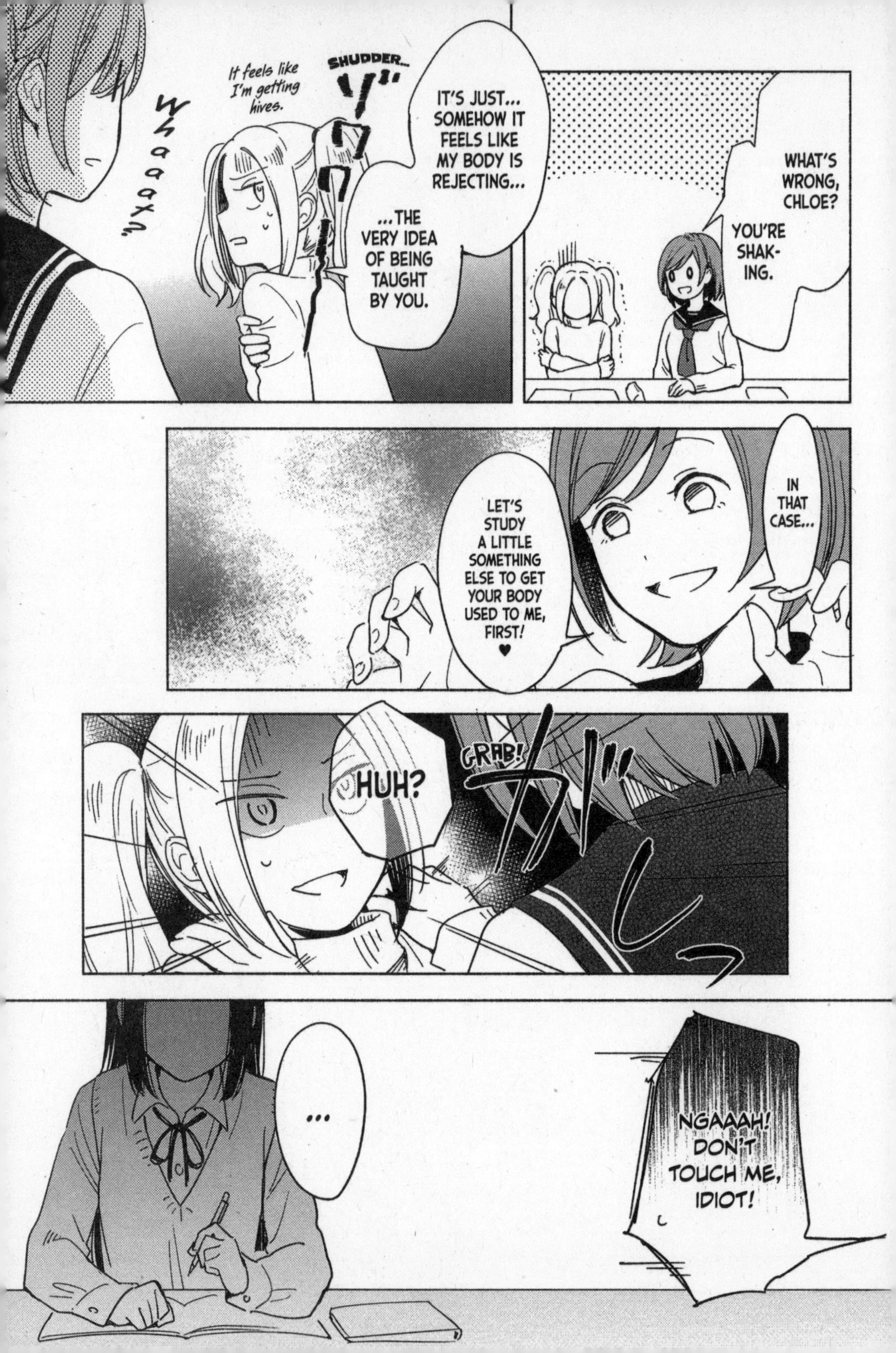
WHAT'S WRONG, CHLOE?
YOU'RE SHAK-ING.
SHUDDER...
IT'S JUST... SOMEHOW IT FEELS LIKE MY BODY IS REJECTING...
...THE VERY IDEA OF BEING TAUGHT BY YOU.
It feels like I'm getting hives.
Whaaaat?
IN THAT CASE...
LET'S STUDY A LITTLE SOMETHING ELSE TO GET YOUR BODY USED TO ME, FIRST! ♥
GRAB!
HUH?
NGAAAH! DON'T TOUCH ME, IDIOT!
...

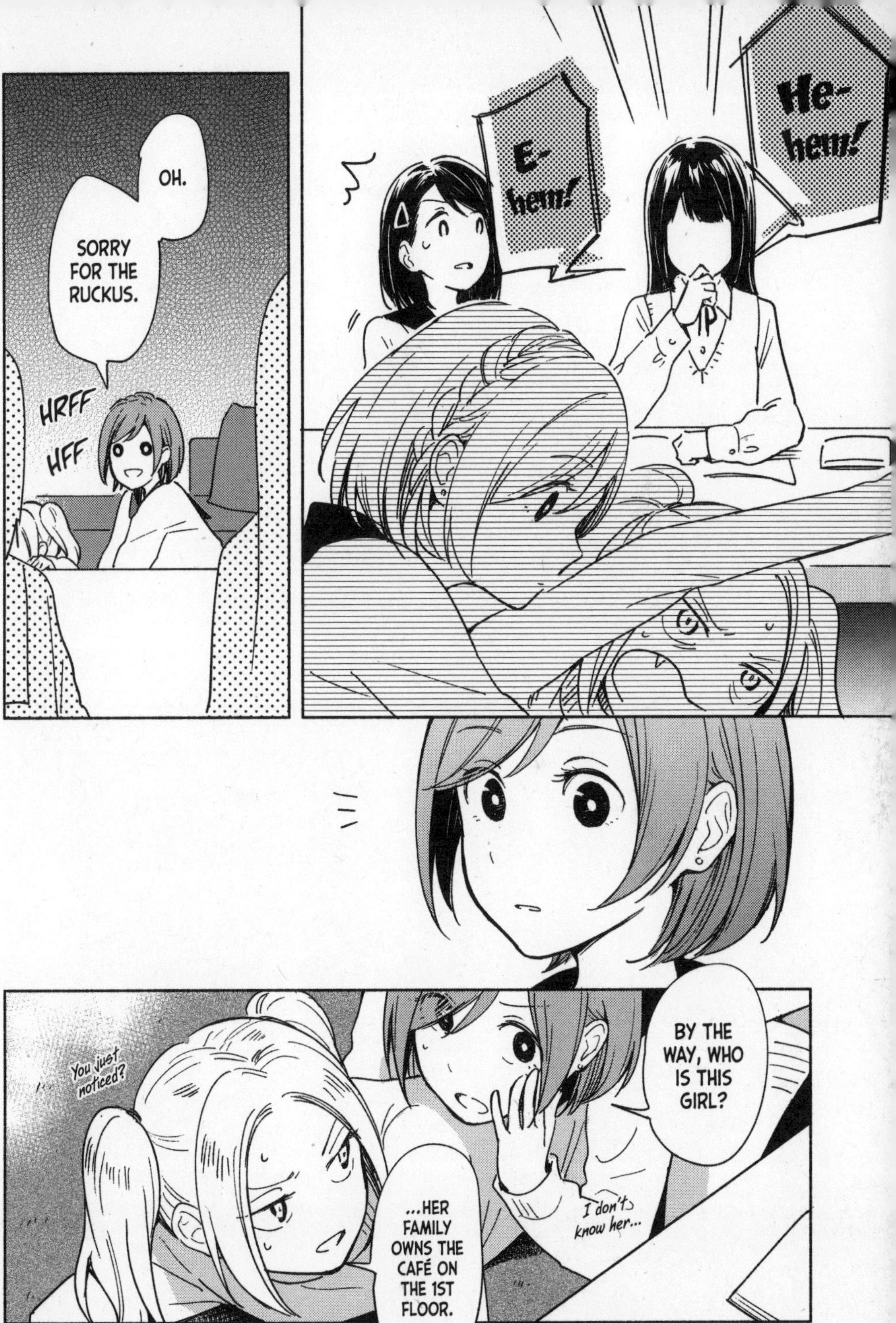
He-hem!
E-hem!
OH.
SORRY FOR THE RUCKUS.
HRFF HFF
BY THE WAY, WHO IS THIS GIRL?
I don't know her...
...HER FAMILY OWNS THE CAFÉ ON THE 1ST FLOOR.
You just noticed?

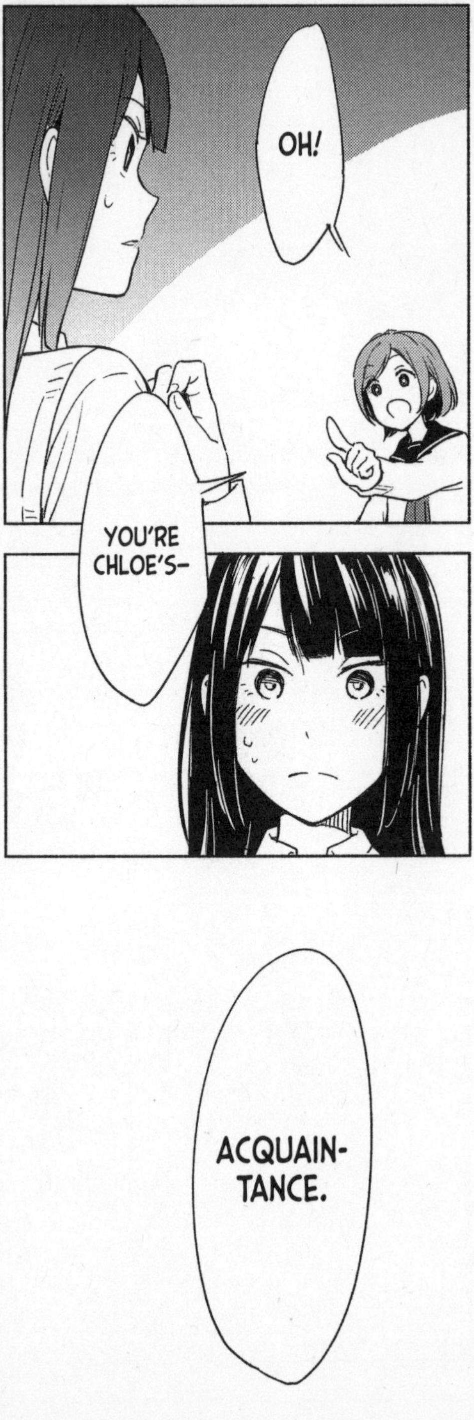
OH!
YOU'RE CHLOE'S-
ACQUAIN-
TANCE.

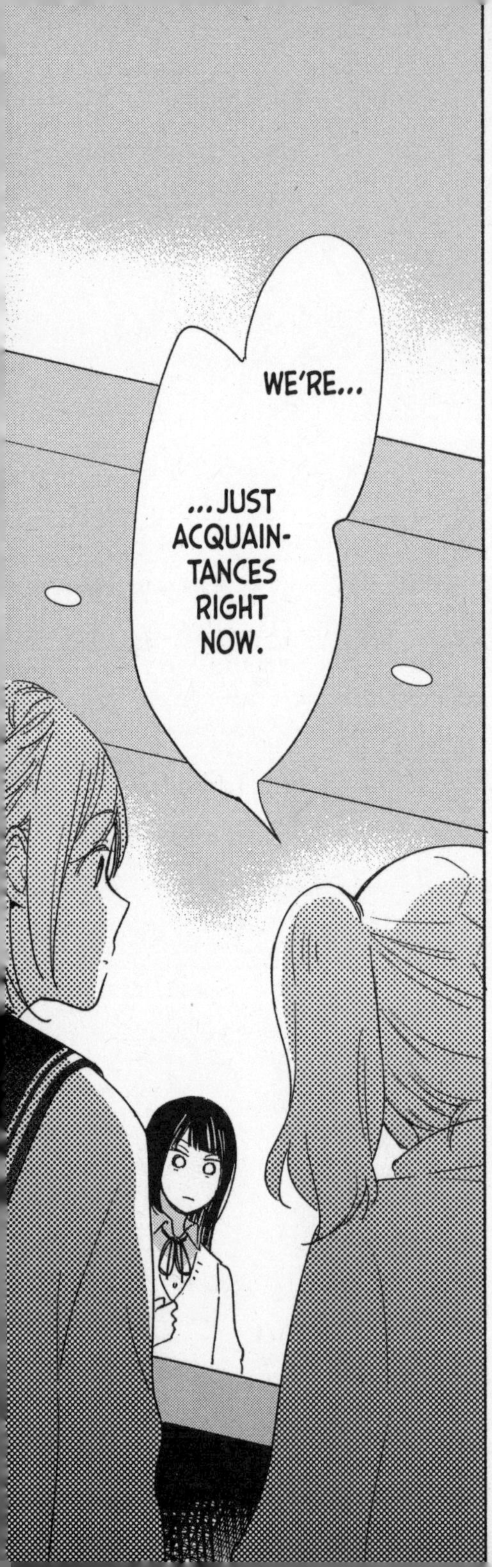
WE'RE...
...JUST ACQUAIN-
TANCES RIGHT NOW.

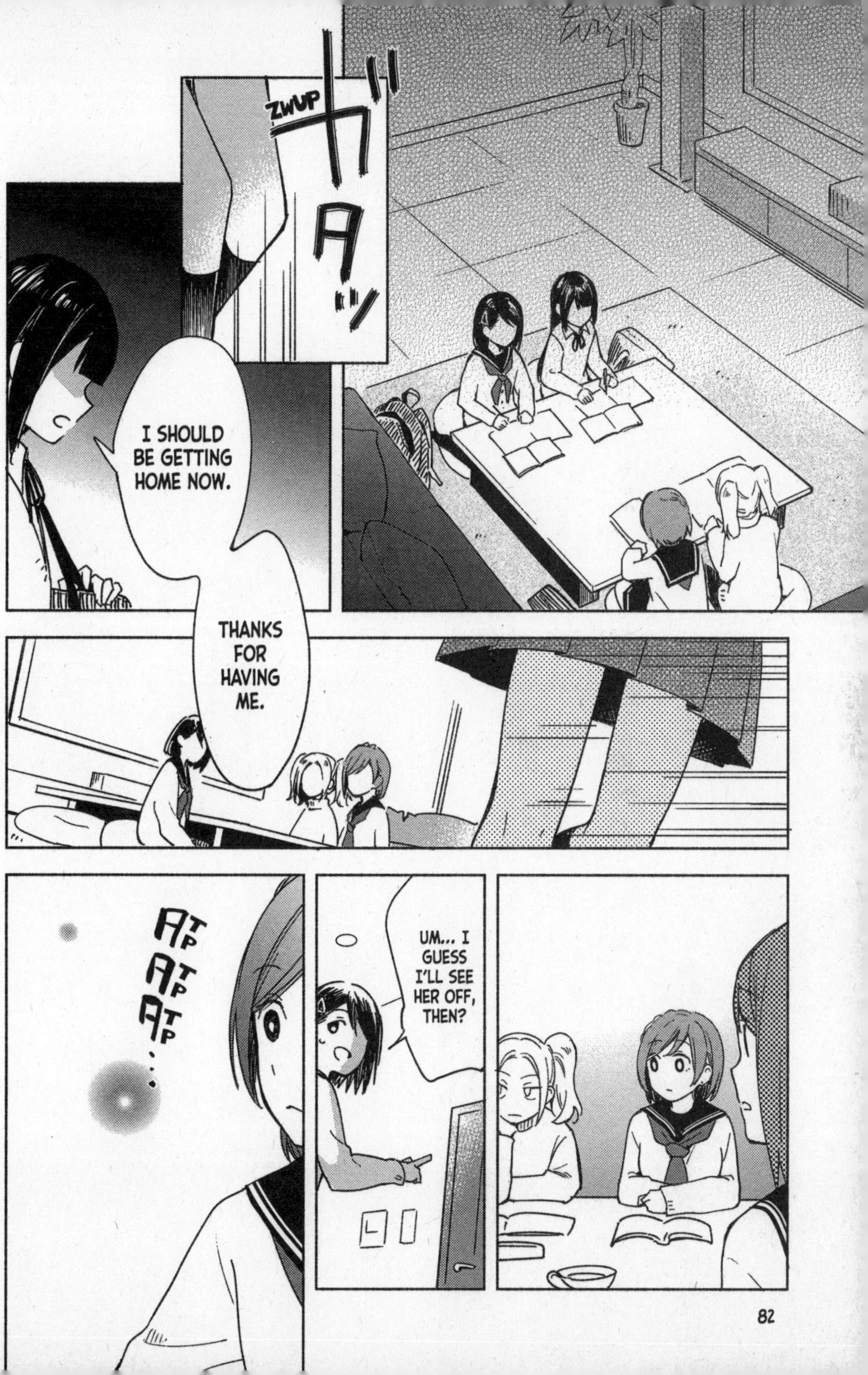
ZWUP
ガタッ
I SHOULD BE GETTING HOME NOW.
THANKS FOR HAVING ME.
UM... I GUESS I'LL SEE HER OFF, THEN?
TAP TAP TAP...

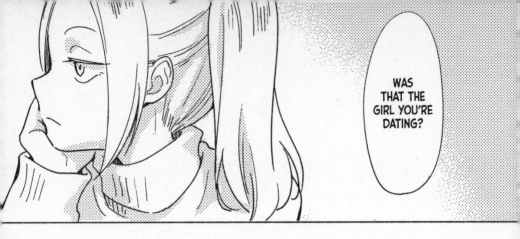

WAS THAT THE GIRL YOU'RE DATING?

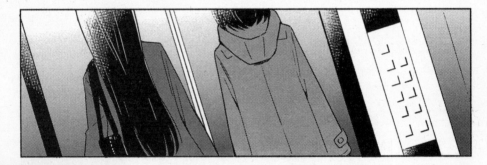

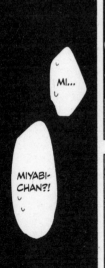

MI...

MIYABI-CHAN?!

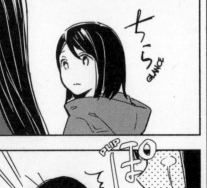

GLANCE

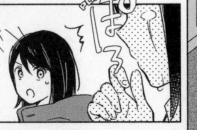

...

WRRR

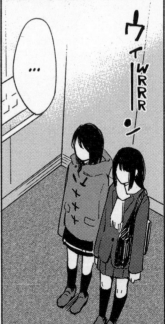

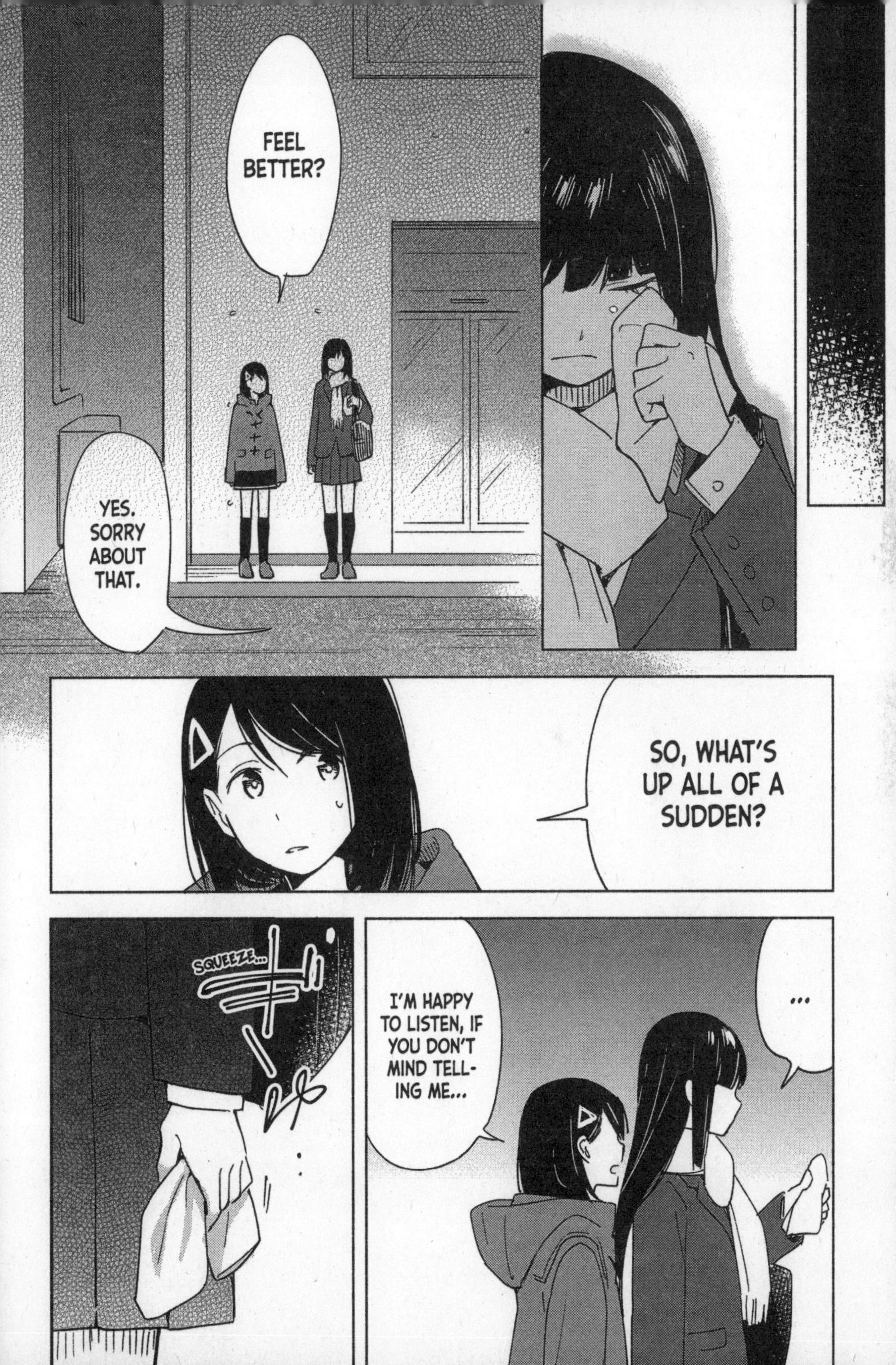
FEEL BETTER?
YES. SORRY ABOUT THAT.
SO, WHAT'S UP ALL OF A SUDDEN?
...
I'M HAPPY TO LISTEN, IF YOU DON'T MIND TELL-ING ME...
SQUEEZE...

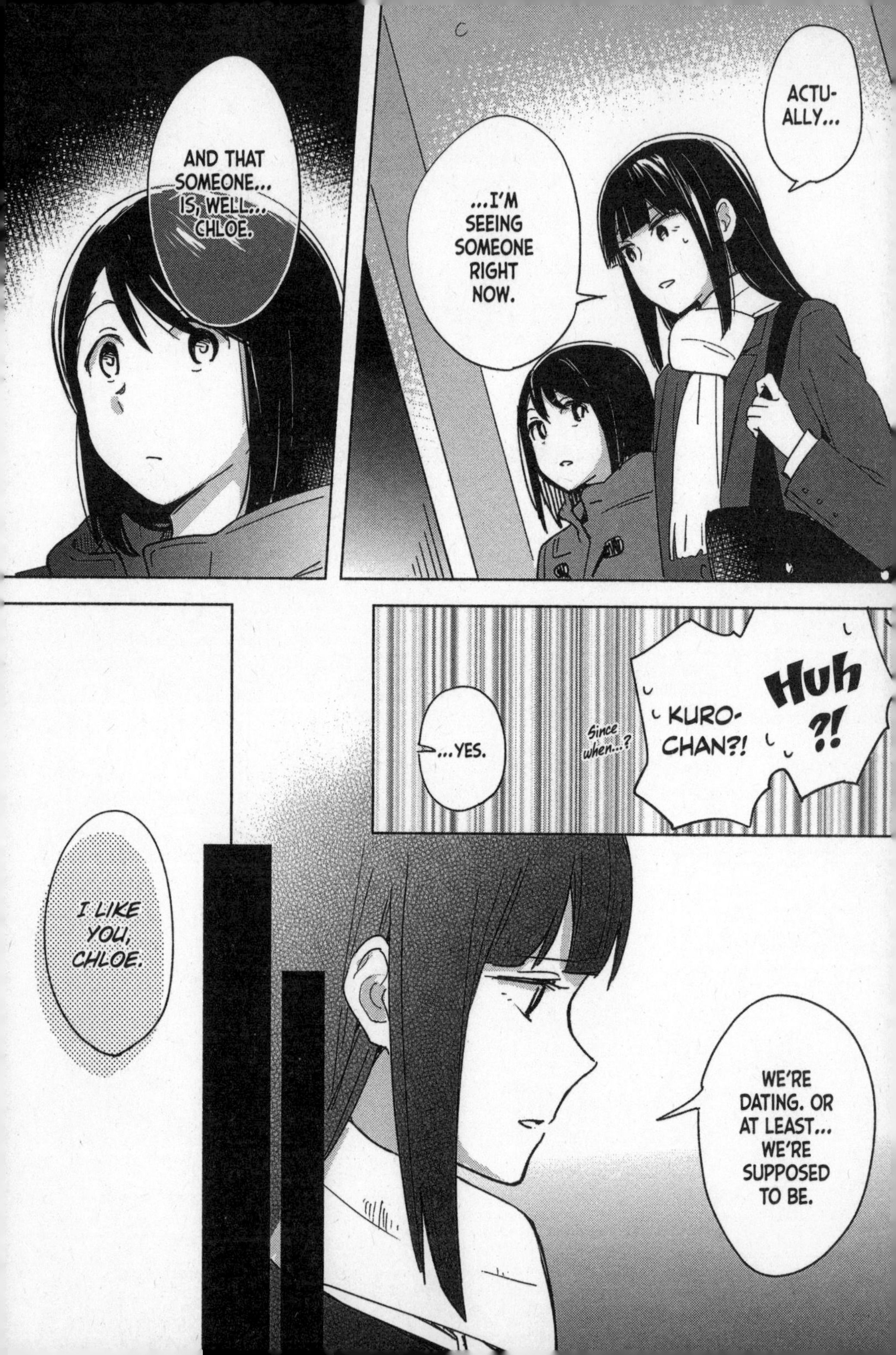
ACTU-ALLY...
...I'M SEEING SOMEONE RIGHT NOW.
AND THAT SOMEONE... IS, WELL... CHLOE.
HUH ?!
KURO-CHAN?!
Since when...?
...YES.
WE'RE DATING. OR AT LEAST... WE'RE SUPPOSED TO BE.
I LIKE YOU, CHLOE.

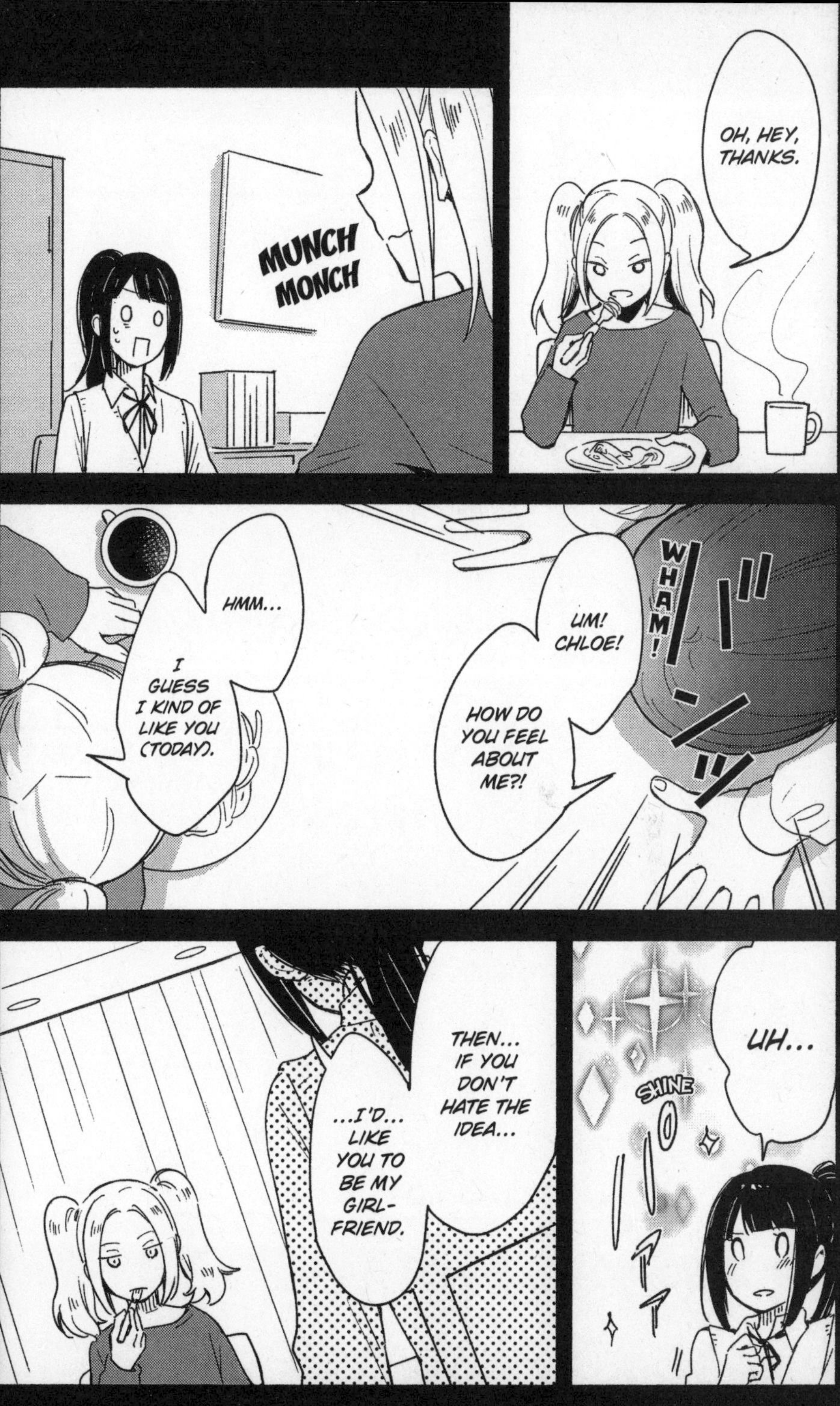
OH, HEY, THANKS.
MUNCH MONCH
UM! CHLOE!
HOW DO YOU FEEL ABOUT ME?!
WHAM!
HMM...
I GUESS I KIND OF LIKE YOU (TODAY).
UH...
SHINE
THEN... IF YOU DON'T HATE THE IDEA...
...I'D... LIKE YOU TO BE MY GIRL-FRIEND.

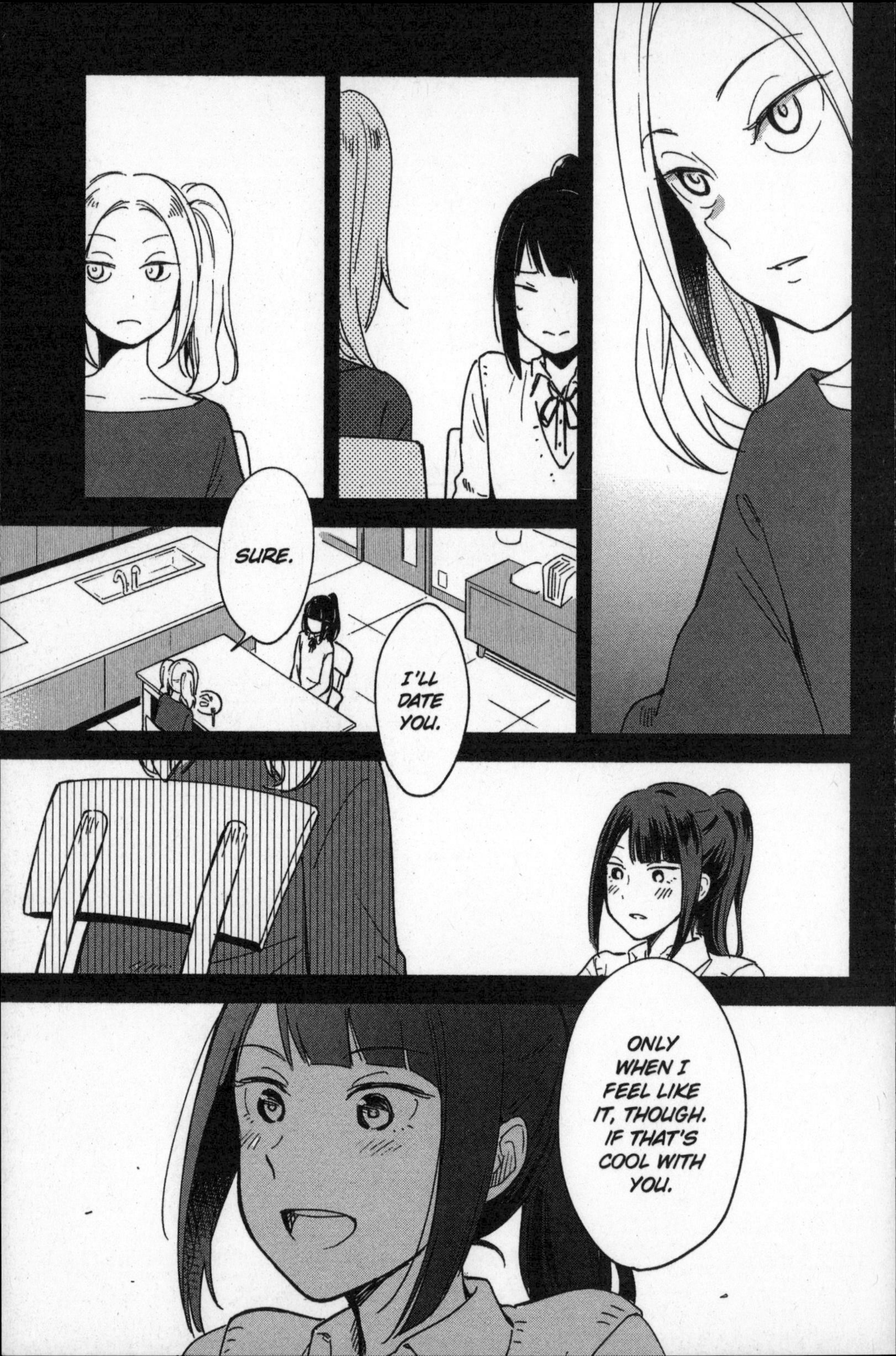
SURE.
I'LL DATE YOU.
ONLY WHEN I FEEL LIKE IT, THOUGH. IF THAT'S COOL WITH YOU.

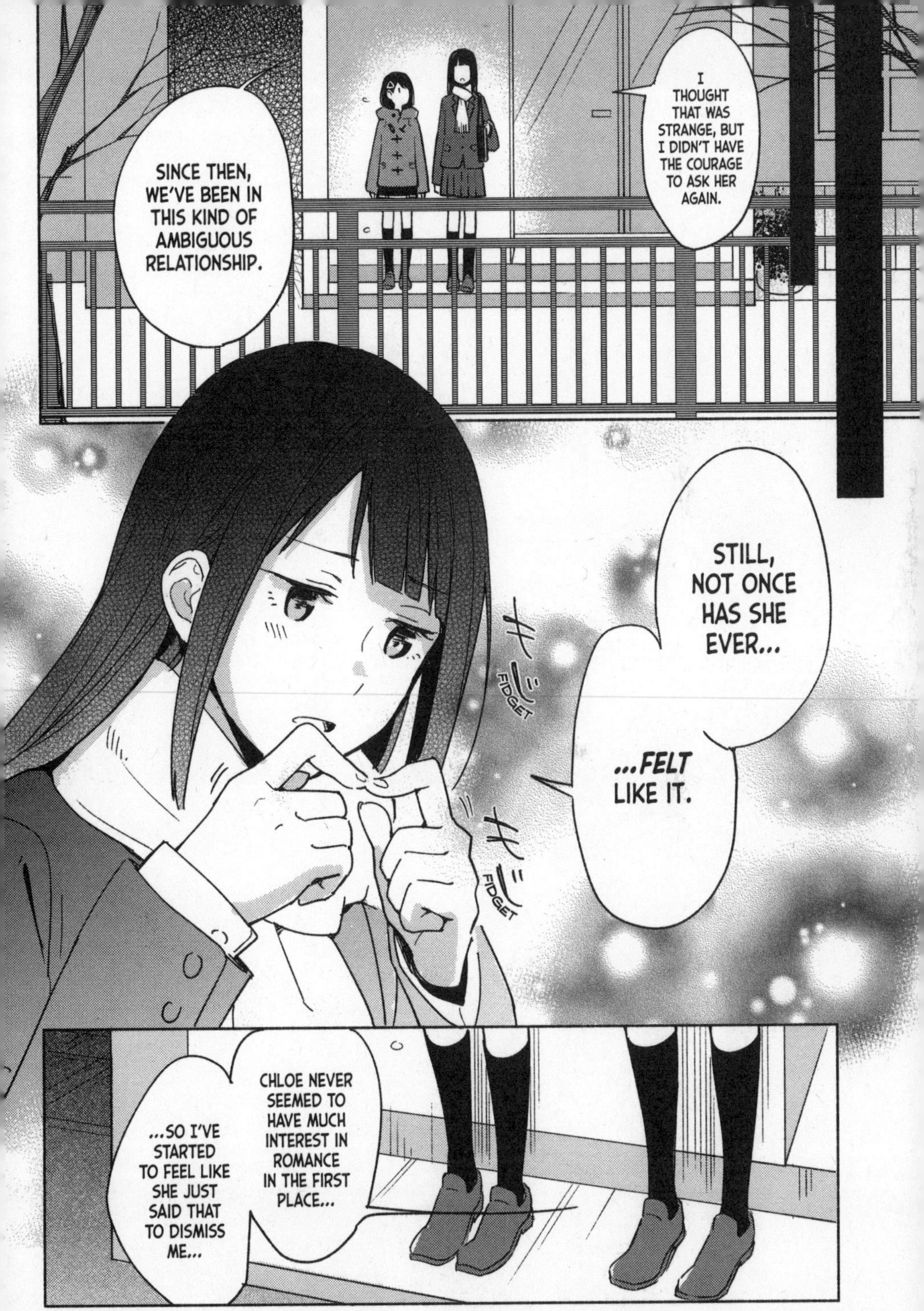
I THOUGHT THAT WAS STRANGE, BUT I DIDN'T HAVE THE COURAGE TO ASK HER AGAIN.
SINCE THEN, WE'VE BEEN IN THIS KIND OF AMBIGUOUS RELATIONSHIP.
STILL, NOT ONCE HAS SHE EVER...
...*FELT* LIKE IT.
FIDGET
FIDGET
CHLOE NEVER SEEMED TO HAVE MUCH INTEREST IN ROMANCE IN THE FIRST PLACE...
...SO I'VE STARTED TO FEEL LIKE SHE JUST SAID THAT TO DISMISS ME...

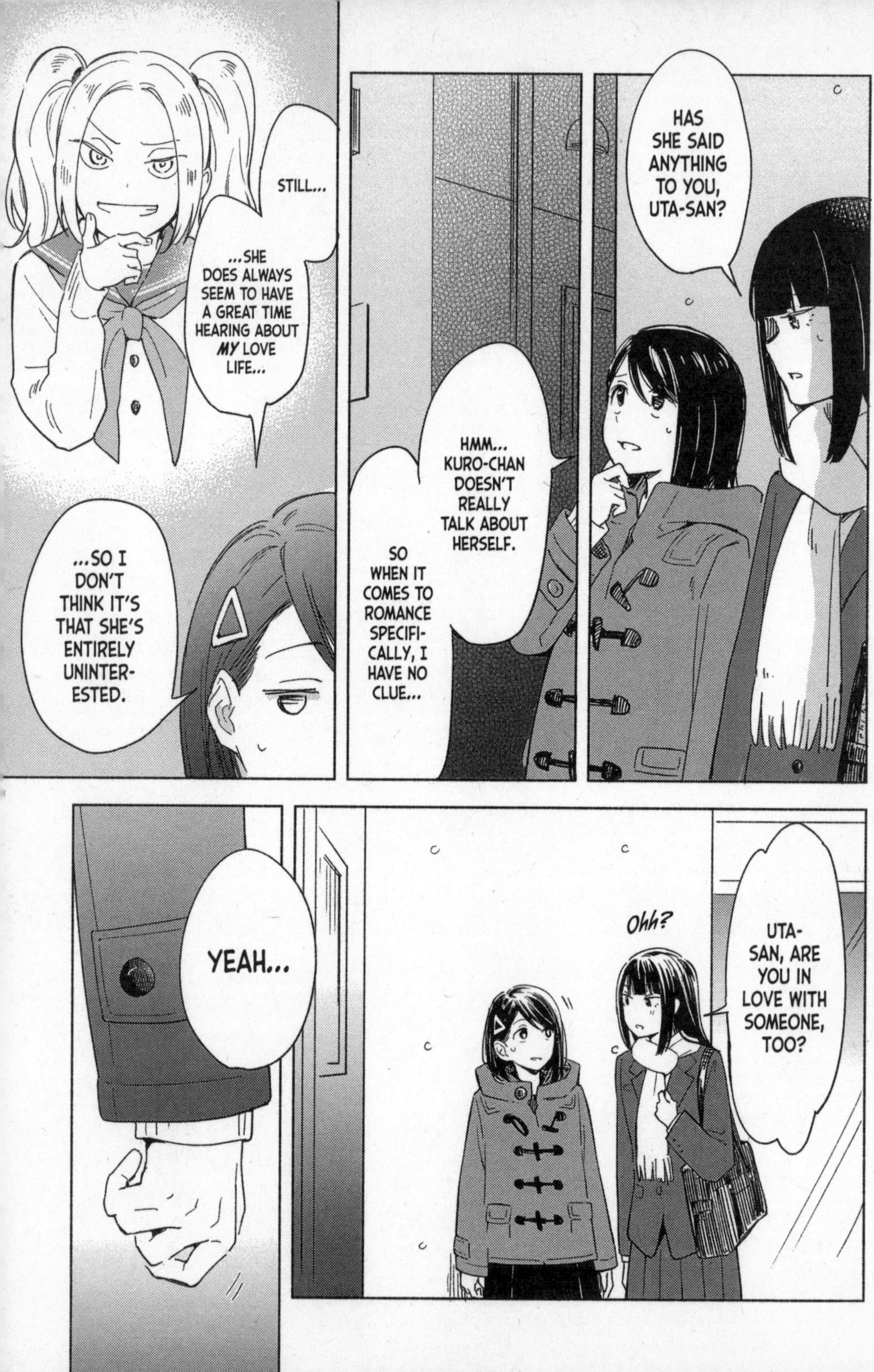
HAS SHE SAID ANYTHING TO YOU, UTA-SAN?
HMM... KURO-CHAN DOESN'T REALLY TALK ABOUT HERSELF.
SO WHEN IT COMES TO ROMANCE SPECIFI-CALLY, I HAVE NO CLUE...
STILL...
...SHE DOES ALWAYS SEEM TO HAVE A GREAT TIME HEARING ABOUT *MY* LOVE LIFE...
...SO I DON'T THINK IT'S THAT SHE'S ENTIRELY UNINTER-ESTED.
UTA-SAN, ARE YOU IN LOVE WITH SOMEONE, TOO?
Ohh?
YEAH...

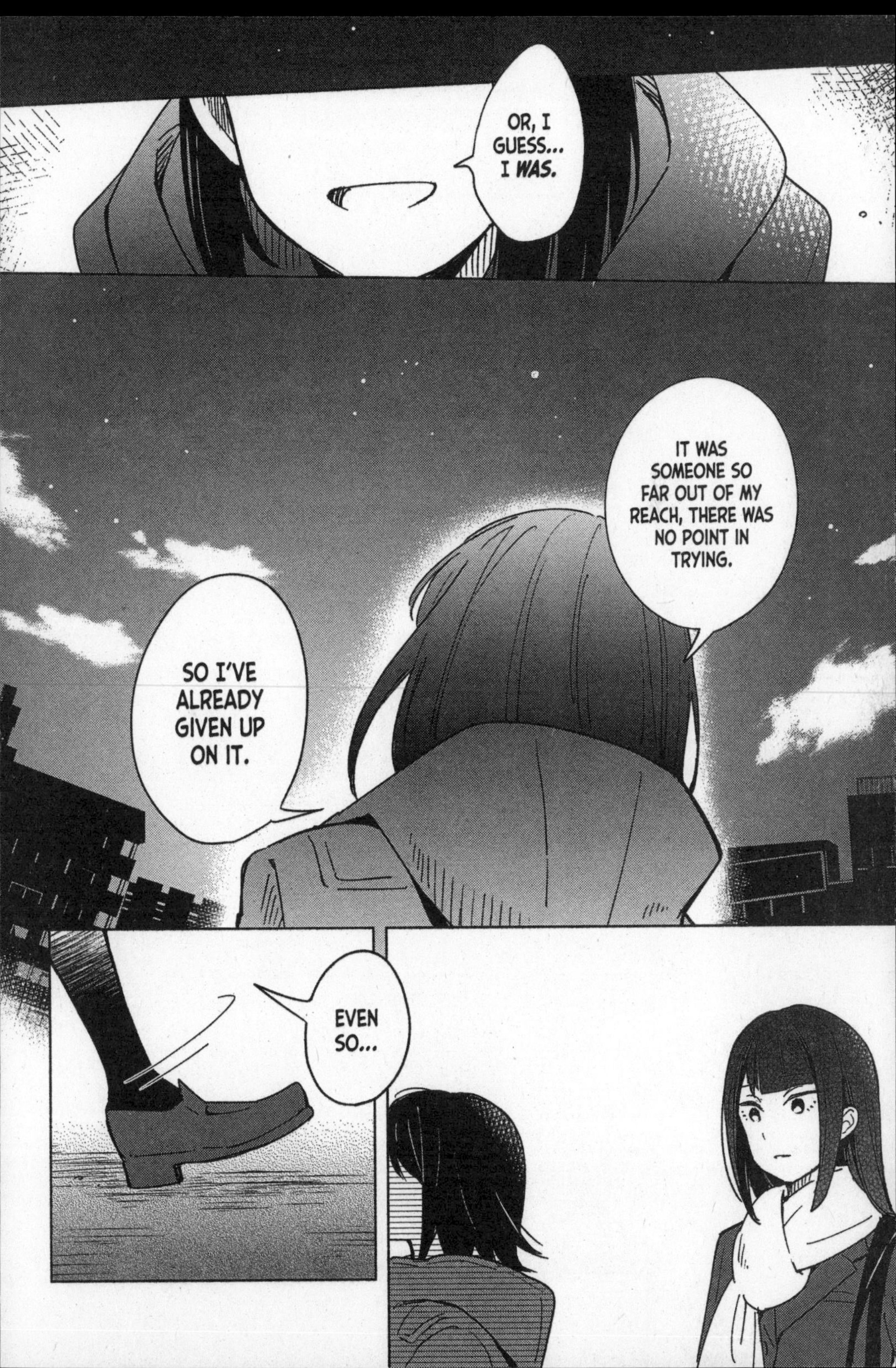
OR, I GUESS... I *WAS.*
IT WAS SOMEONE SO FAR OUT OF MY REACH, THERE WAS NO POINT IN TRYING.
SO I'VE ALREADY GIVEN UP ON IT.
EVEN SO...

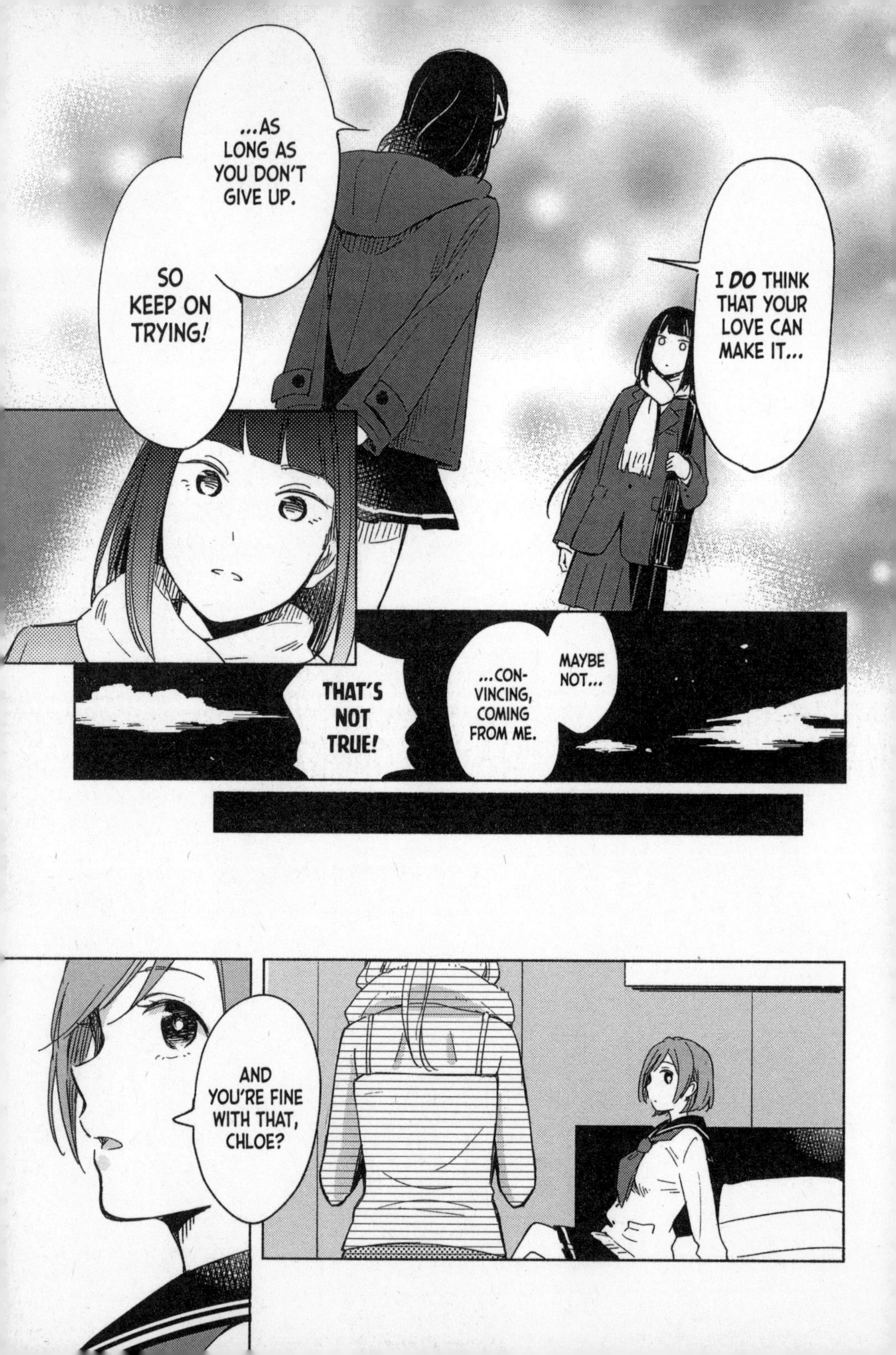
I DO THINK THAT YOUR LOVE CAN MAKE IT...
...AS LONG AS YOU DON'T GIVE UP.
SO KEEP ON TRYING!
MAYBE NOT...
...CON-VINCING, COMING FROM ME.
THAT'S NOT TRUE!
AND YOU'RE FINE WITH THAT, CHLOE?

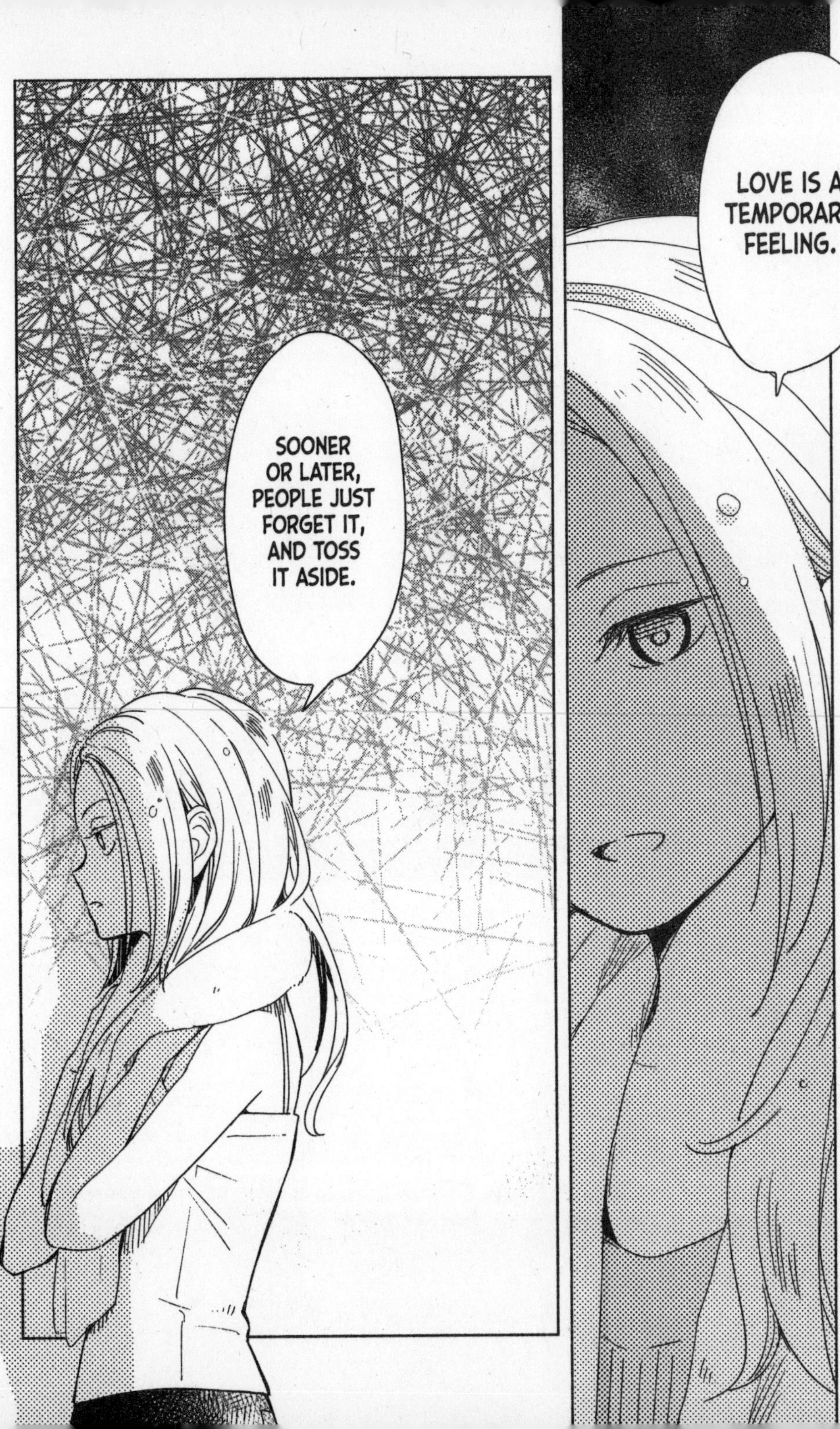
LOVE IS A TEMPORARY FEELING.
SOONER OR LATER, PEOPLE JUST FORGET IT, AND TOSS IT ASIDE.

If I Could
Reach You

If I Could
Reach You

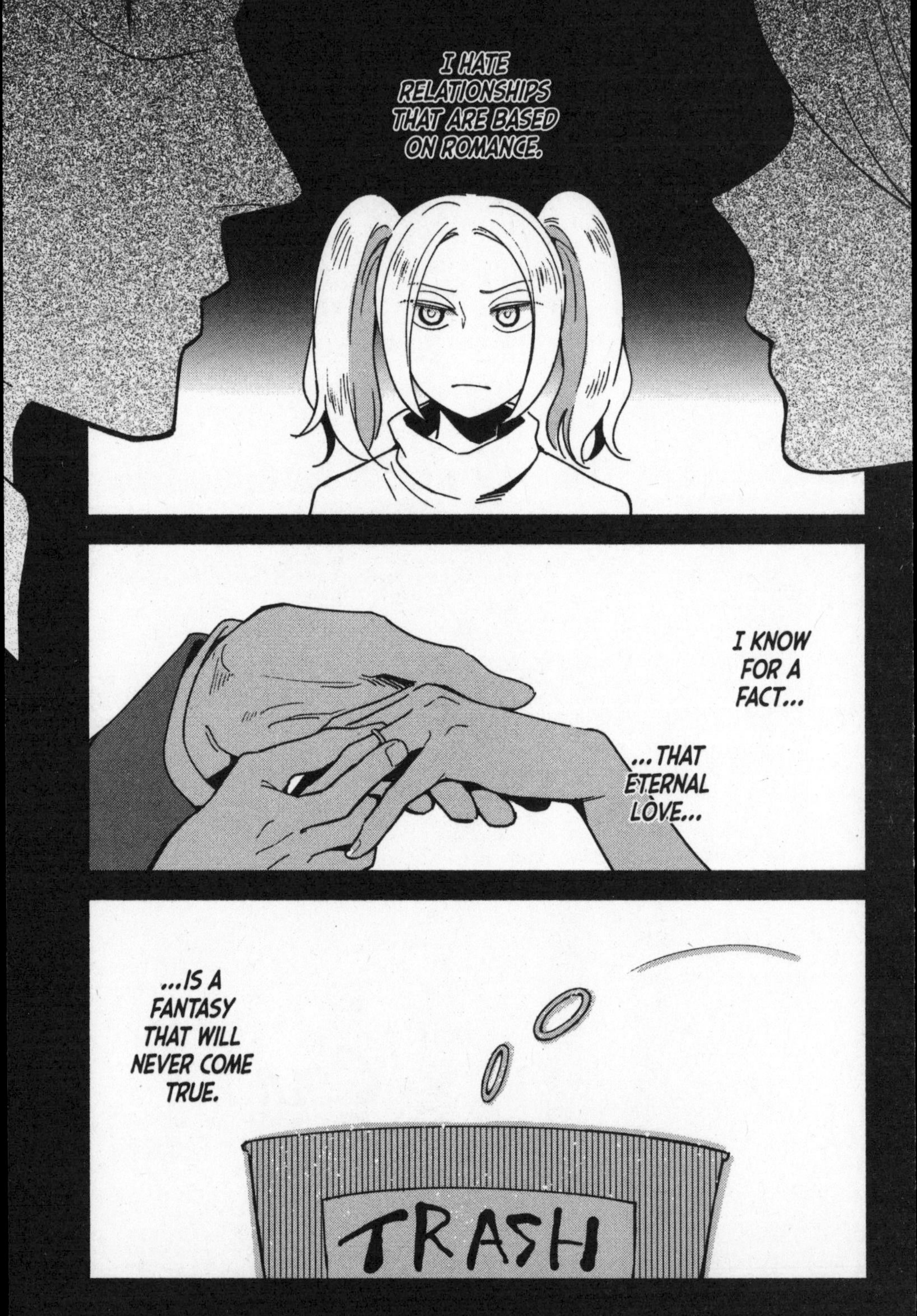
I HATE RELATIONSHIPS THAT ARE BASED ON ROMANCE.
I KNOW FOR A FACT...
...THAT ETERNAL LOVE...
...IS A FANTASY THAT WILL NEVER COME TRUE.
TRASH

Chapter 9

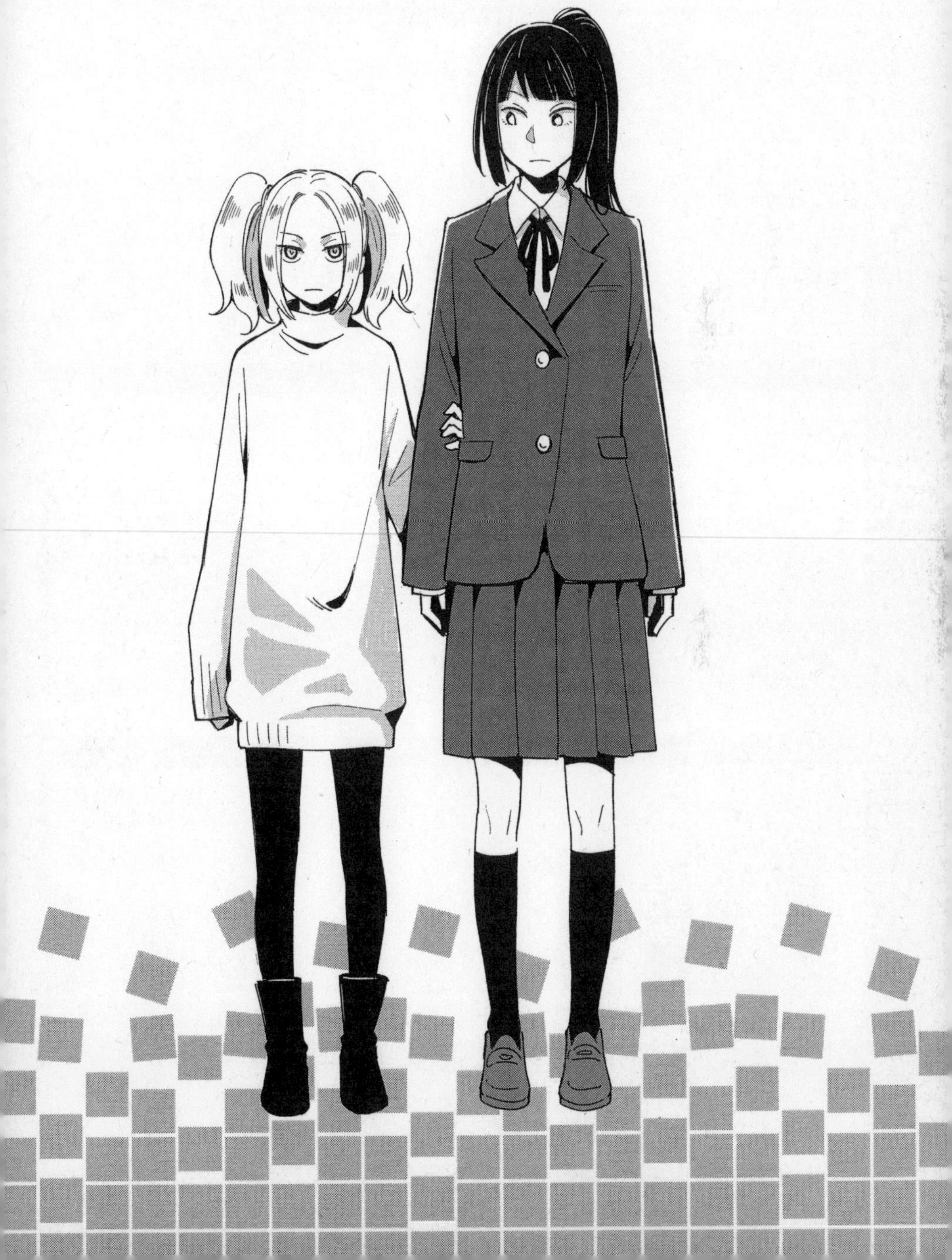

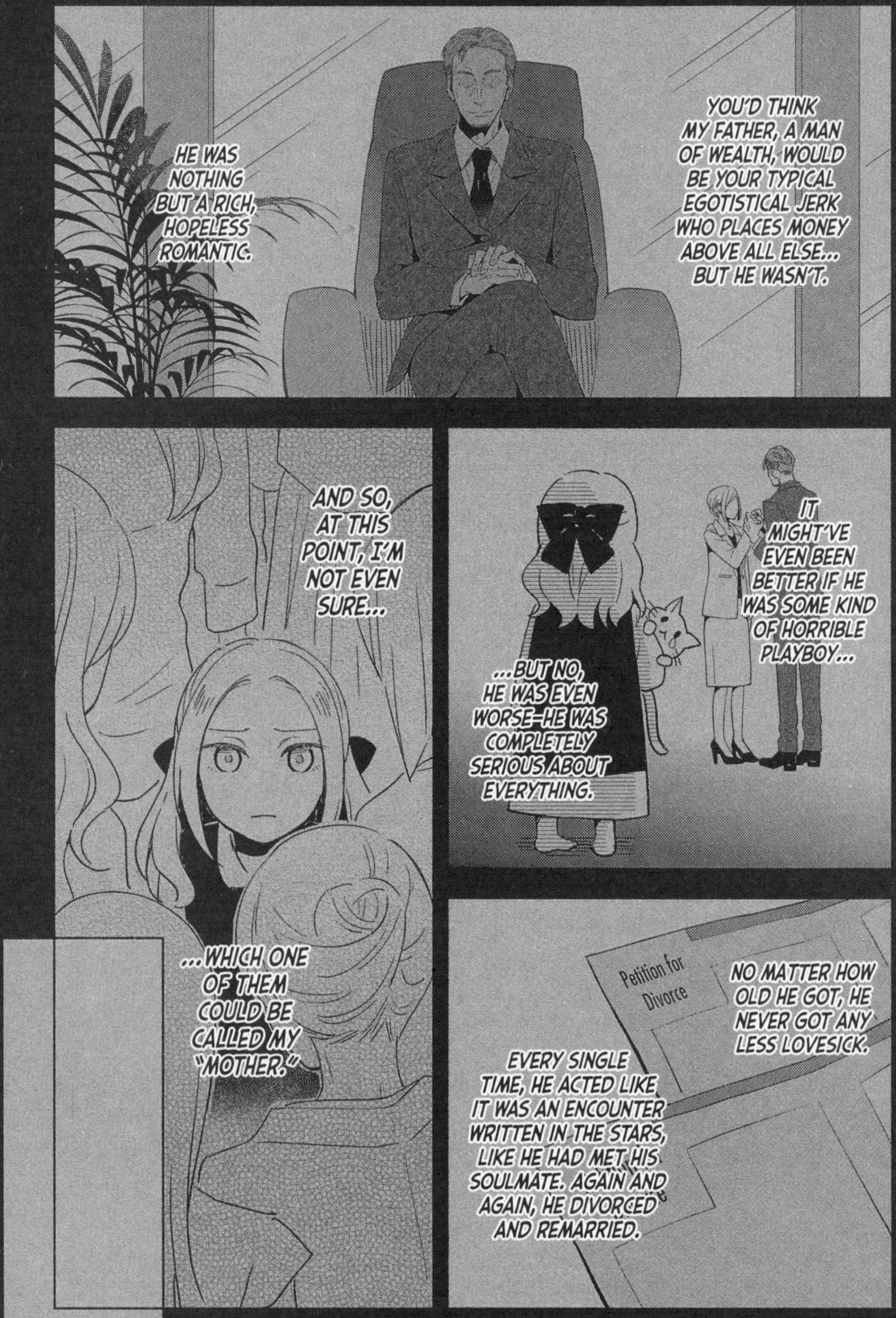
YOU'D THINK MY FATHER, A MAN OF WEALTH, WOULD BE YOUR TYPICAL EGOTISTICAL JERK WHO PLACES MONEY ABOVE ALL ELSE... BUT HE WASN'T.
HE WAS NOTHING BUT A RICH, HOPELESS ROMANTIC.
IT MIGHT'VE EVEN BEEN BETTER IF HE WAS SOME KIND OF HORRIBLE PLAYBOY...
...BUT NO, HE WAS EVEN WORSE—HE WAS COMPLETELY SERIOUS ABOUT EVERYTHING.
NO MATTER HOW OLD HE GOT, HE NEVER GOT ANY LESS LOVESICK.
Petition for Divorce
EVERY SINGLE TIME, HE ACTED LIKE IT WAS AN ENCOUNTER WRITTEN IN THE STARS, LIKE HE HAD MET HIS SOULMATE. AGAIN AND AGAIN, HE DIVORCED AND REMARRIED.
AND SO, AT THIS POINT, I'M NOT EVEN SURE...
...WHICH ONE OF THEM COULD BE CALLED MY "MOTHER."

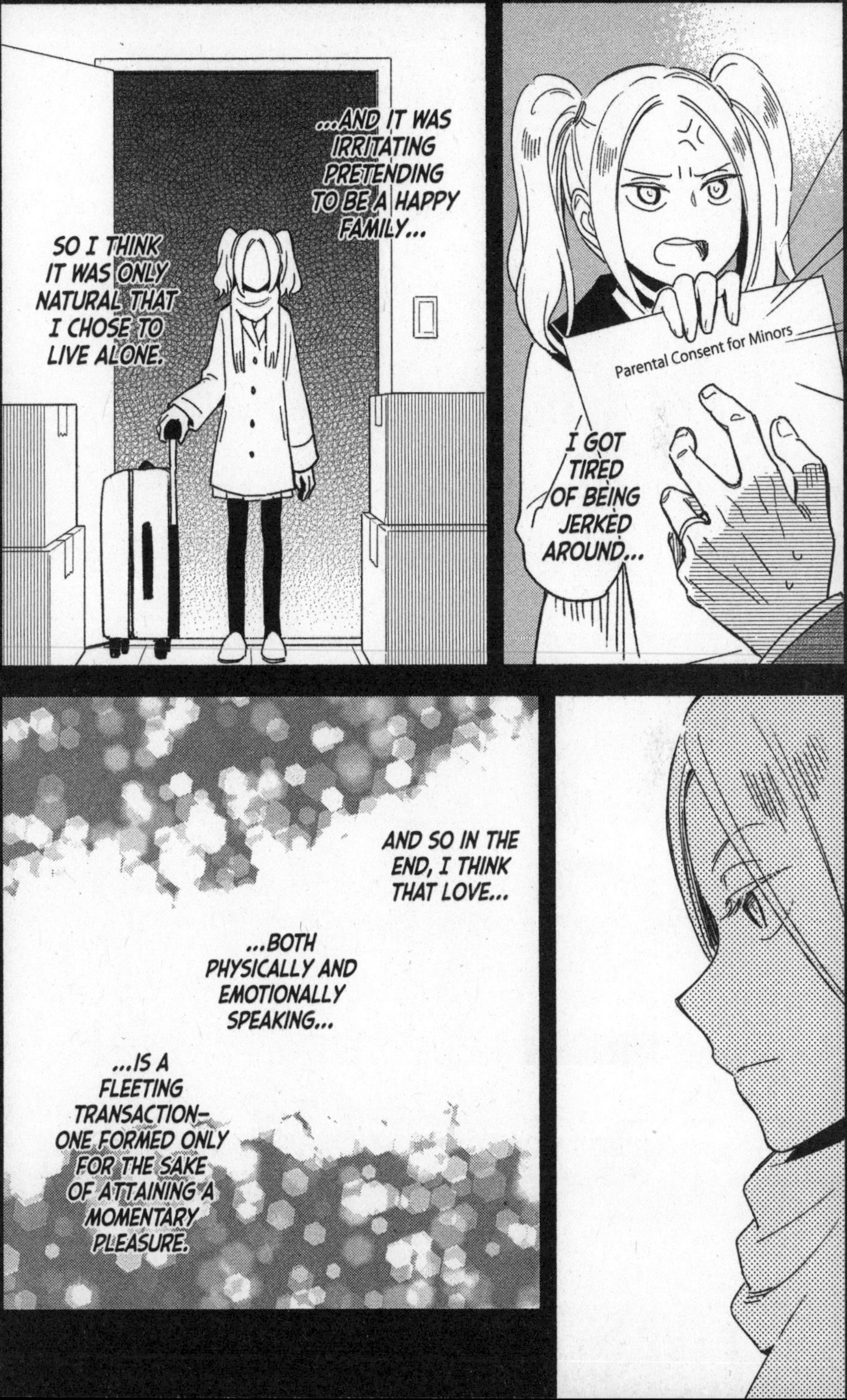
Parental Consent for Minors
I GOT TIRED OF BEING JERKED AROUND...
...AND IT WAS IRRITATING PRETENDING TO BE A HAPPY FAMILY...
SO I THINK IT WAS ONLY NATURAL THAT I CHOSE TO LIVE ALONE.
AND SO IN THE END, I THINK THAT LOVE...
...BOTH PHYSICALLY AND EMOTIONALLY SPEAKING...
...IS A FLEETING TRANSACTION– ONE FORMED ONLY FOR THE SAKE OF ATTAINING A MOMENTARY PLEASURE.

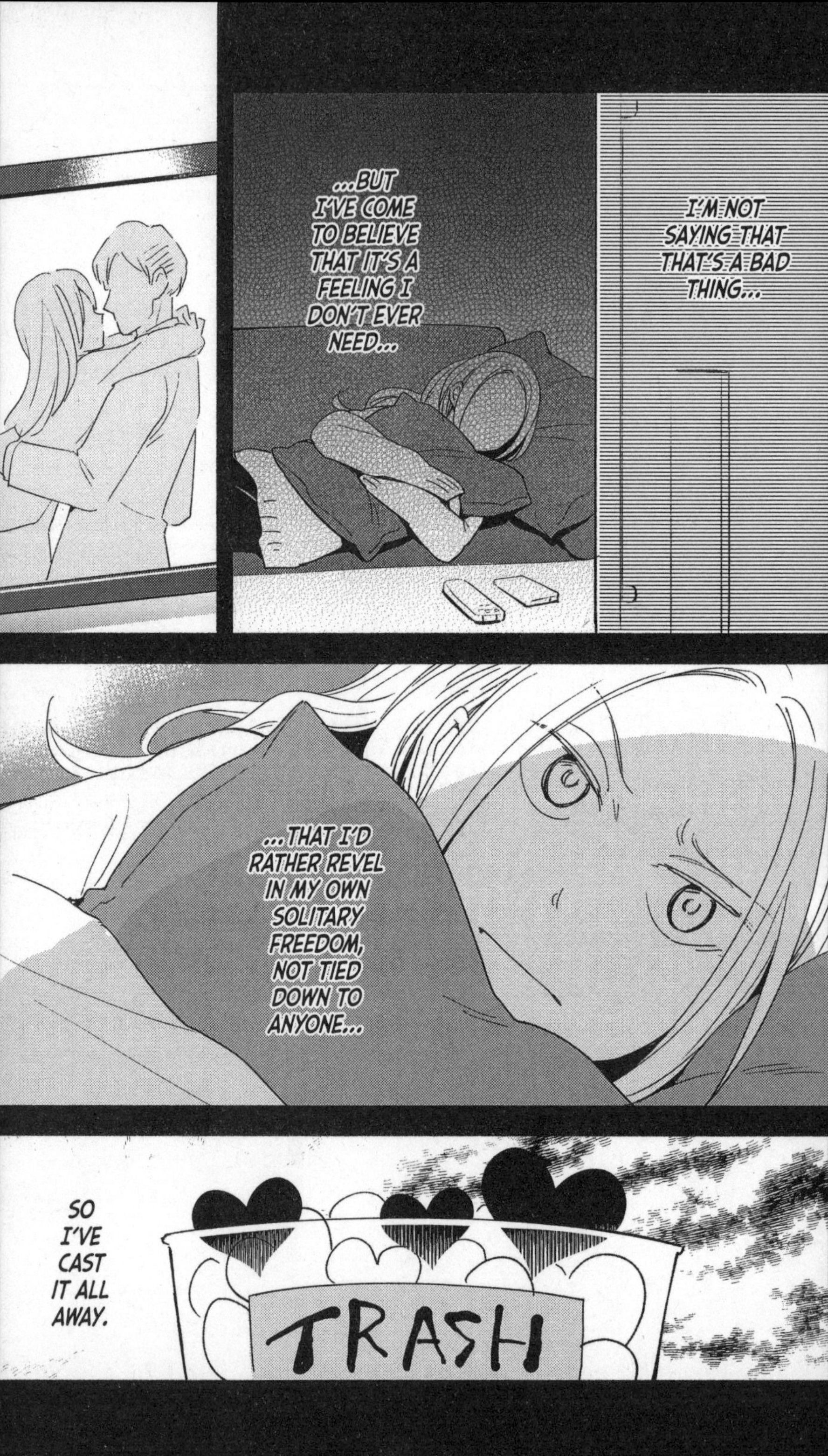
I'M NOT SAYING THAT THAT'S A BAD THING...
...BUT I'VE COME TO BELIEVE THAT IT'S A FEELING I DON'T EVER NEED...
...THAT I'D RATHER REVEL IN MY OWN SOLITARY FREEDOM, NOT TIED DOWN TO ANYONE...
SO I'VE CAST IT ALL AWAY.
TRASH

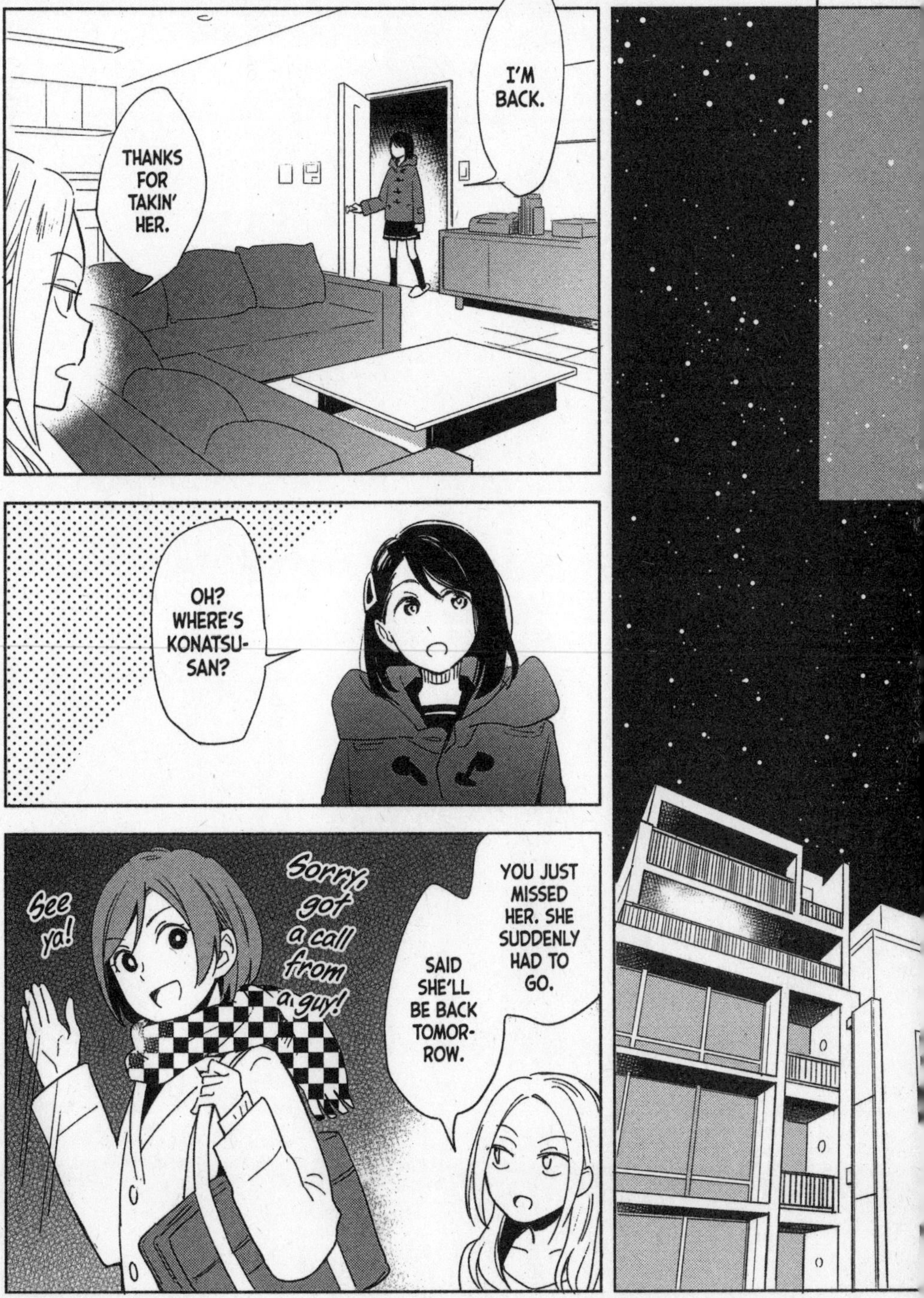
I'M BACK.
THANKS FOR TAKIN' HER.
OH? WHERE'S KONATSU-SAN?
YOU JUST MISSED HER. SHE SUDDENLY HAD TO GO.
SAID SHE'LL BE BACK TOMOR-ROW.
Sorry, got a call from a guy!
See ya!

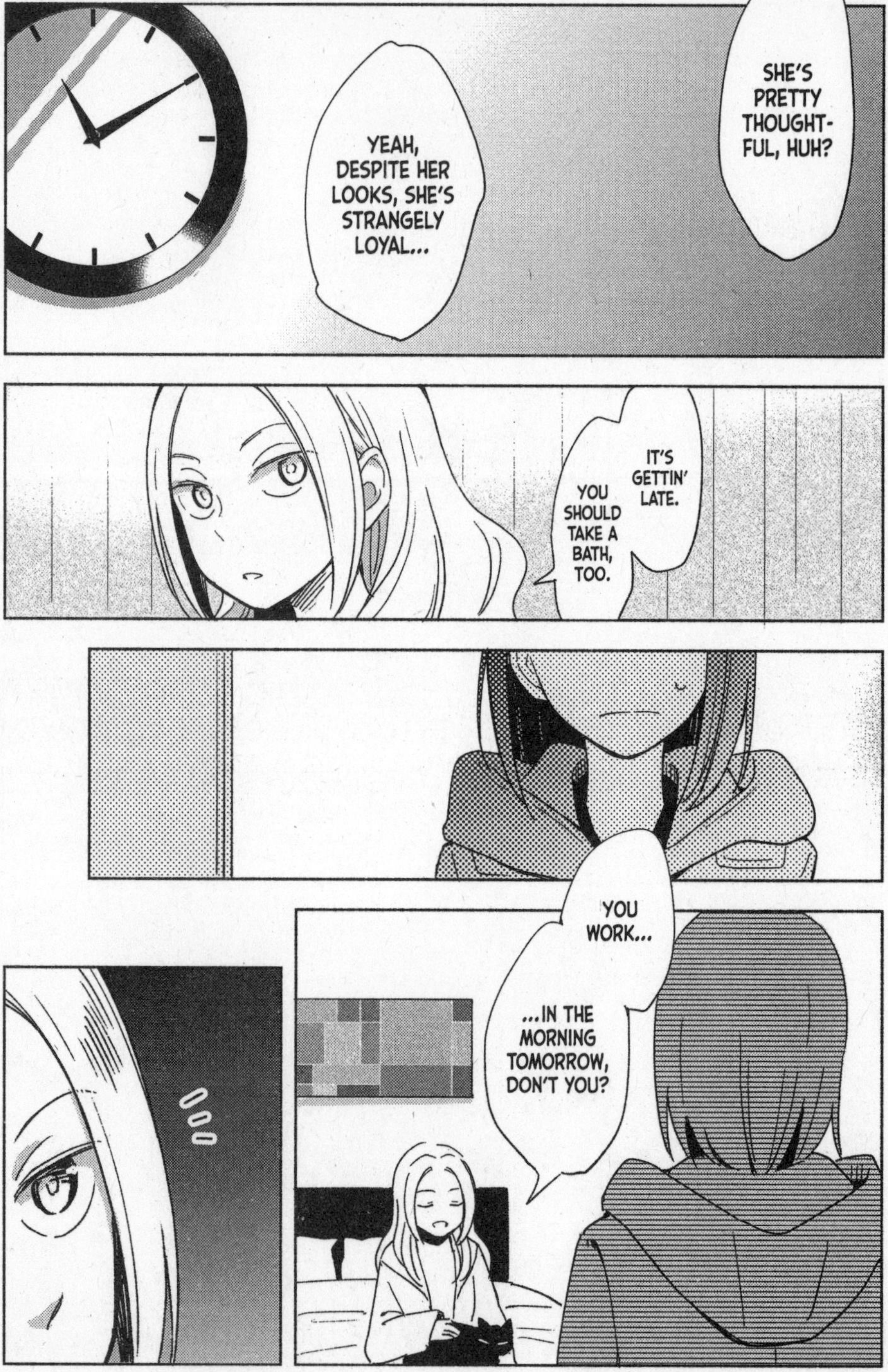
SHE'S PRETTY THOUGHT-FUL, HUH?
YEAH, DESPITE HER LOOKS, SHE'S STRANGELY LOYAL...
IT'S GETTIN' LATE. YOU SHOULD TAKE A BATH, TOO.
YOU WORK...
...IN THE MORNING TOMORROW, DON'T YOU?

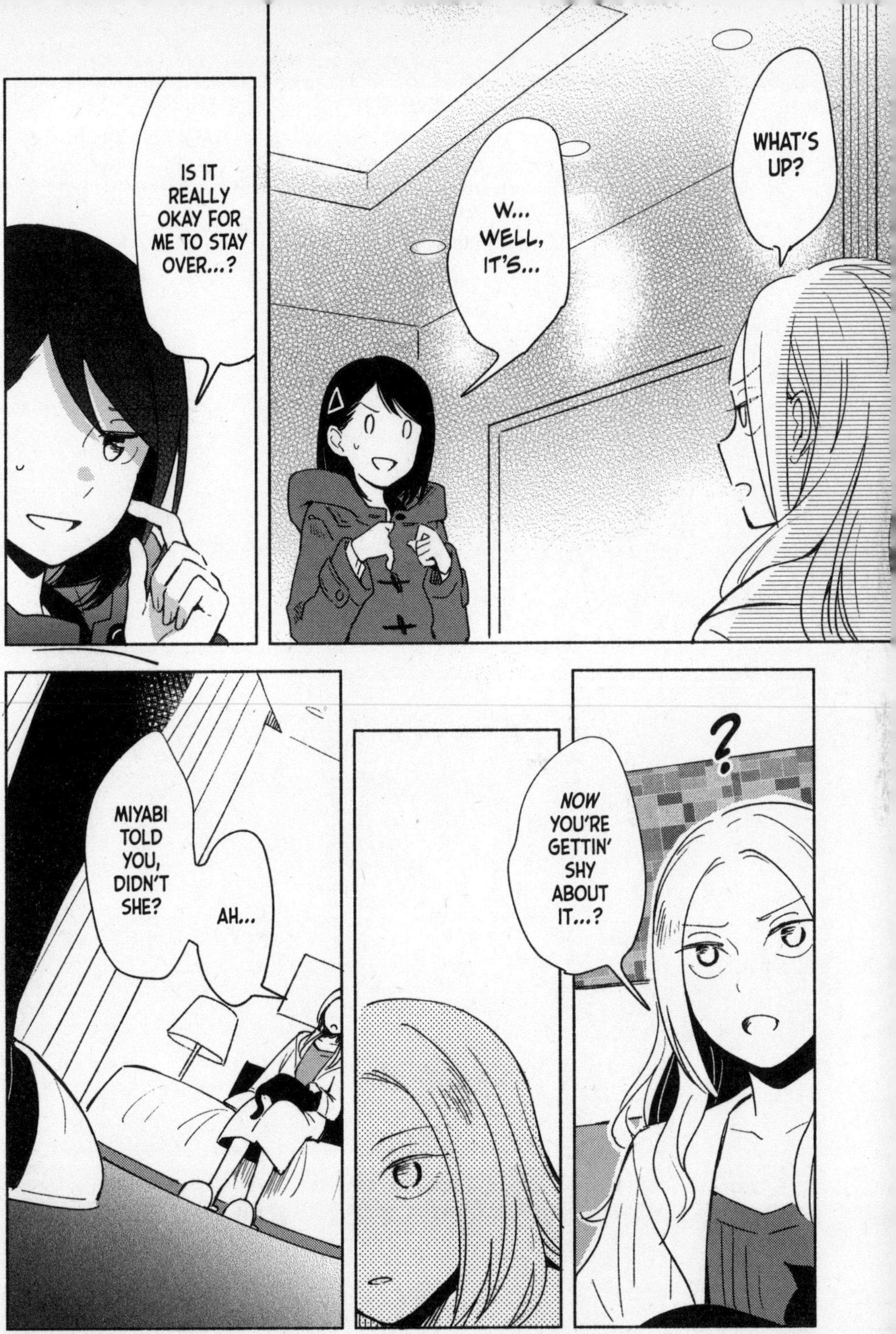
WHAT'S UP?
W... WELL, IT'S...
IS IT REALLY OKAY FOR ME TO STAY OVER...?
?
NOW YOU'RE GETTIN' SHY ABOUT IT...?
MIYABI TOLD YOU, DIDN'T SHE?
AH...

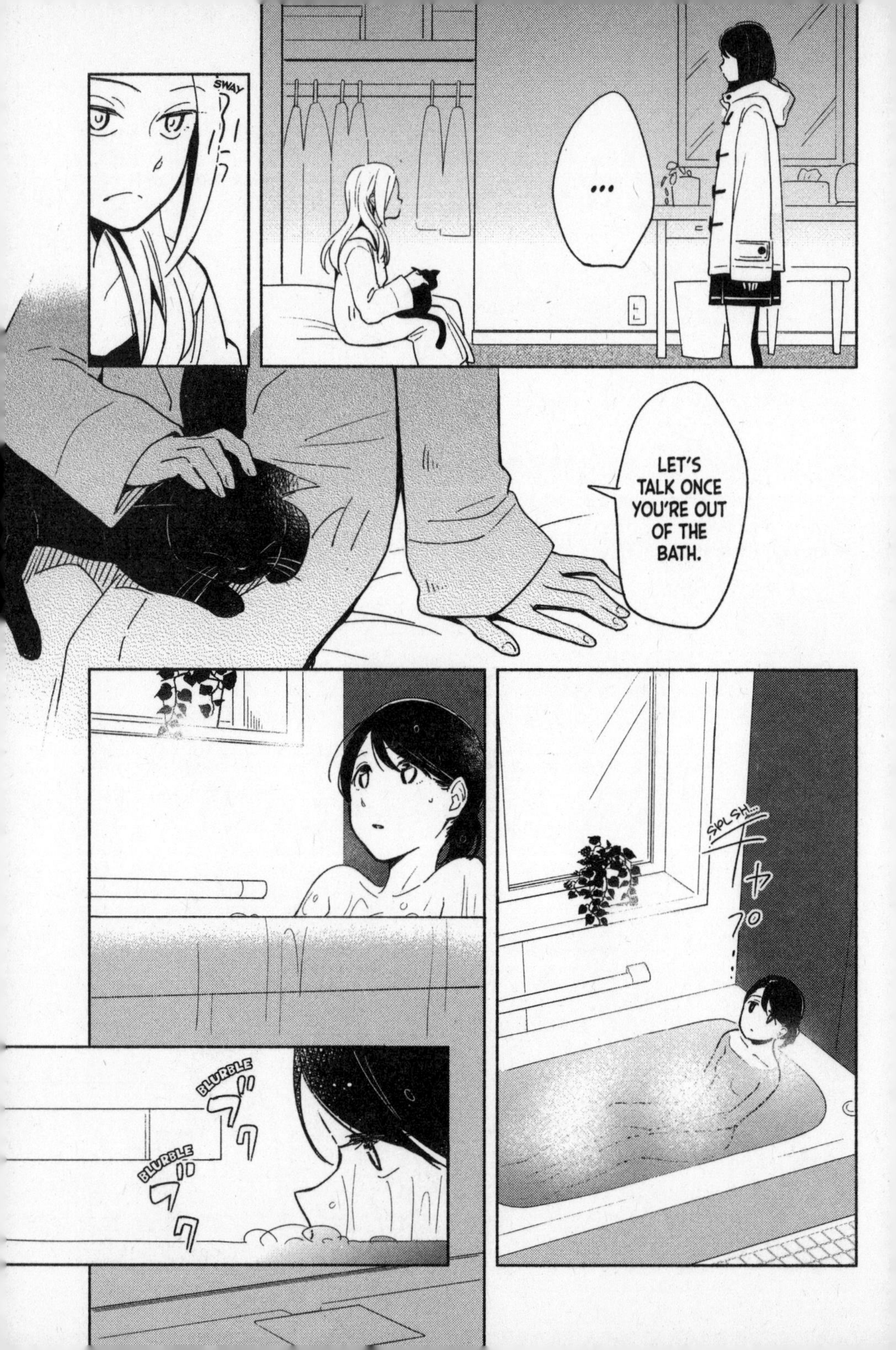
...
SWAY
LET'S TALK ONCE YOU'RE OUT OF THE BATH.
SPLSH...
BLURBLE
BLURBLE

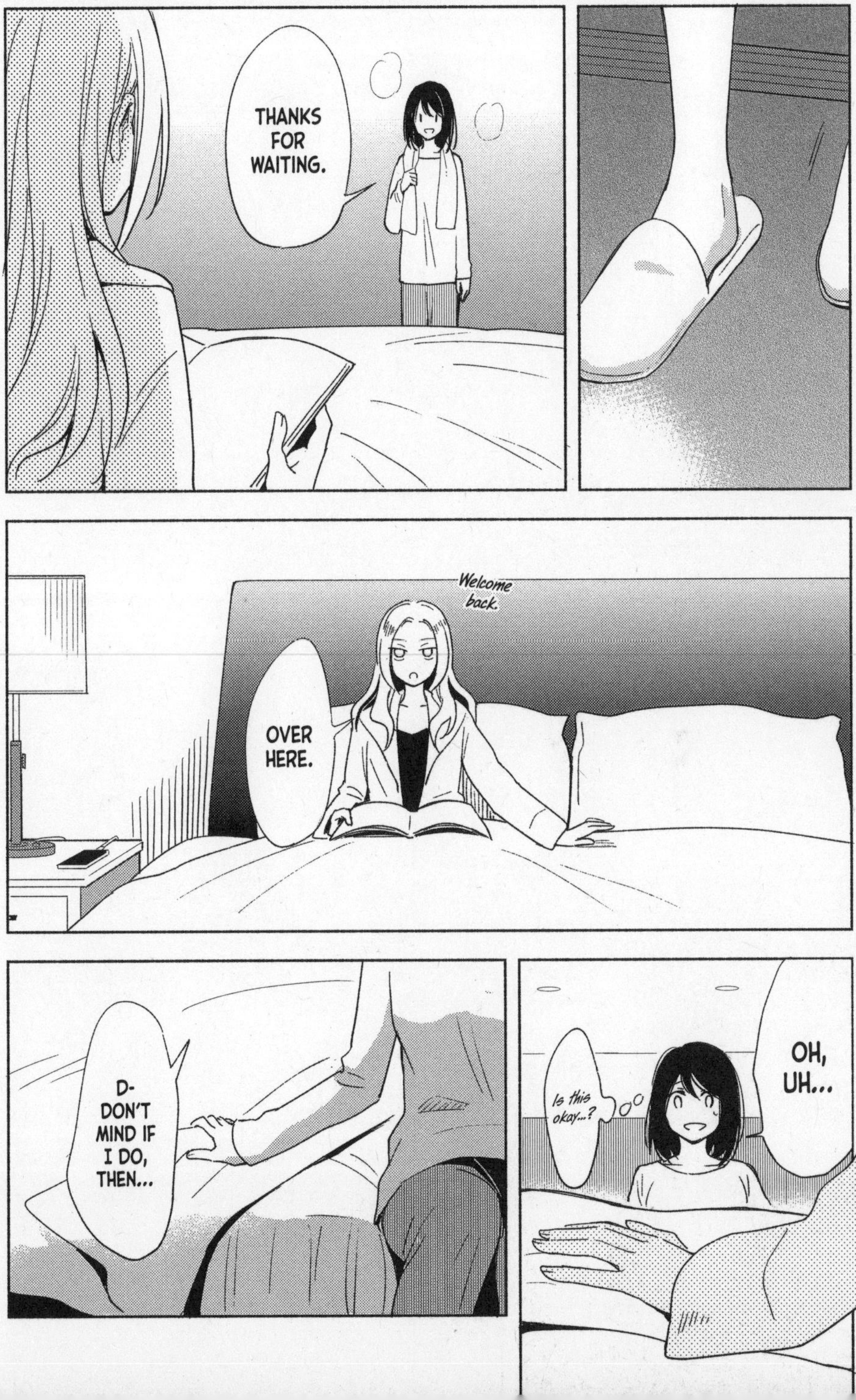
THANKS FOR WAITING.
Welcome back.
OVER HERE.
OH, UH...
Is this okay...?
D-DON'T MIND IF I DO, THEN...

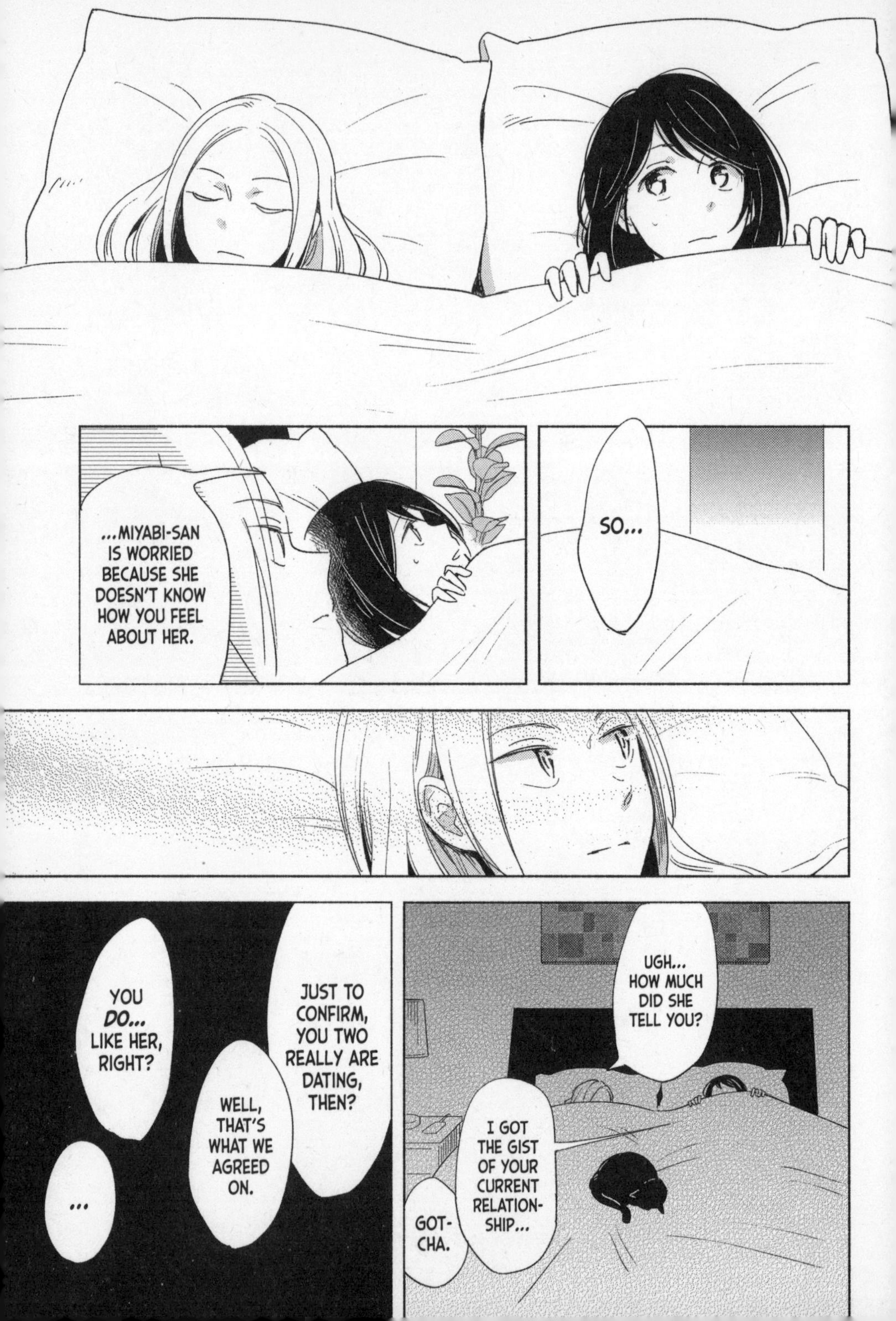
SO...
...MIYABI-SAN IS WORRIED BECAUSE SHE DOESN'T KNOW HOW YOU FEEL ABOUT HER.
UGH... HOW MUCH DID SHE TELL YOU?
I GOT THE GIST OF YOUR CURRENT RELATIONSHIP...
GOT-CHA.
JUST TO CONFIRM, YOU TWO REALLY ARE DATING, THEN?
WELL, THAT'S WHAT WE AGREED ON.
YOU *DO*... LIKE HER, RIGHT?
...

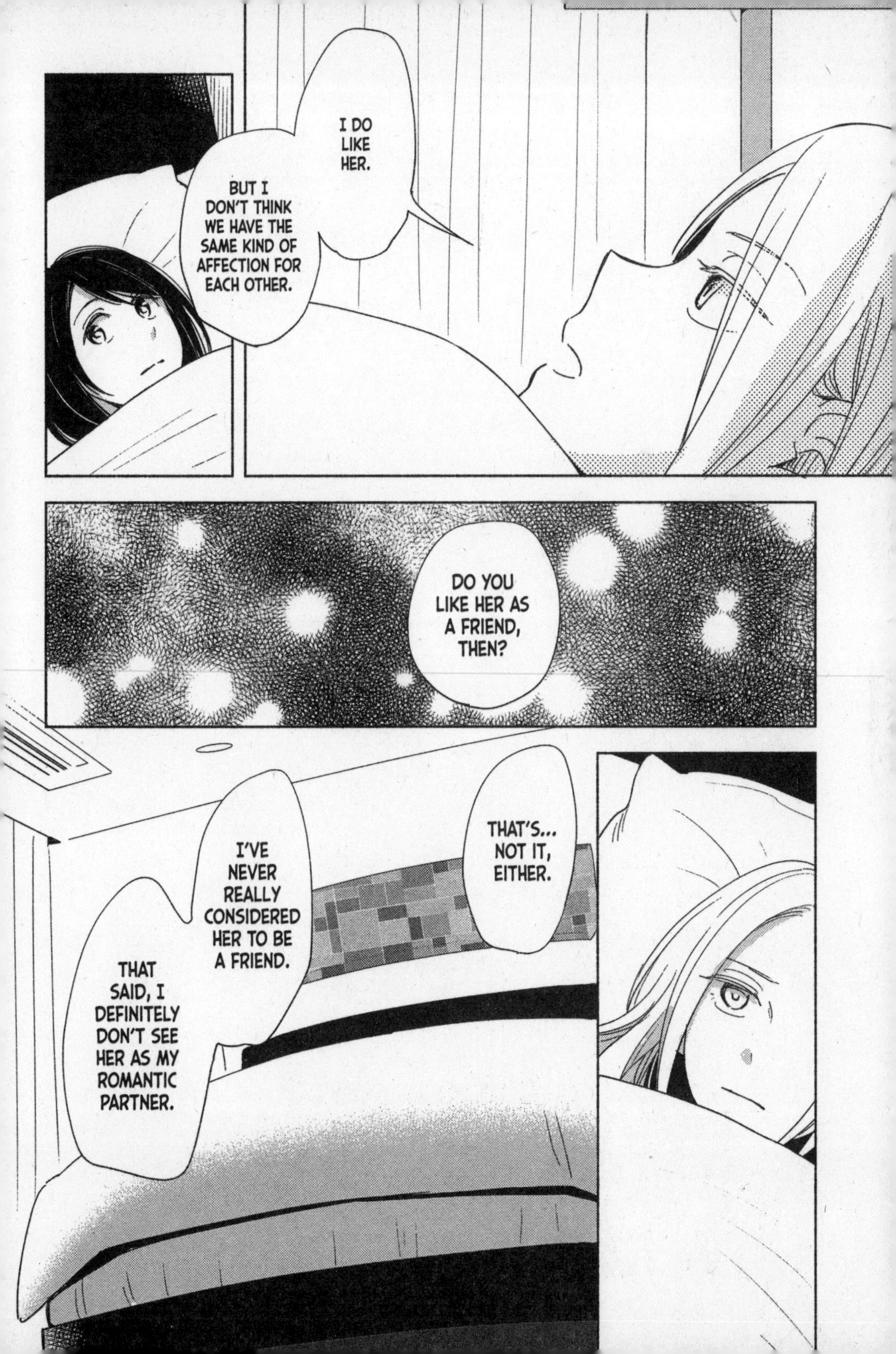
I DO LIKE HER.
BUT I DON'T THINK WE HAVE THE SAME KIND OF AFFECTION FOR EACH OTHER.
DO YOU LIKE HER AS A FRIEND, THEN?
THAT'S... NOT IT, EITHER.
I'VE NEVER REALLY CONSIDERED HER TO BE A FRIEND.
THAT SAID, I DEFINITELY DON'T SEE HER AS MY ROMANTIC PARTNER.

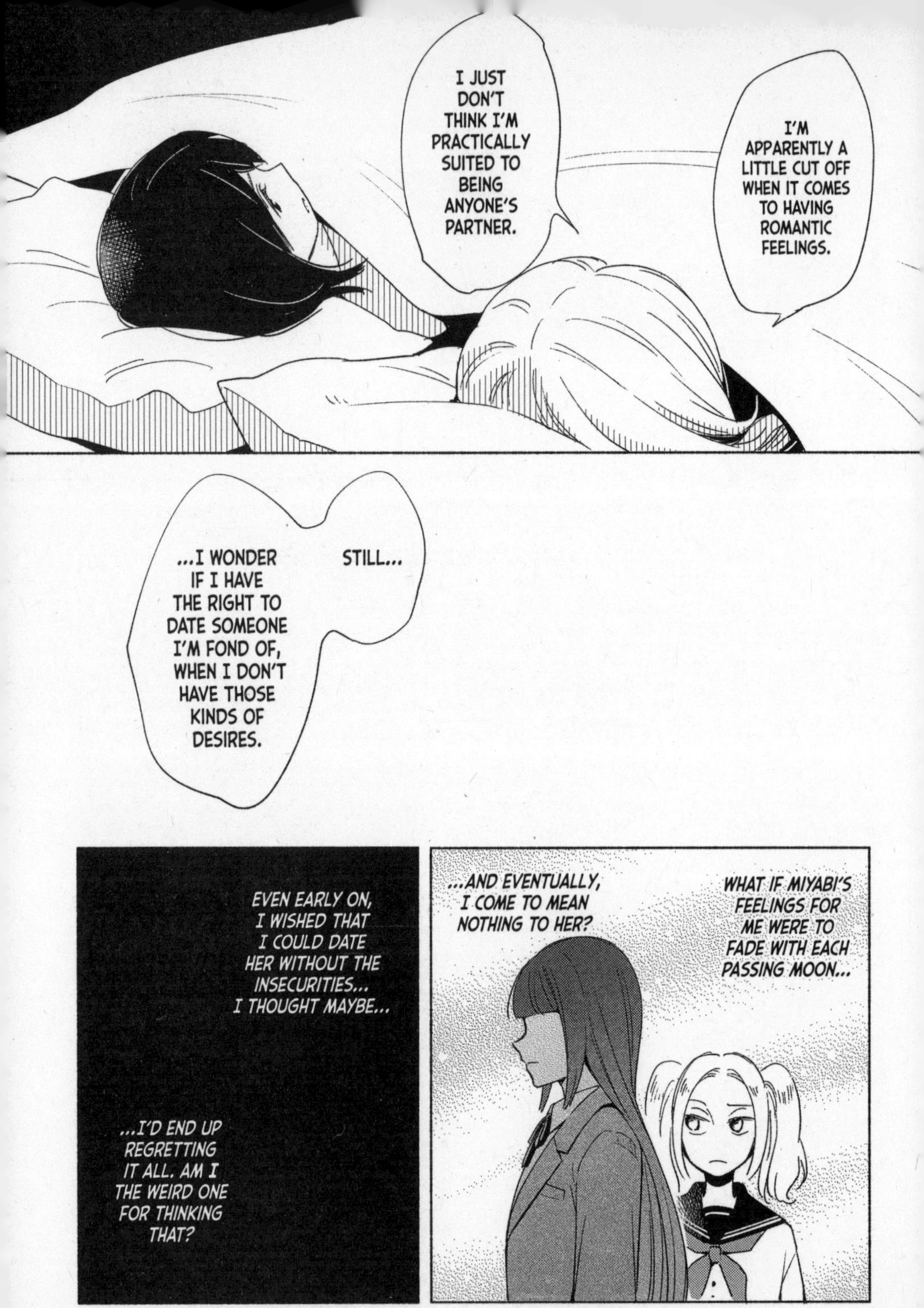
I'M APPARENTLY A LITTLE CUT OFF WHEN IT COMES TO HAVING ROMANTIC FEELINGS.
I JUST DON'T THINK I'M PRACTICALLY SUITED TO BEING ANYONE'S PARTNER.
STILL...
...I WONDER IF I HAVE THE RIGHT TO DATE SOMEONE I'M FOND OF, WHEN I DON'T HAVE THOSE KINDS OF DESIRES.
WHAT IF MIYABI'S FEELINGS FOR ME WERE TO FADE WITH EACH PASSING MOON...
...AND EVENTUALLY, I COME TO MEAN NOTHING TO HER?
EVEN EARLY ON, I WISHED THAT I COULD DATE HER WITHOUT THE INSECURITIES... I THOUGHT MAYBE...
...I'D END UP REGRETTING IT ALL. AM I THE WEIRD ONE FOR THINKING THAT?

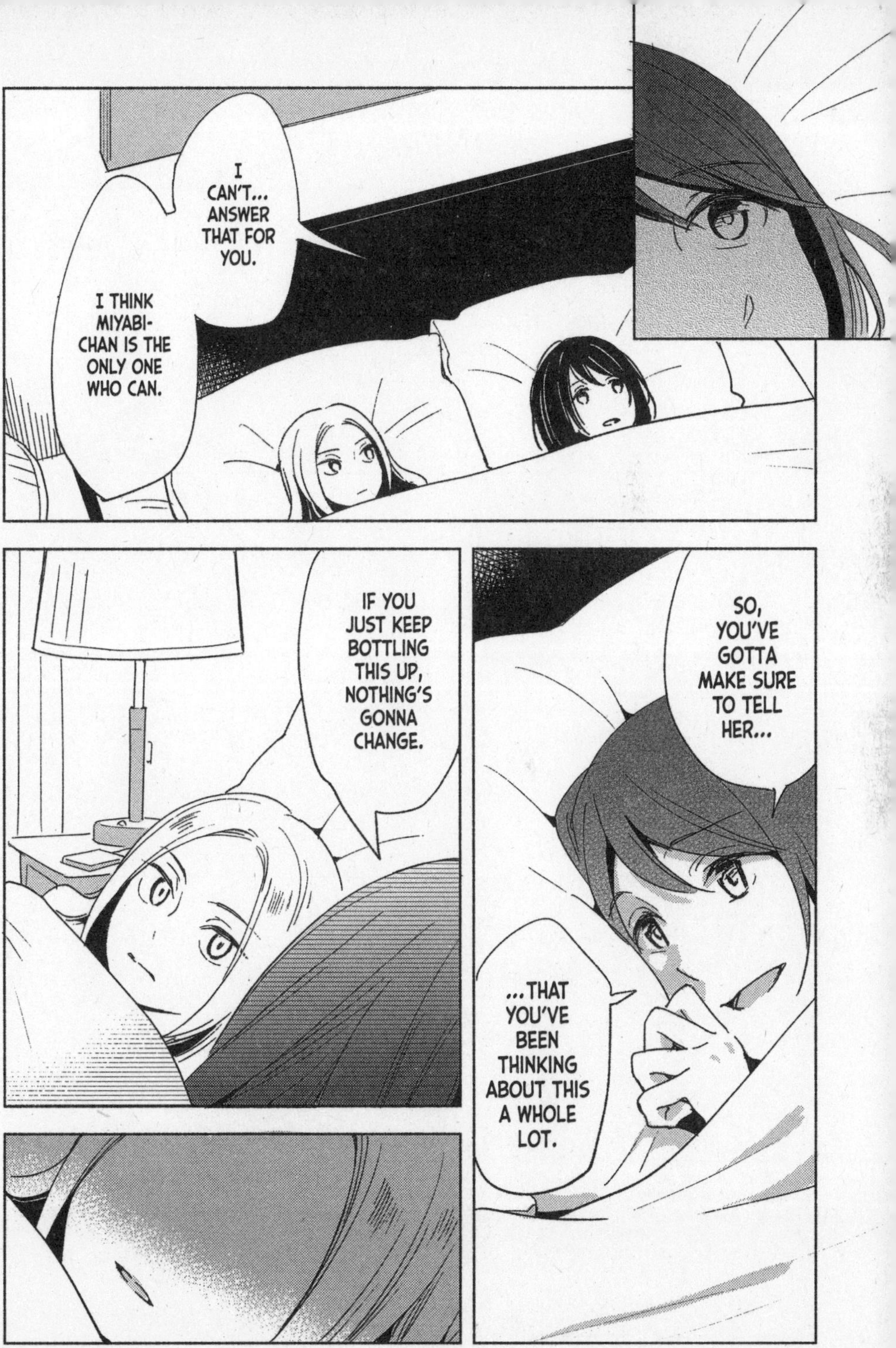
I CAN'T... ANSWER THAT FOR YOU.
I THINK MIYABI-CHAN IS THE ONLY ONE WHO CAN.
SO, YOU'VE GOTTA MAKE SURE TO TELL HER...
...THAT YOU'VE BEEN THINKING ABOUT THIS A WHOLE LOT.
IF YOU JUST KEEP BOTTLING THIS UP, NOTHING'S GONNA CHANGE.

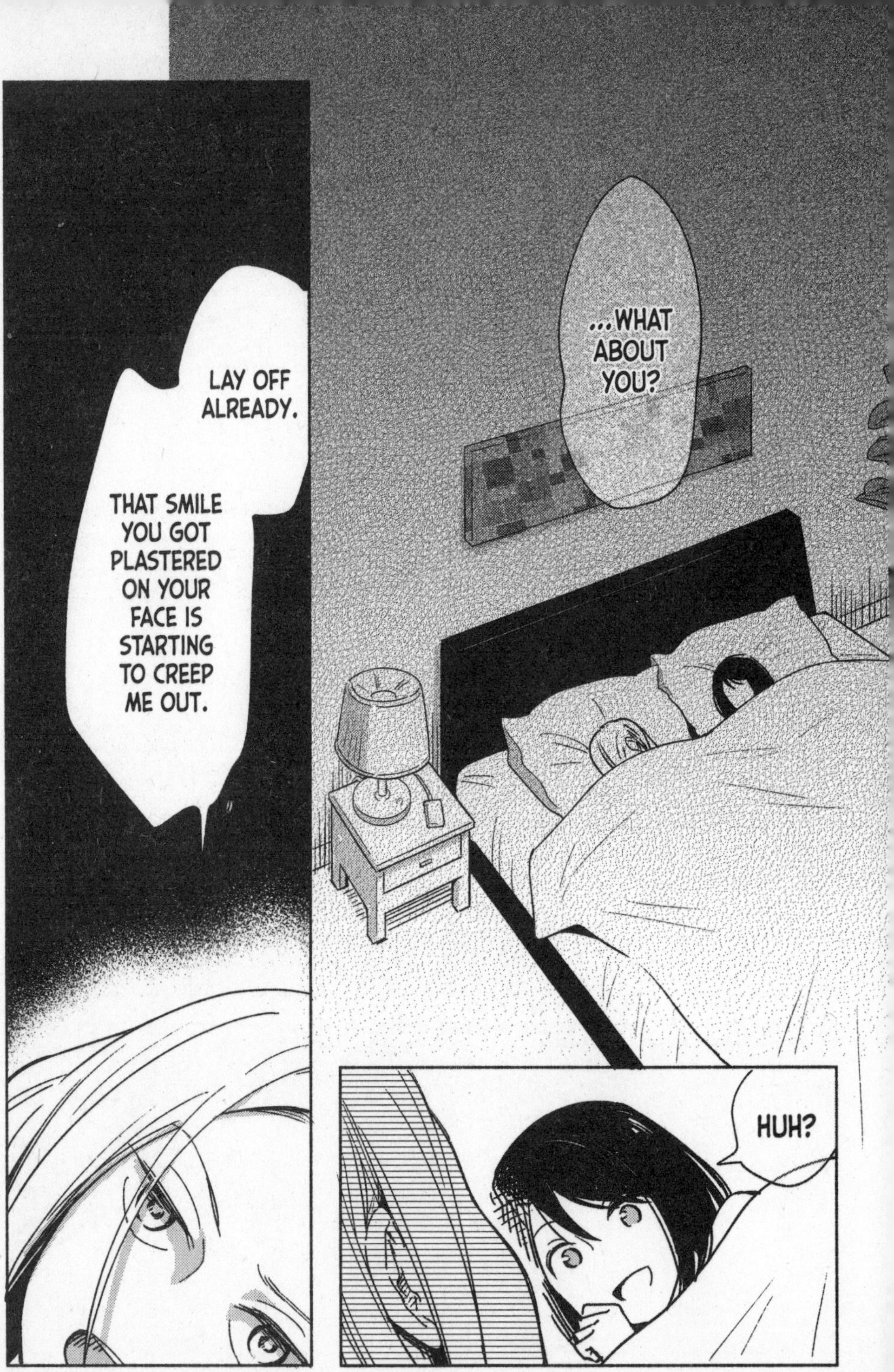
...WHAT ABOUT YOU?
HUH?
LAY OFF ALREADY.
THAT SMILE YOU GOT PLASTERED ON YOUR FACE IS STARTING TO CREEP ME OUT.

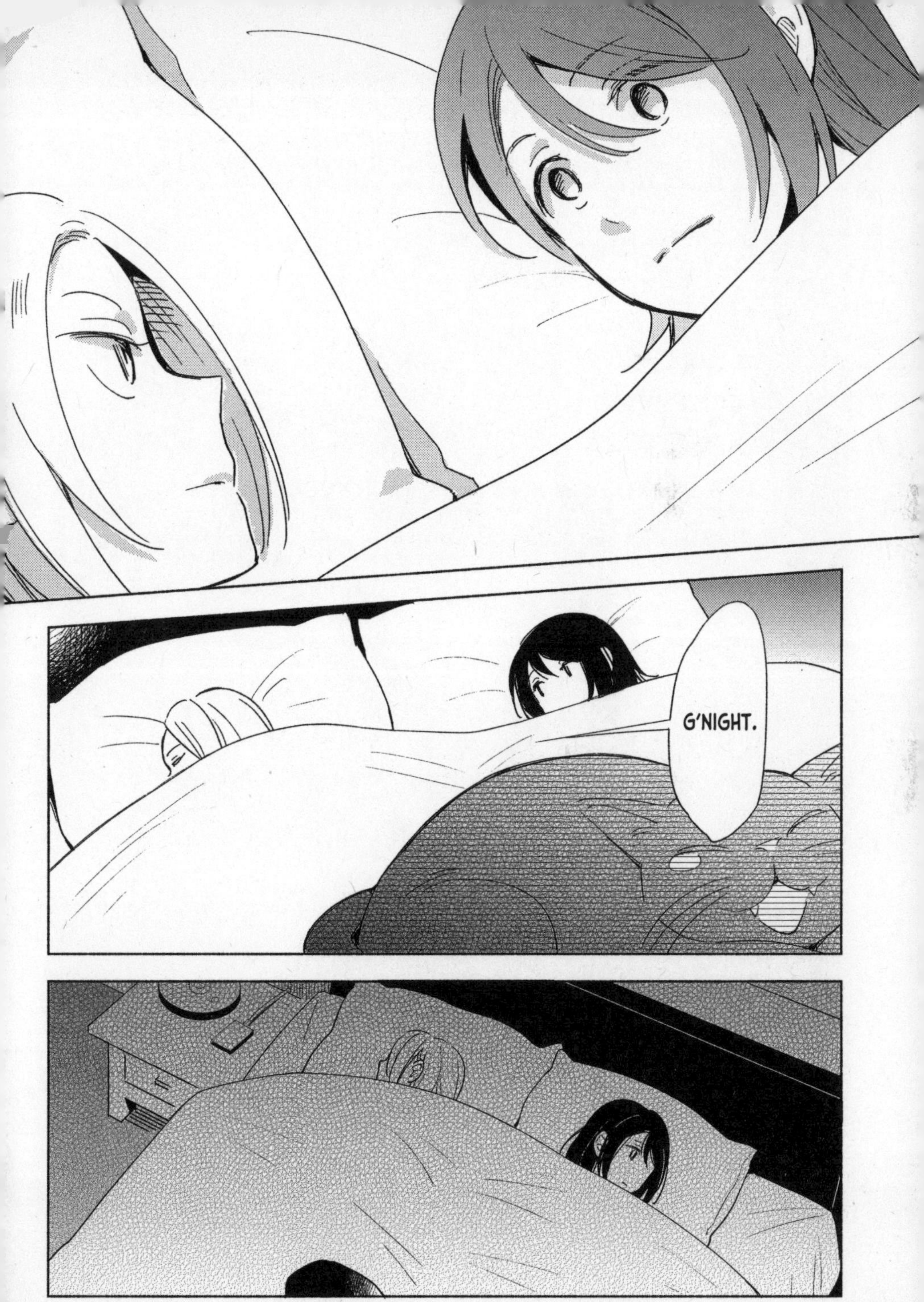
G'NIGHT.

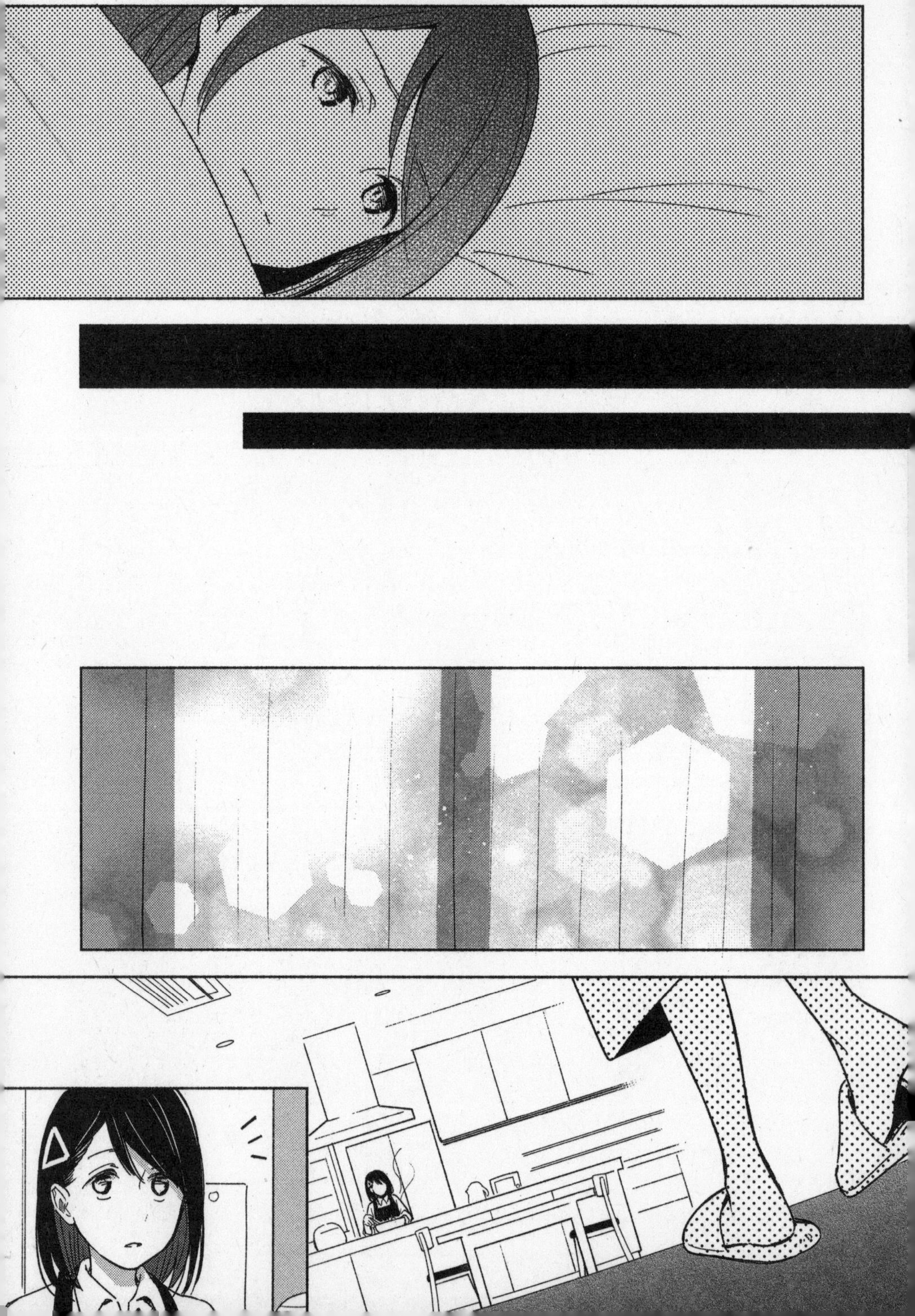

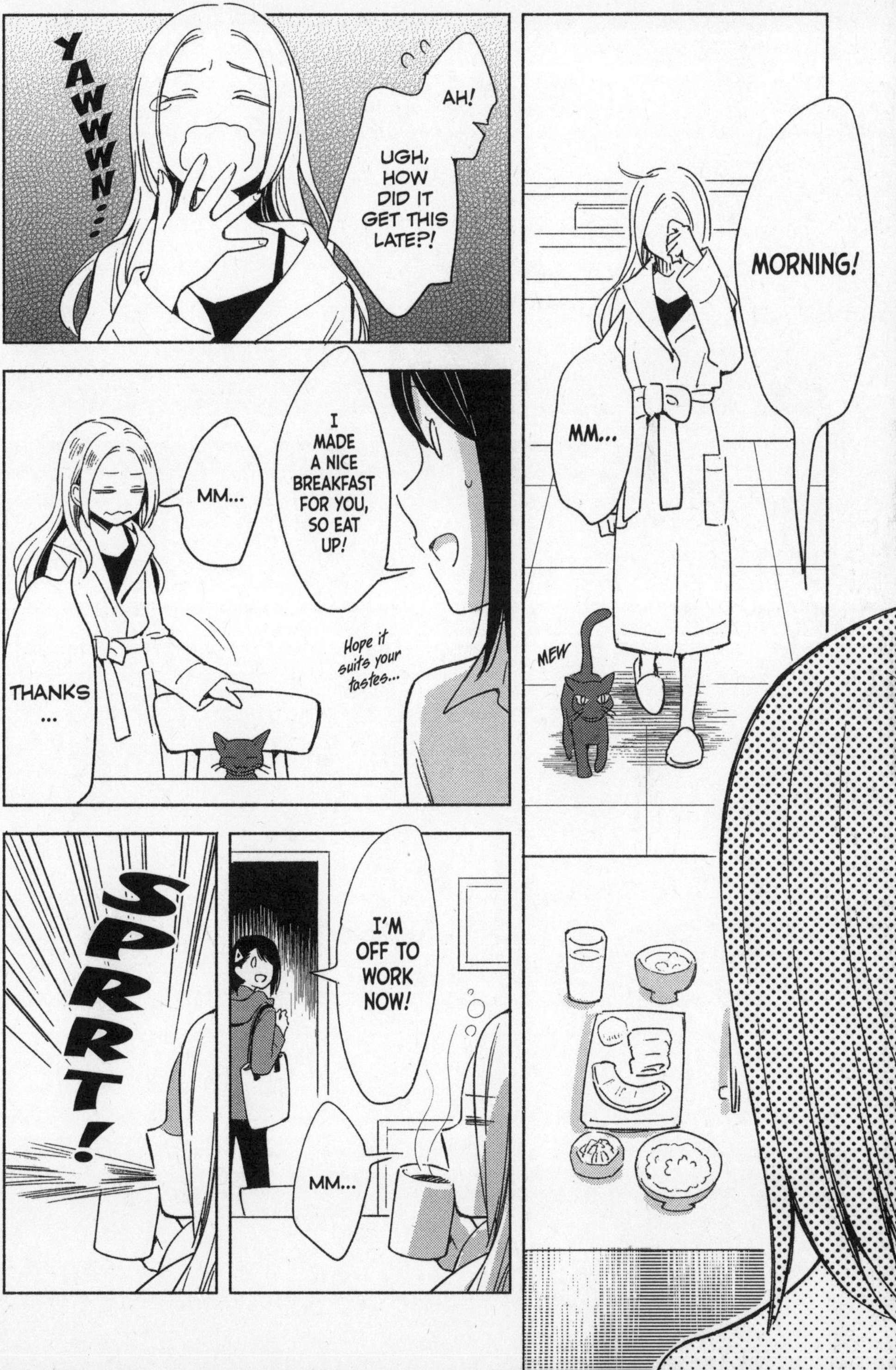
MORNING!
MM...
MEW
YAWWWN...
AH!
UGH, HOW DID IT GET THIS LATE?!
I MADE A NICE BREAKFAST FOR YOU, SO EAT UP!
Hope it suits your tastes...
MM...
THANKS...
I'M OFF TO WORK NOW!
MM...
SPRRT!

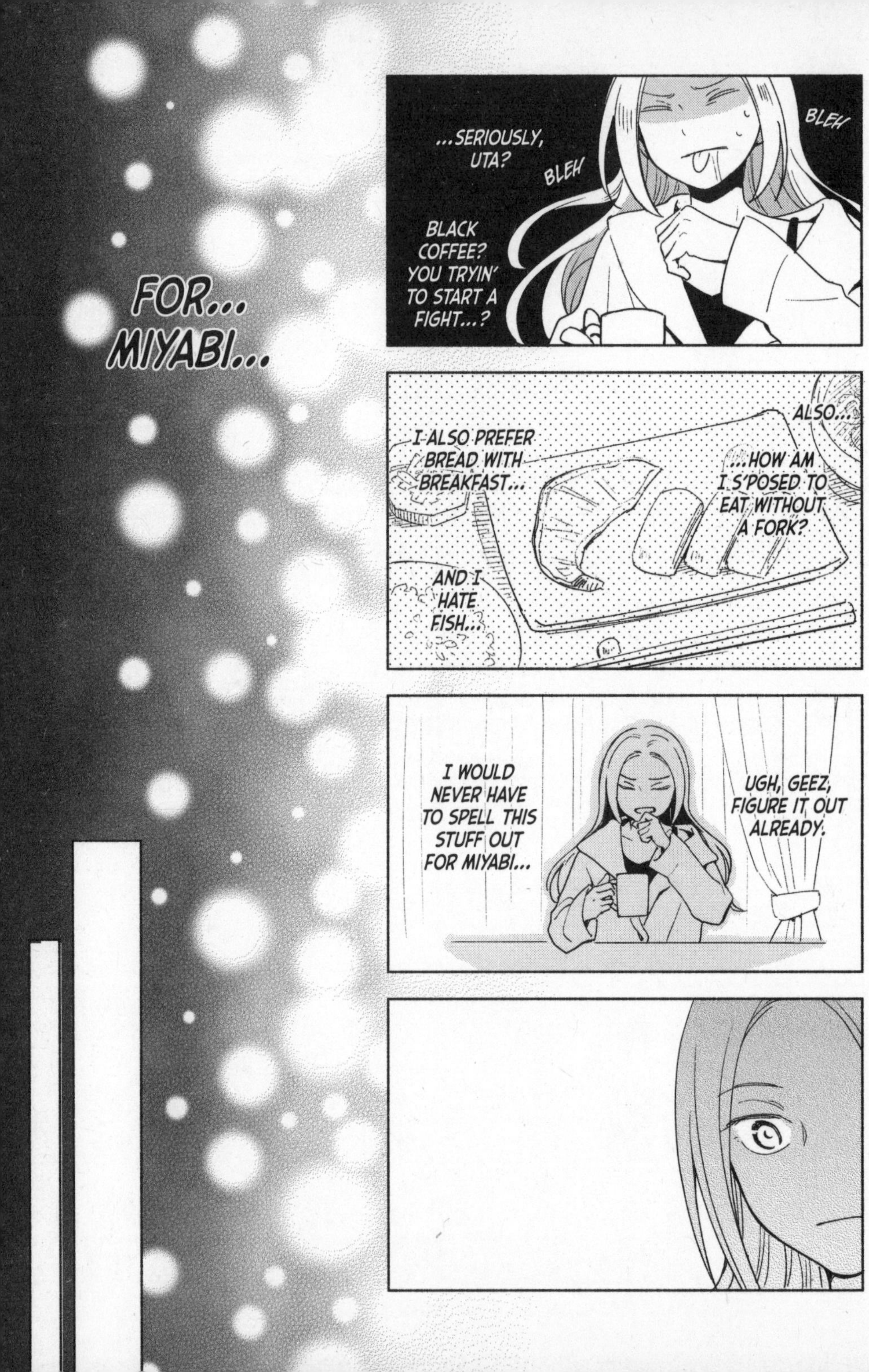
BLEH
...SERIOUSLY, UTA?
BLEH
BLACK COFFEE? YOU TRYIN' TO START A FIGHT...?
ALSO...
...HOW AM I S'POSED TO EAT WITHOUT A FORK?
I ALSO PREFER BREAD WITH BREAKFAST...
AND I HATE FISH...
UGH, GEEZ, FIGURE IT OUT ALREADY.
I WOULD NEVER HAVE TO SPELL THIS STUFF OUT FOR MIYABI...
FOR... MIYABI...

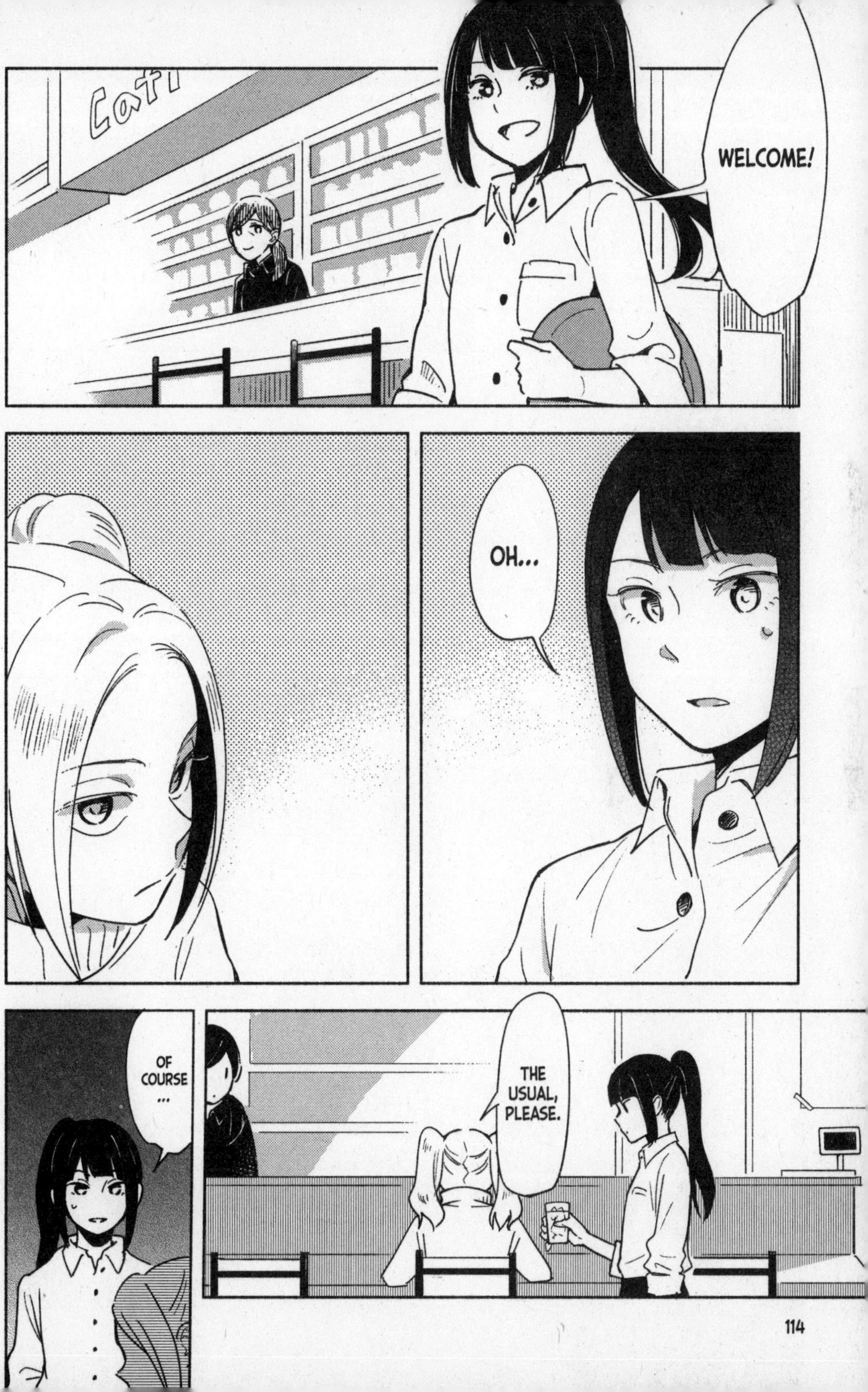
WELCOME!
OH...
THE USUAL, PLEASE.
OF COURSE ...

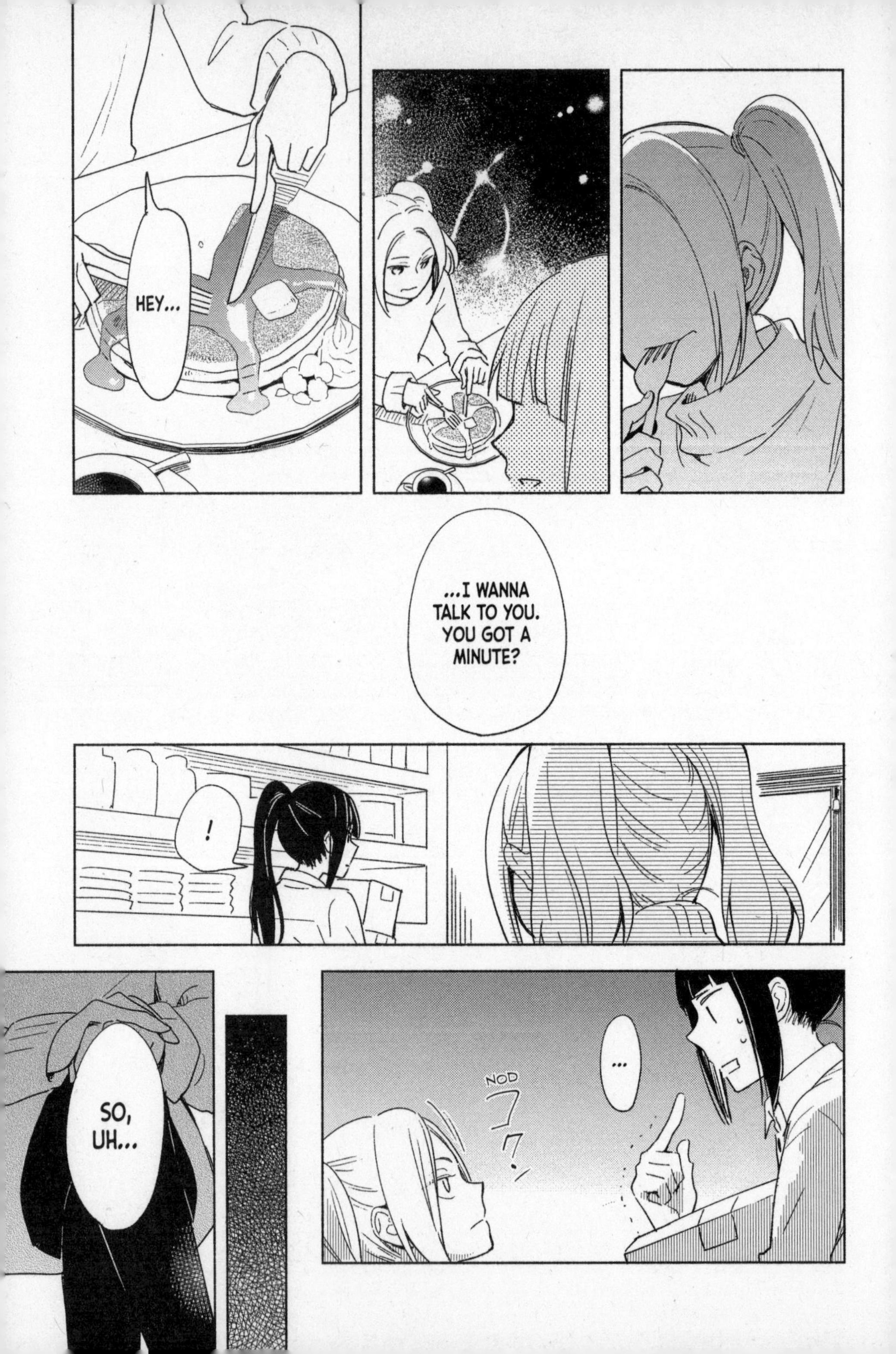
HEY...
...I WANNA TALK TO YOU. YOU GOT A MINUTE?
!
...
NOD
SO, UH...

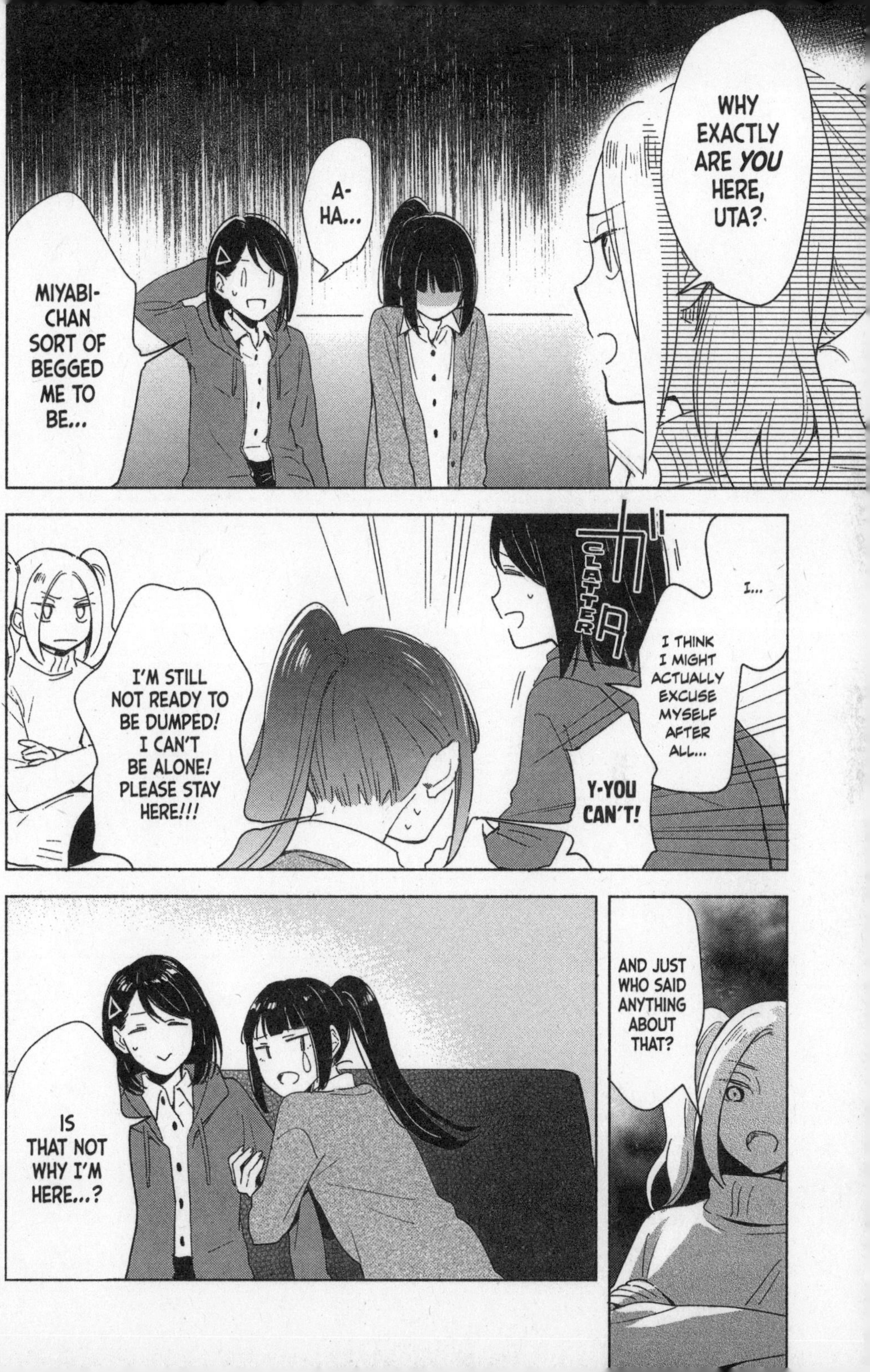
WHY EXACTLY ARE YOU HERE, UTA?
A-HA...
MIYABI-CHAN SORT OF BEGGED ME TO BE...
CLATTER
I...
I THINK I MIGHT ACTUALLY EXCUSE MYSELF AFTER ALL...
Y-YOU CAN'T!
I'M STILL NOT READY TO BE DUMPED! I CAN'T BE ALONE! PLEASE STAY HERE!!!
AND JUST WHO SAID ANYTHING ABOUT THAT?
IS THAT NOT WHY I'M HERE...?

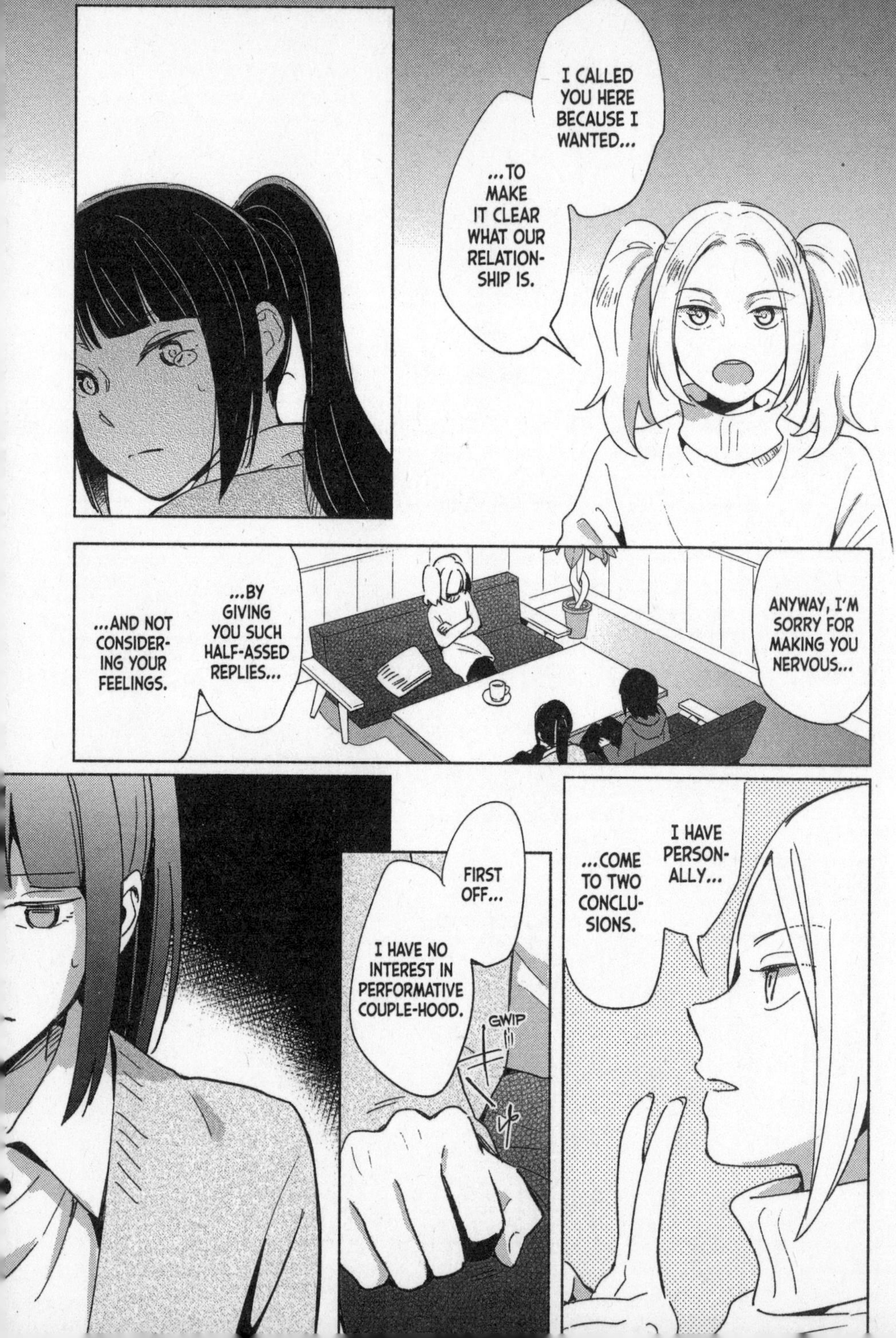
I CALLED YOU HERE BECAUSE I WANTED...
...TO MAKE IT CLEAR WHAT OUR RELATIONSHIP IS.
ANYWAY, I'M SORRY FOR MAKING YOU NERVOUS...
...BY GIVING YOU SUCH HALF-ASSED REPLIES...
...AND NOT CONSIDERING YOUR FEELINGS.
I HAVE PERSONALLY...
...COME TO TWO CONCLUSIONS.
FIRST OFF...
I HAVE NO INTEREST IN PERFORMATIVE COUPLE-HOOD.
GWIP

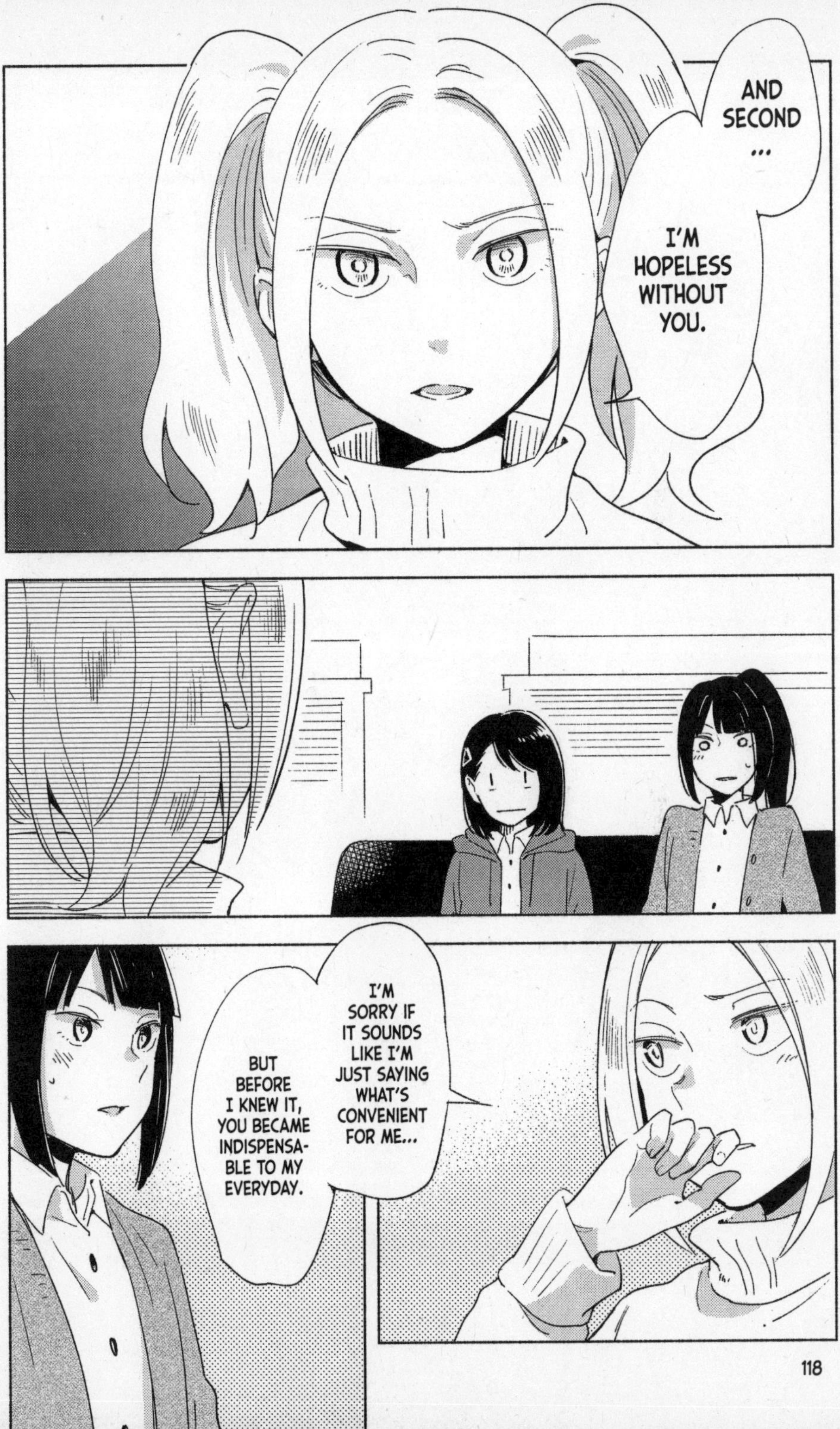
AND SECOND ...
I'M HOPELESS WITHOUT YOU.
I'M SORRY IF IT SOUNDS LIKE I'M JUST SAYING WHAT'S CONVENIENT FOR ME...
BUT BEFORE I KNEW IT, YOU BECAME INDISPENSA-BLE TO MY EVERYDAY.

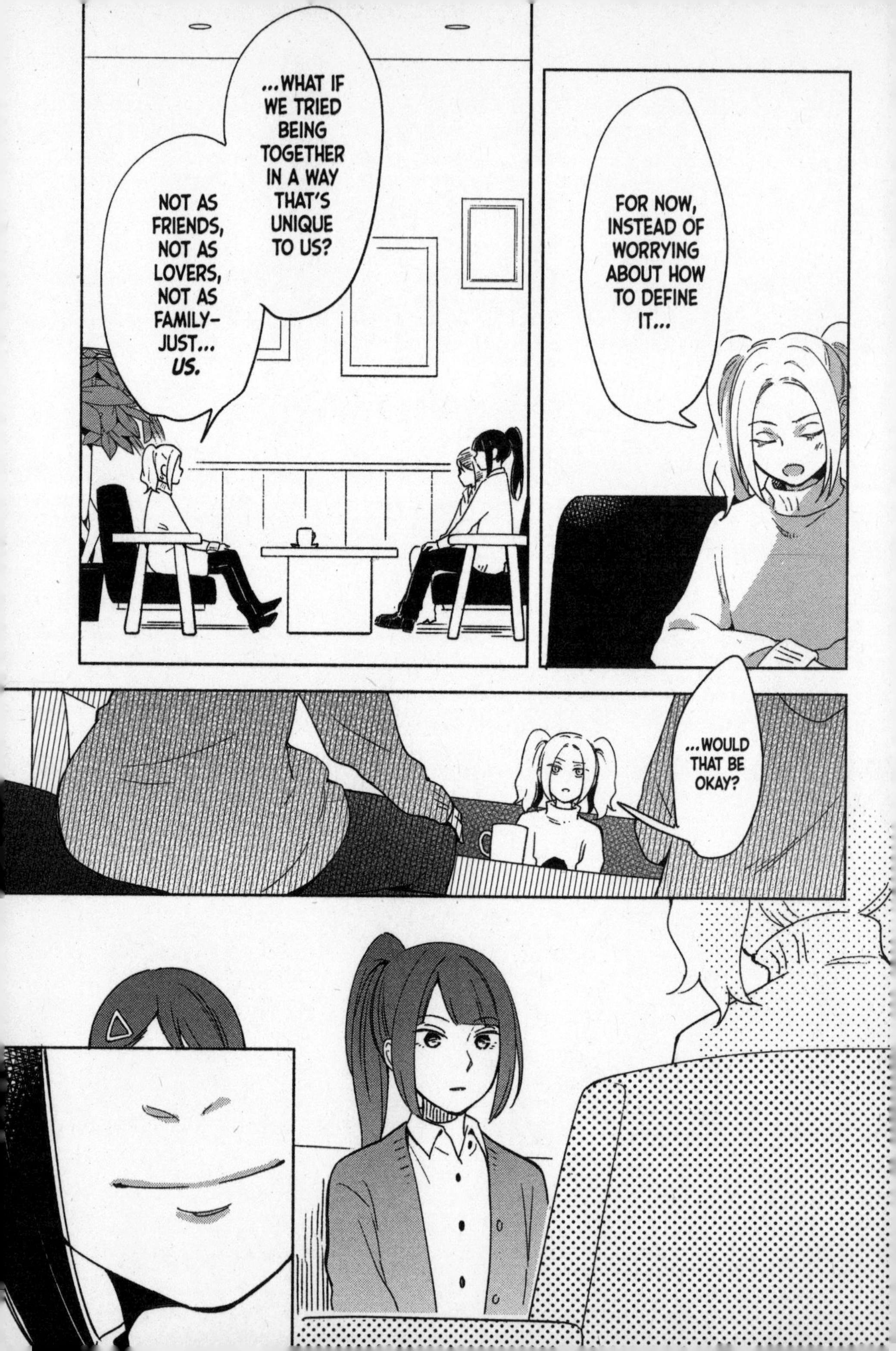
FOR NOW, INSTEAD OF WORRYING ABOUT HOW TO DEFINE IT...
...WHAT IF WE TRIED BEING TOGETHER IN A WAY THAT'S UNIQUE TO US?
NOT AS FRIENDS, NOT AS LOVERS, NOT AS FAMILY–JUST... *US.*
...WOULD THAT BE OKAY?

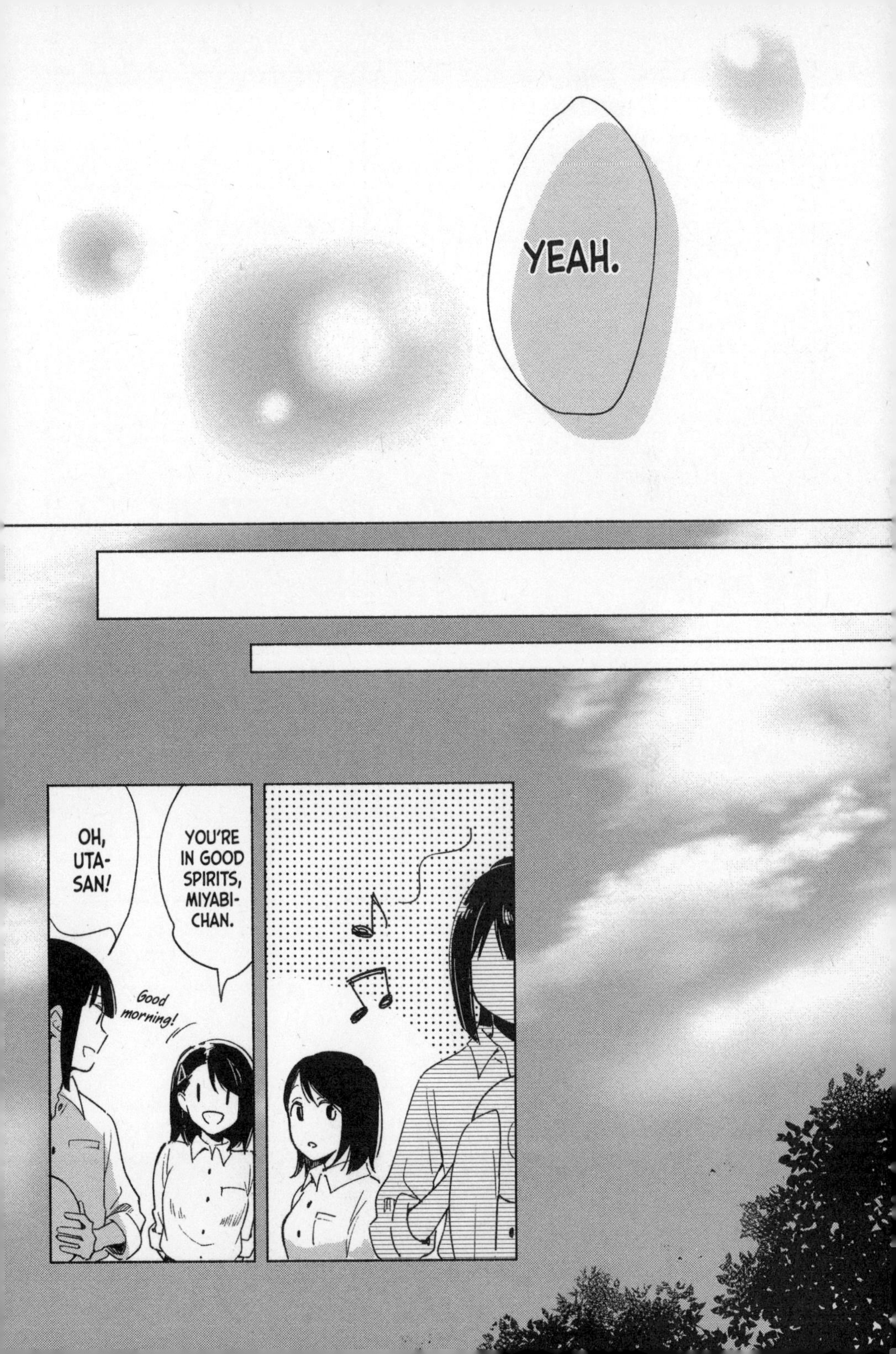
YEAH.
YOU'RE IN GOOD SPIRITS, MIYABI-CHAN.
OH, UTA-SAN!
Good morning!

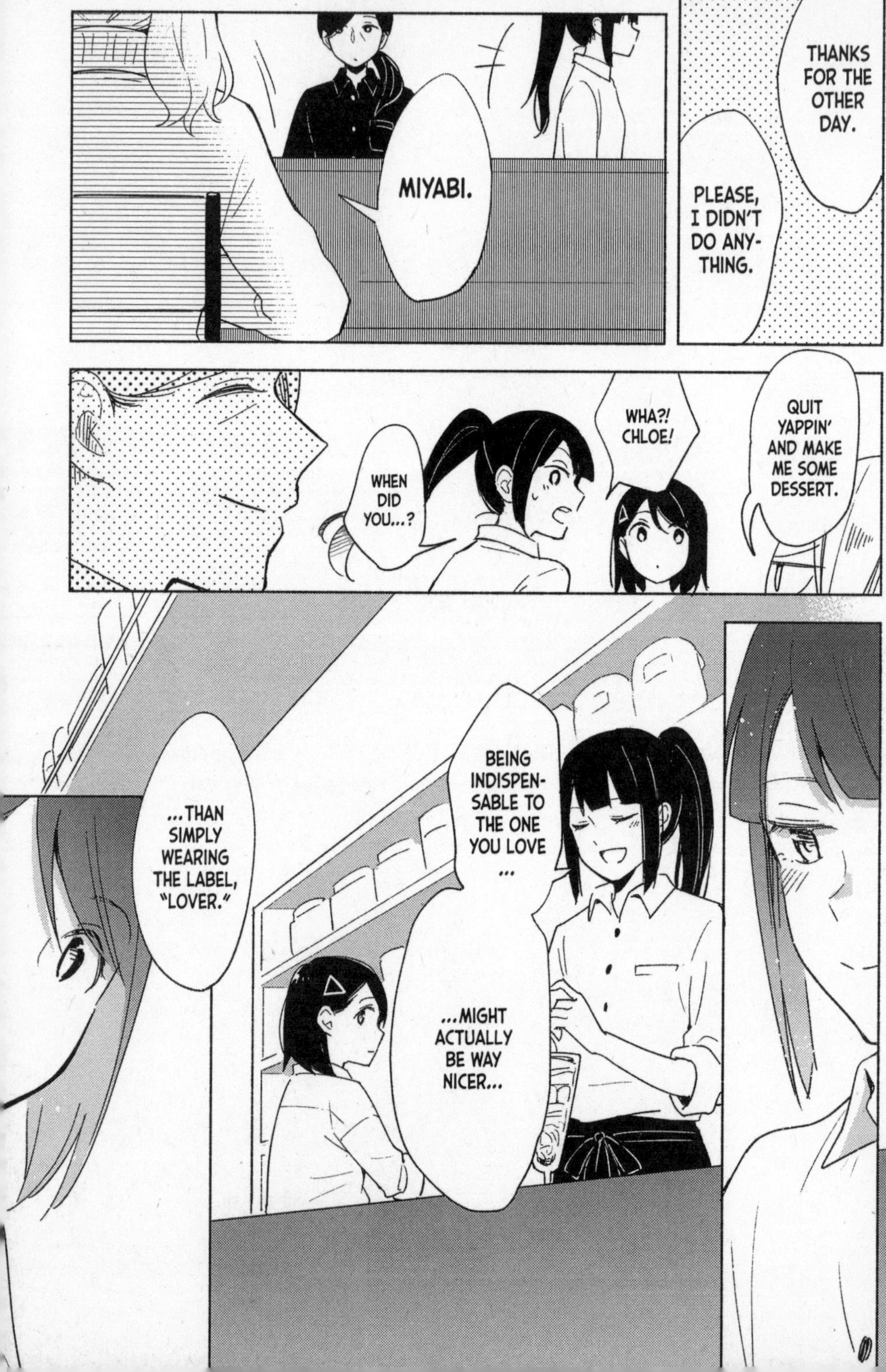
THANKS FOR THE OTHER DAY.
PLEASE, I DIDN'T DO ANY-THING.
MIYABI.
QUIT YAPPIN' AND MAKE ME SOME DESSERT.
WHA?! CHLOE!
WHEN DID YOU...?
BEING INDISPEN-SABLE TO THE ONE YOU LOVE ...
...MIGHT ACTUALLY BE WAY NICER...
...THAN SIMPLY WEARING THE LABEL, "LOVER."

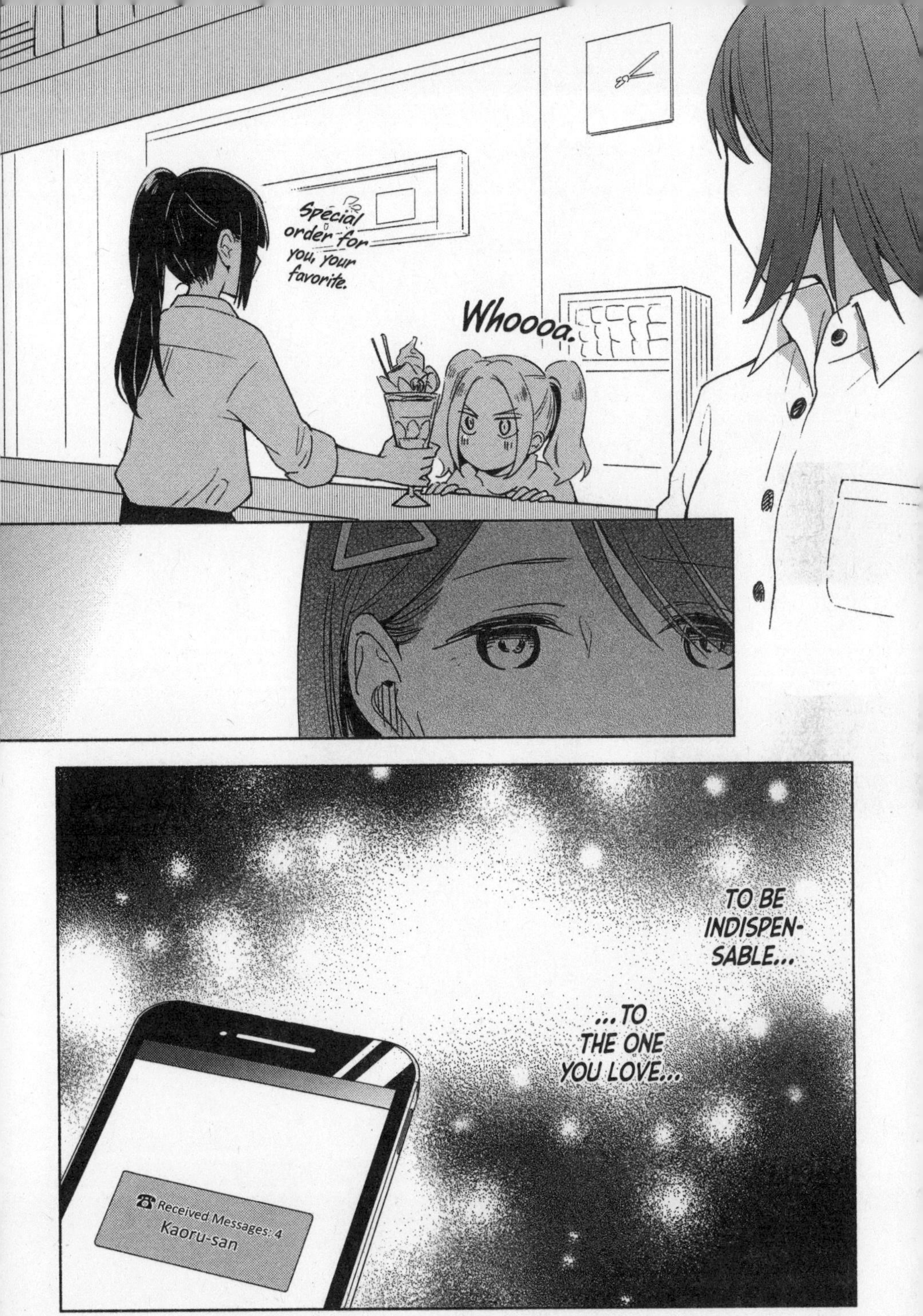
Special order for you, your favorite.
Whoooa.
TO BE INDISPEN-SABLE...
...TO THE ONE YOU LOVE...
Received Messages: 4
Kaoru-san

If I Could
Reach You

If I Could
Reach You

Chapter 10

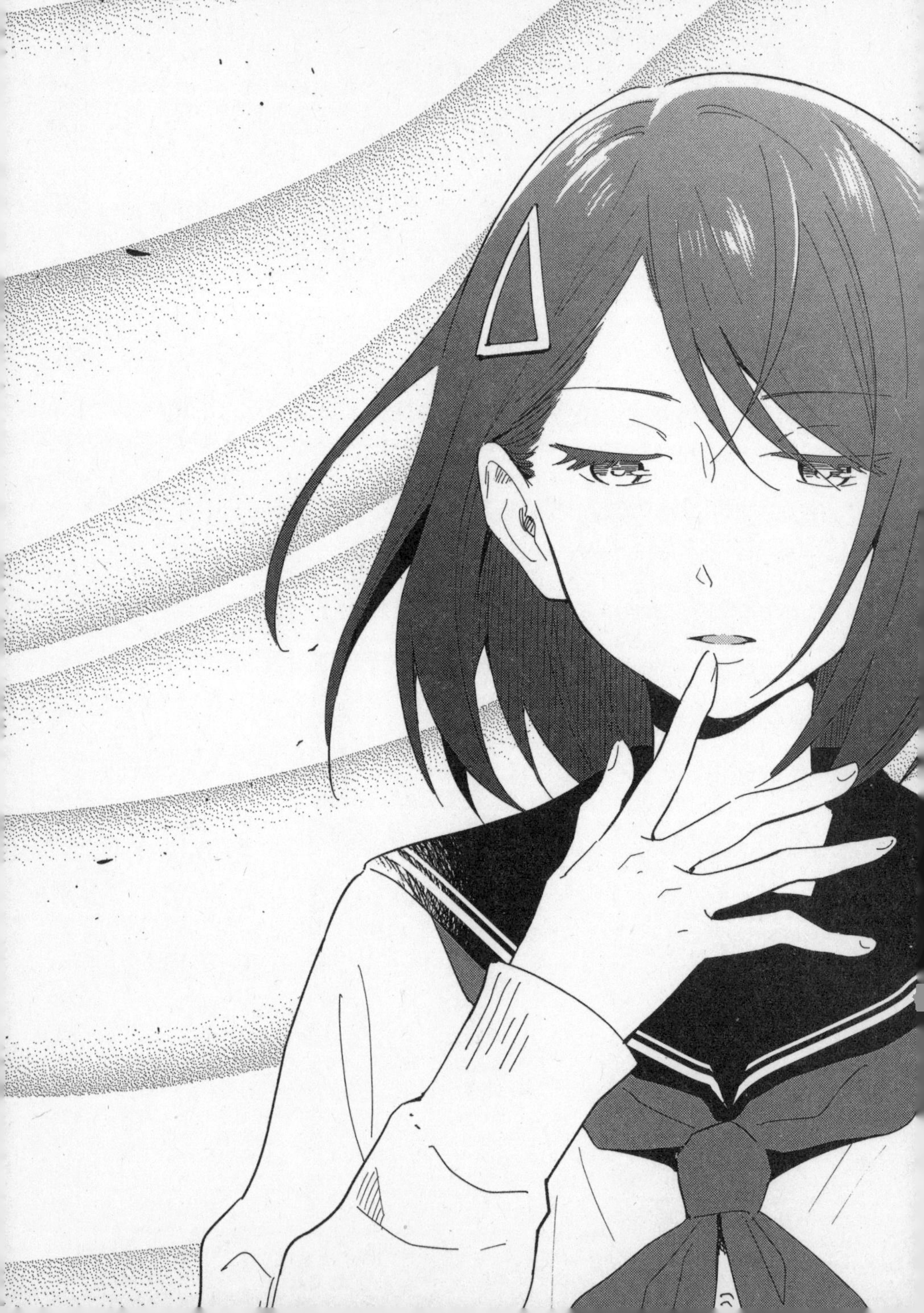

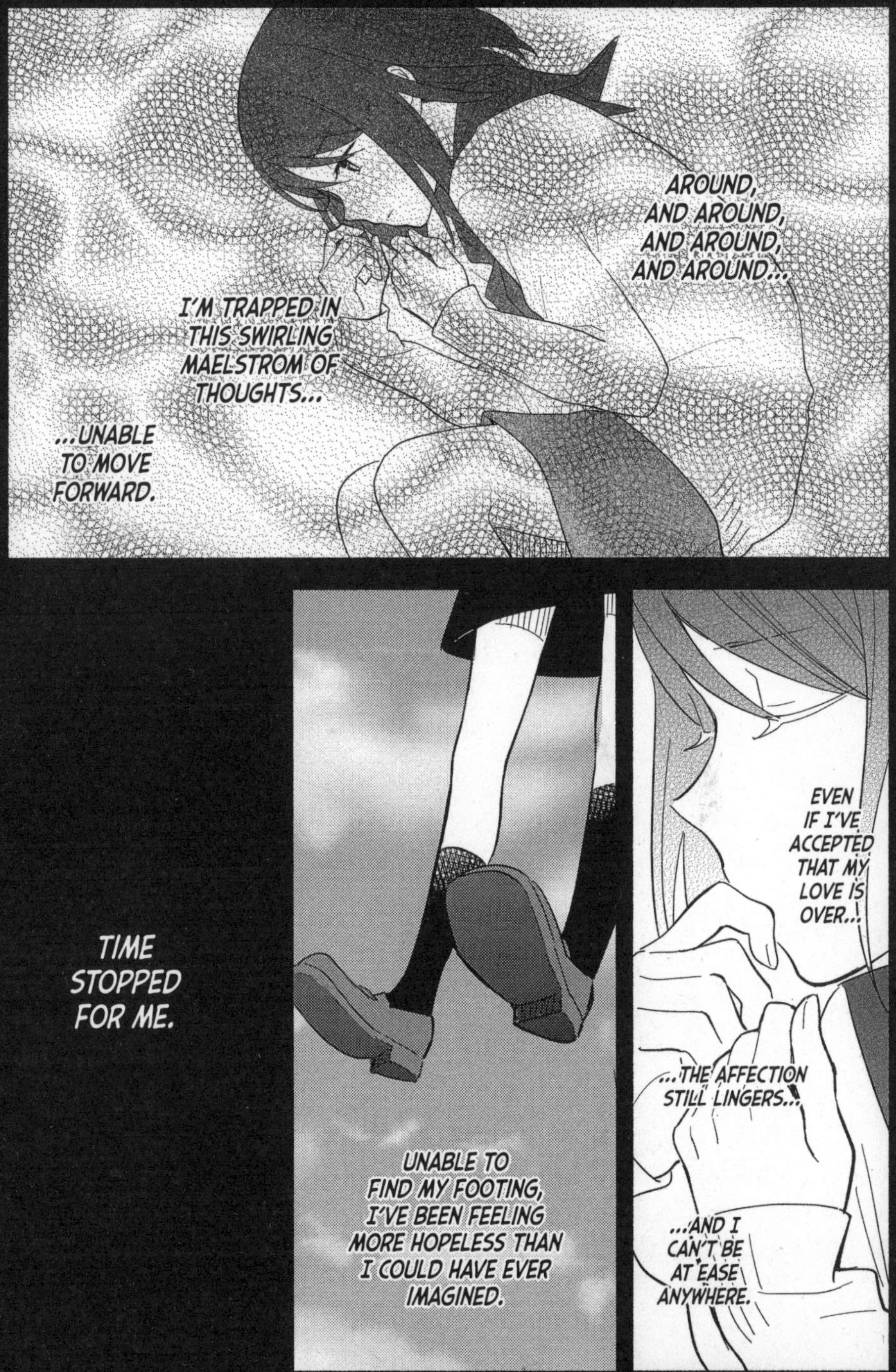
AROUND, AND AROUND, AND AROUND, AND AROUND...
I'M TRAPPED IN THIS SWIRLING MAELSTROM OF THOUGHTS...
...UNABLE TO MOVE FORWARD.
EVEN IF I'VE ACCEPTED THAT MY LOVE IS OVER...
...THE AFFECTION STILL LINGERS...
...AND I CAN'T BE AT EASE ANYWHERE.
UNABLE TO FIND MY FOOTING, I'VE BEEN FEELING MORE HOPELESS THAN I COULD HAVE EVER IMAGINED.
TIME STOPPED FOR ME.

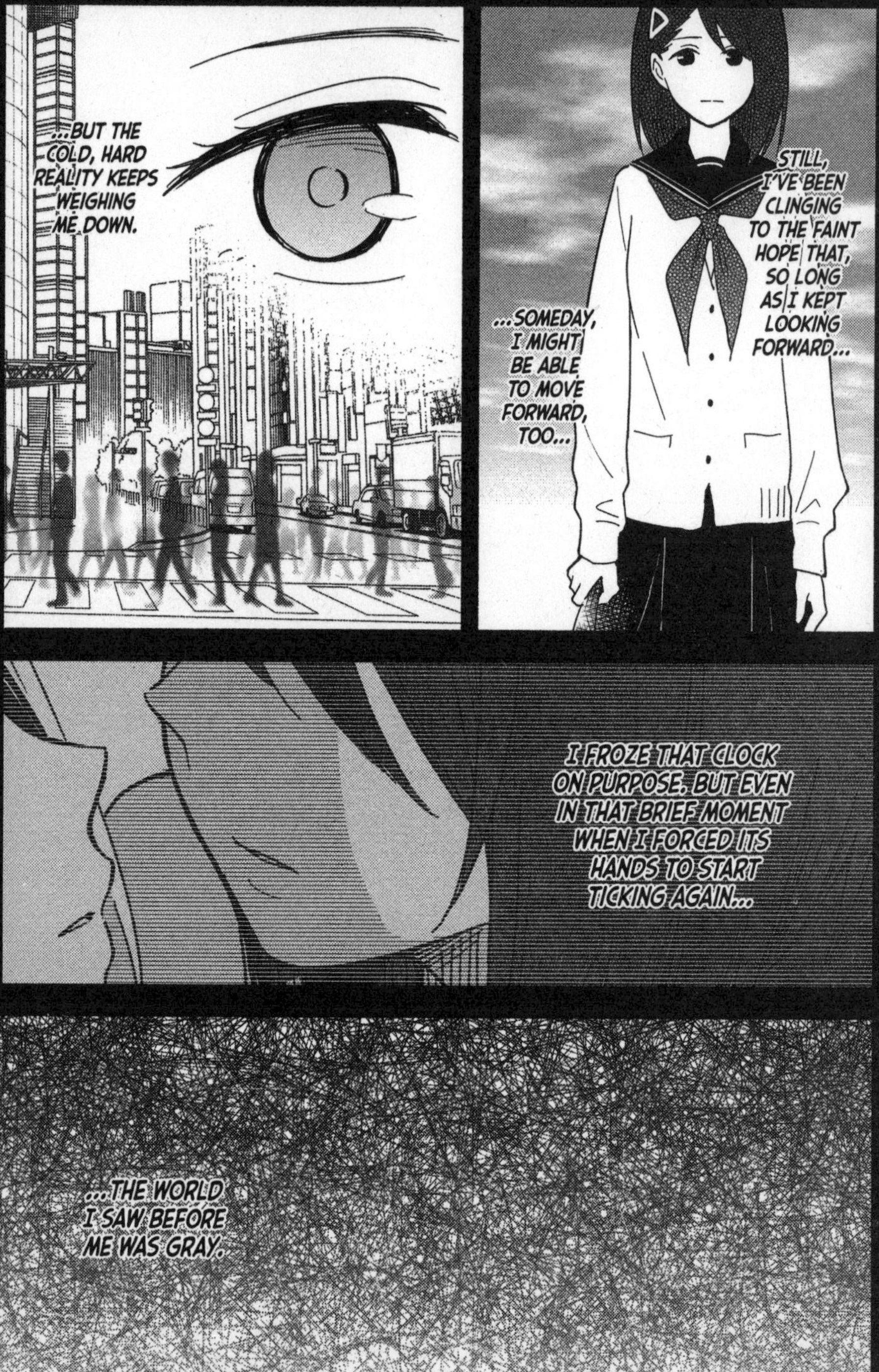
STILL, I'VE BEEN CLINGING TO THE FAINT HOPE THAT, SO LONG AS I KEPT LOOKING FORWARD...
...SOMEDAY, I MIGHT BE ABLE TO MOVE FORWARD, TOO...
...BUT THE COLD, HARD REALITY KEEPS WEIGHING ME DOWN.
I FROZE THAT CLOCK ON PURPOSE. BUT EVEN IN THAT BRIEF MOMENT WHEN I FORCED ITS HANDS TO START TICKING AGAIN...
...THE WORLD I SAW BEFORE ME WAS GRAY.

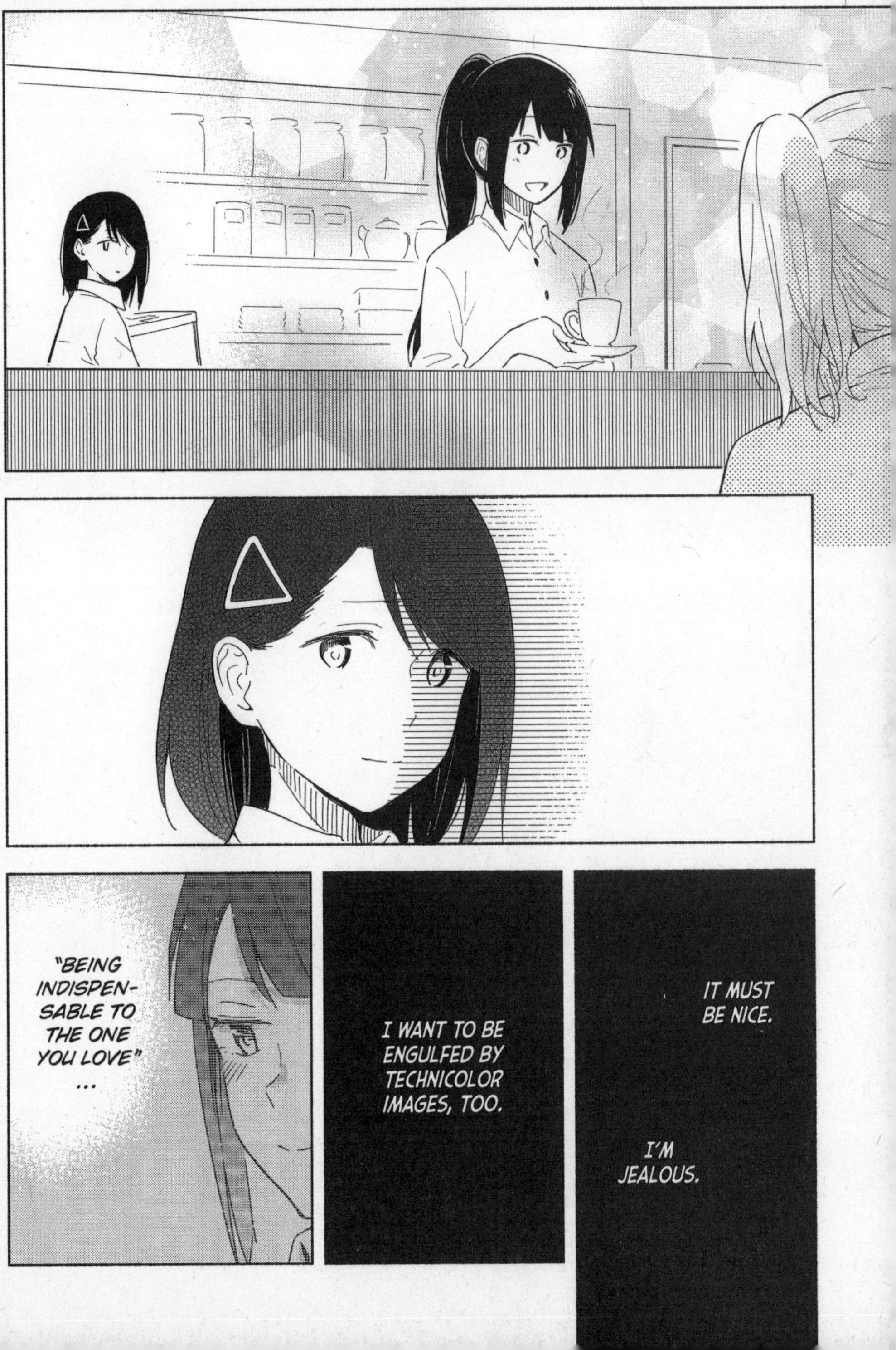
IT MUST BE NICE.
I'M JEALOUS.
I WANT TO BE ENGULFED BY TECHNICOLOR IMAGES, TOO.
"BEING INDISPEN-SABLE TO THE ONE YOU LOVE" ...

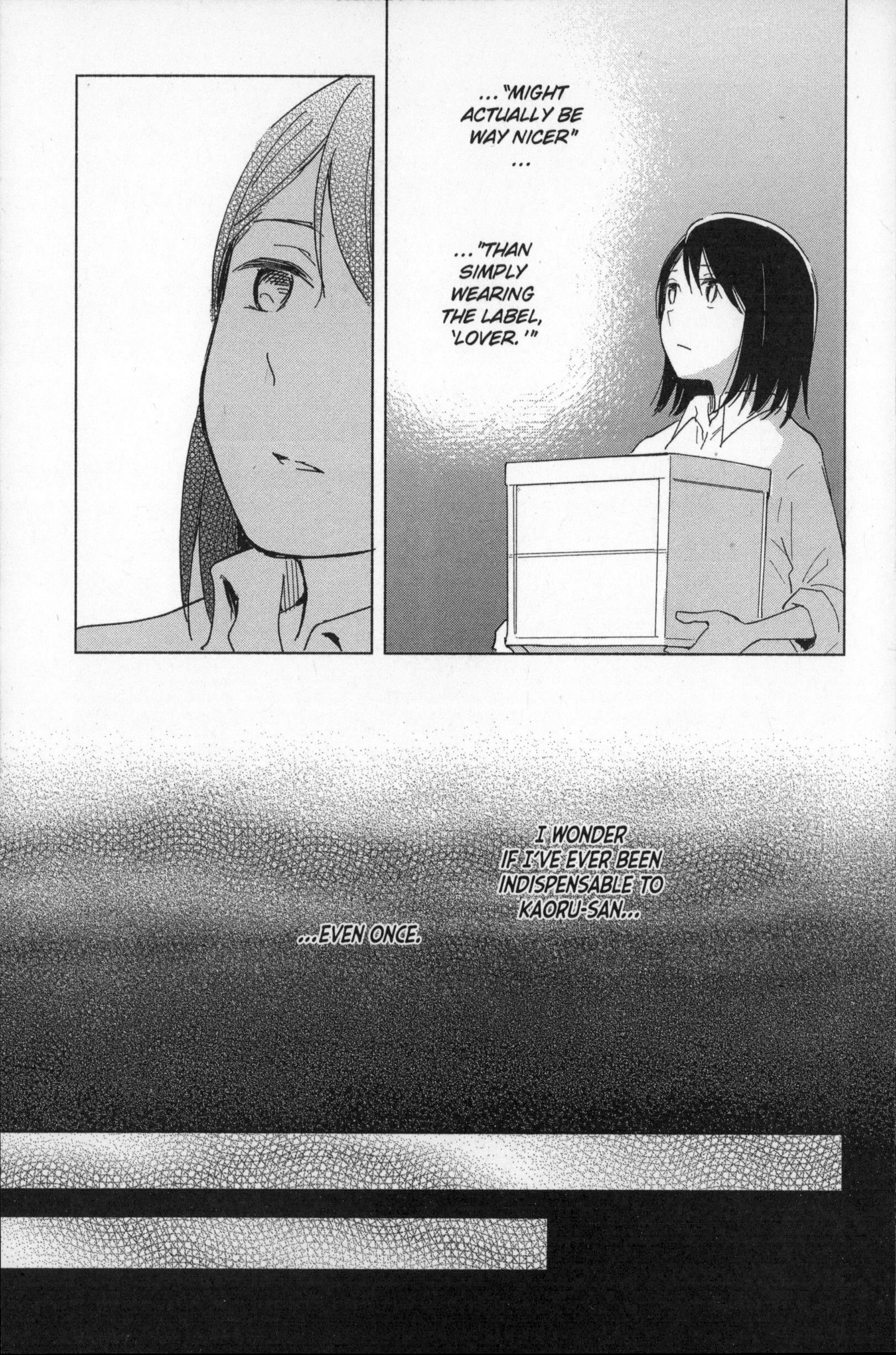
..."MIGHT ACTUALLY BE WAY NICER" ...
..."THAN SIMPLY WEARING THE LABEL, 'LOVER.'"
I WONDER IF I'VE EVER BEEN INDISPENSABLE TO KAORU-SAN...
...EVEN ONCE.

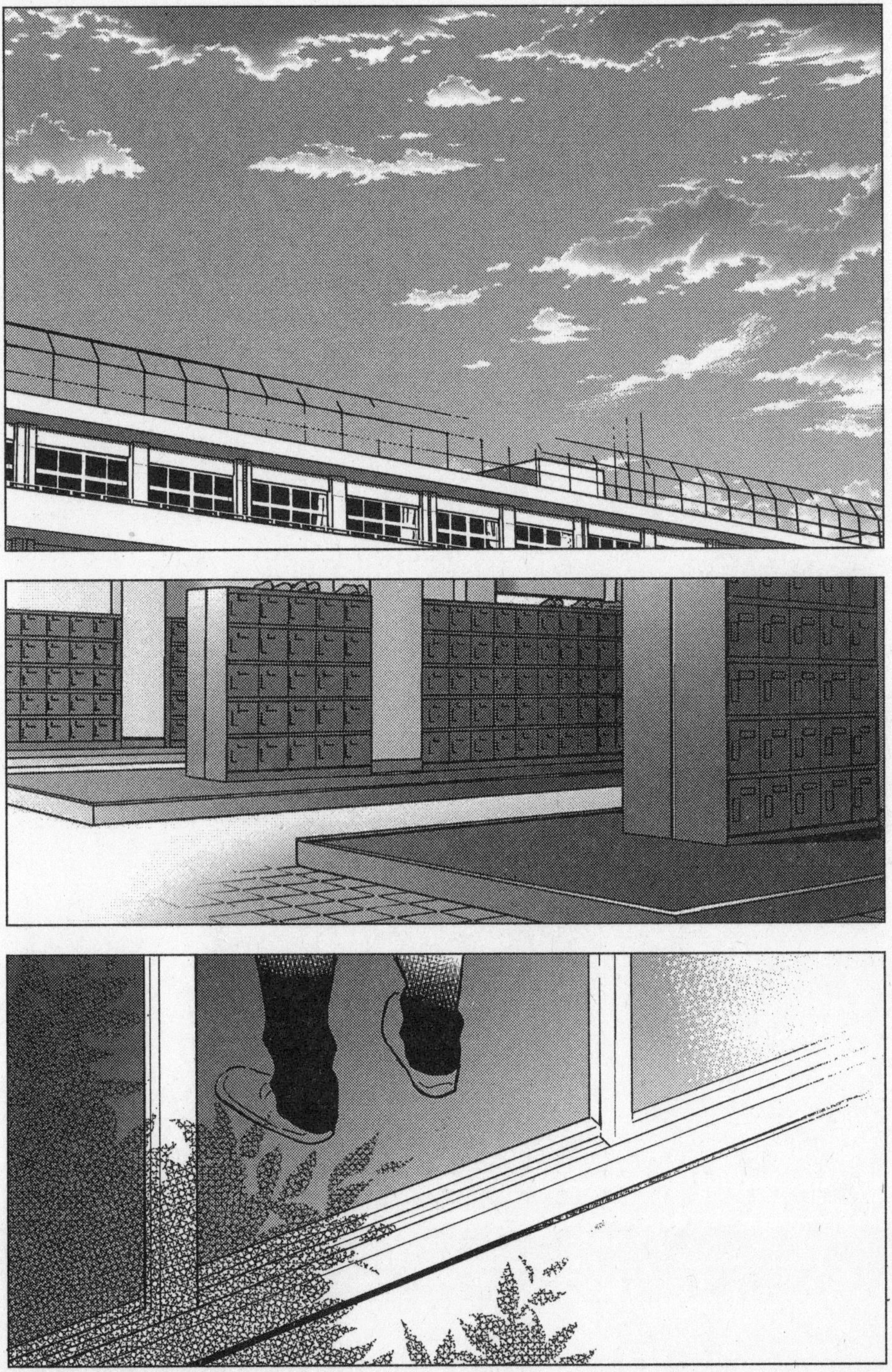

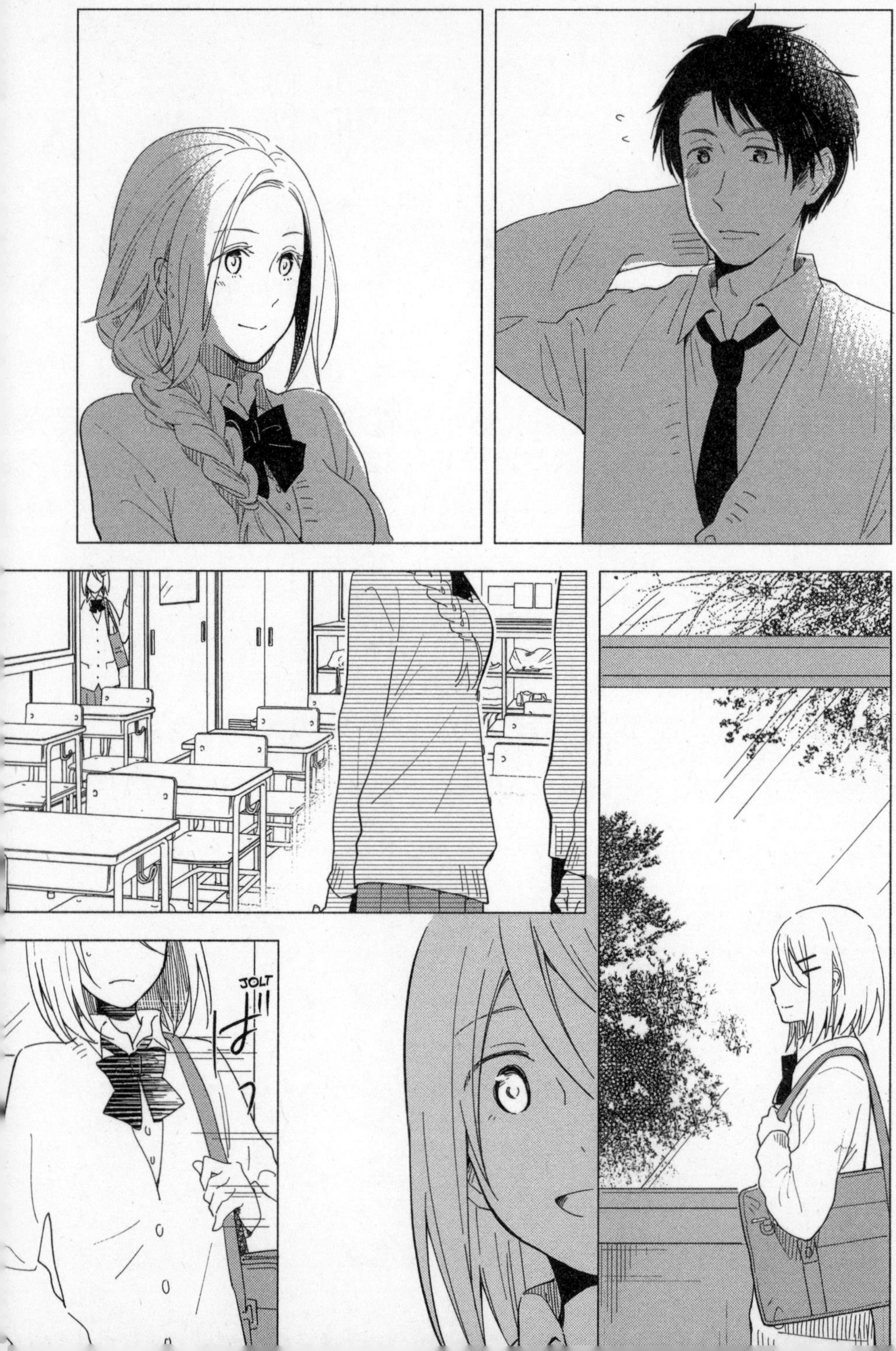
JOLT
ばっ

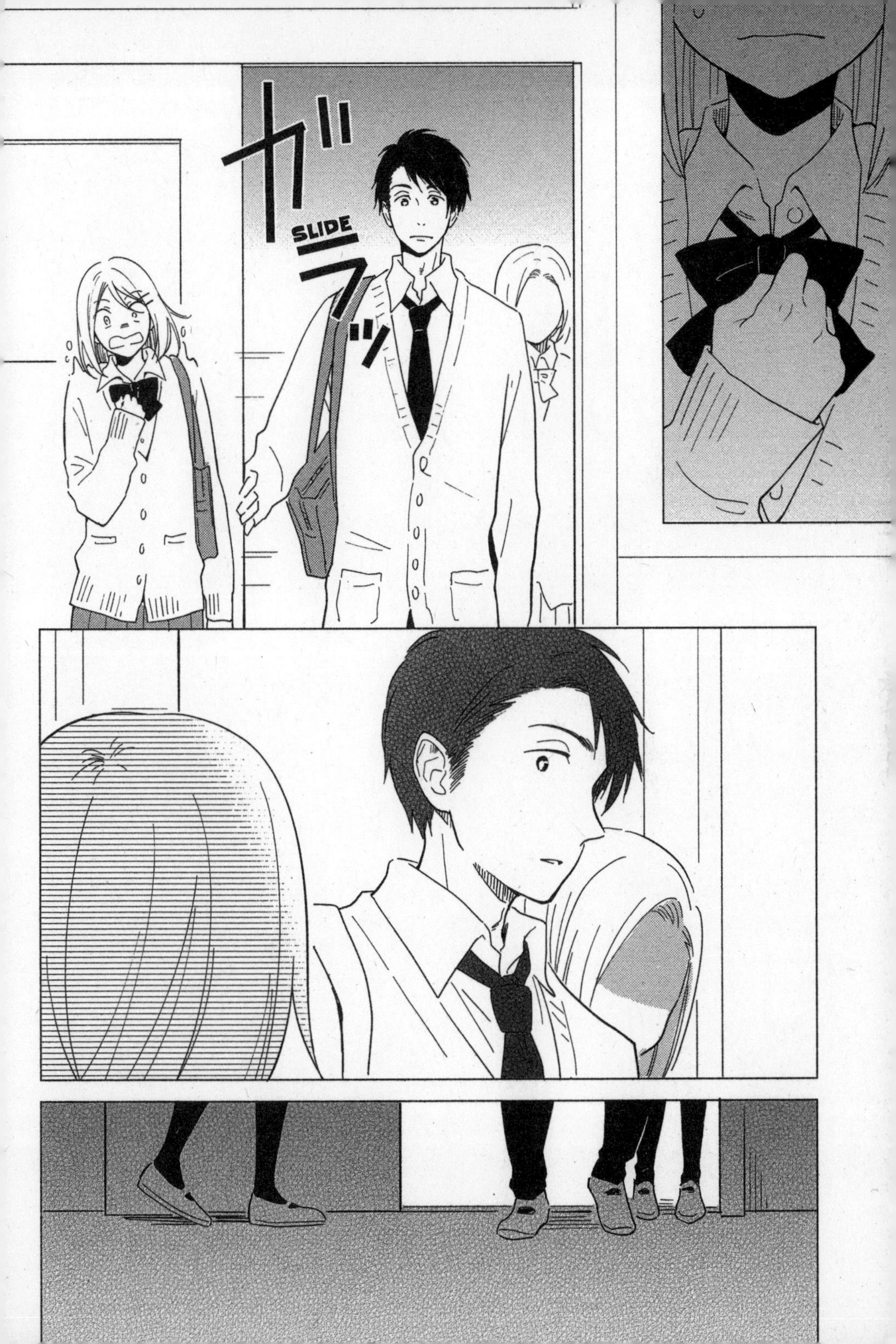
ガラッ
SLIDE

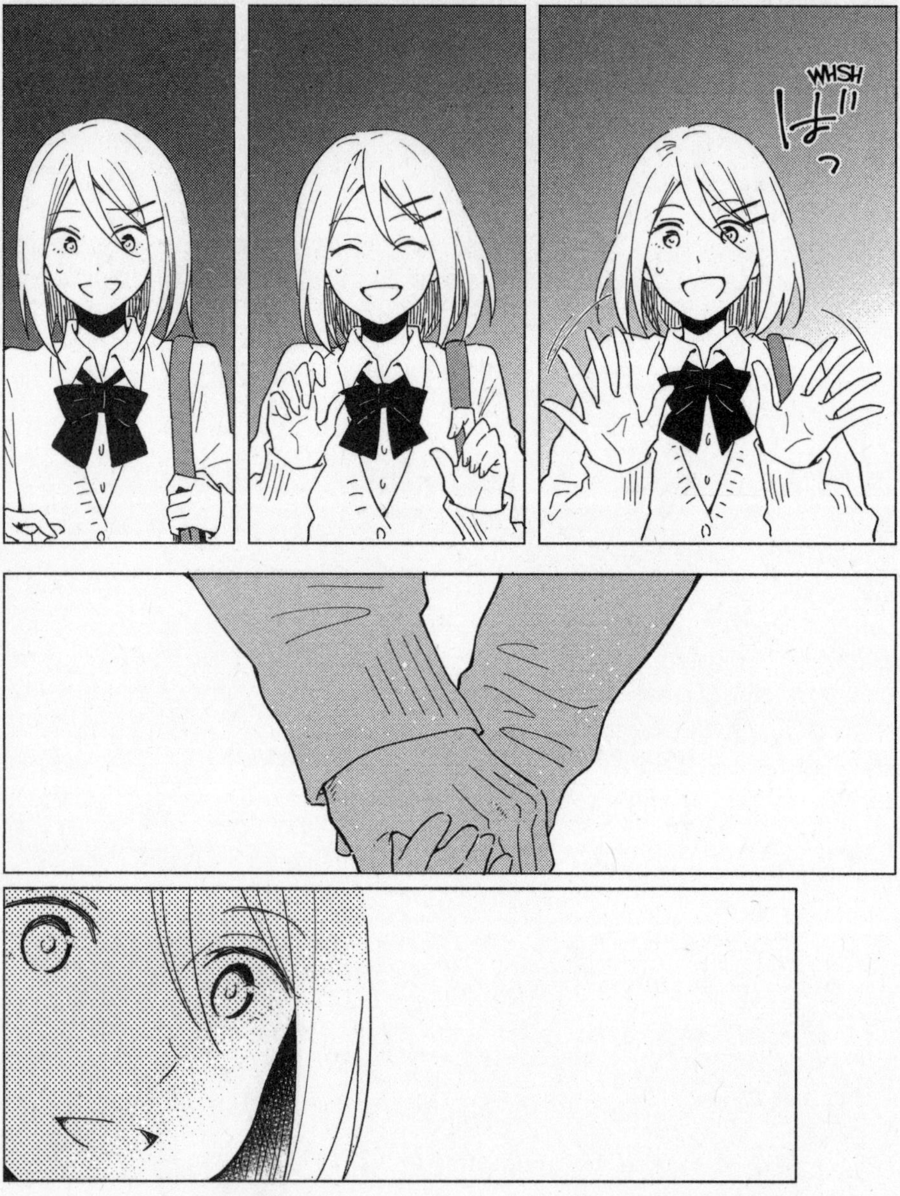
WHSH
ばっ

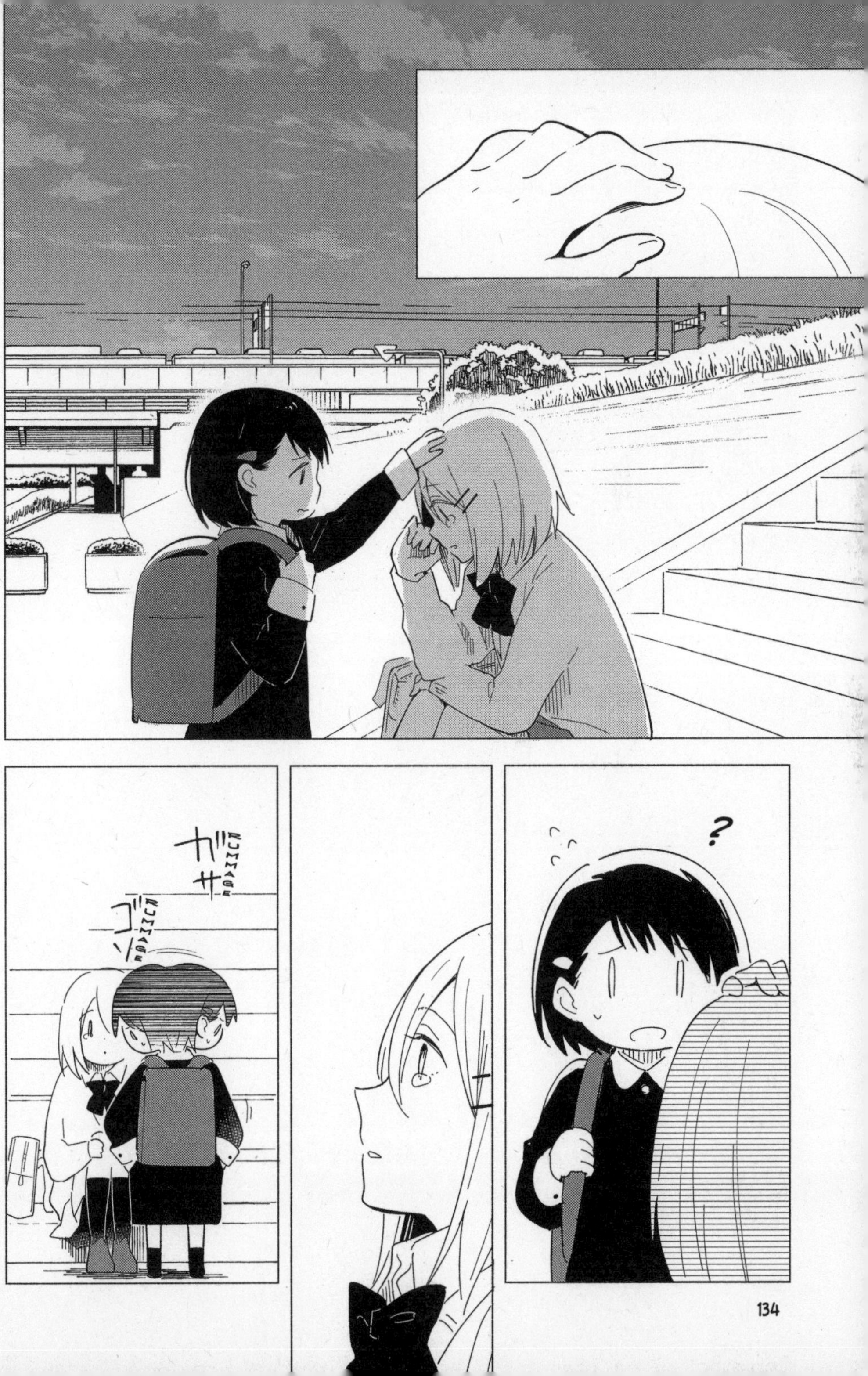
?
ガサ
RUMMAGE
ゴソ
RUMMAGE

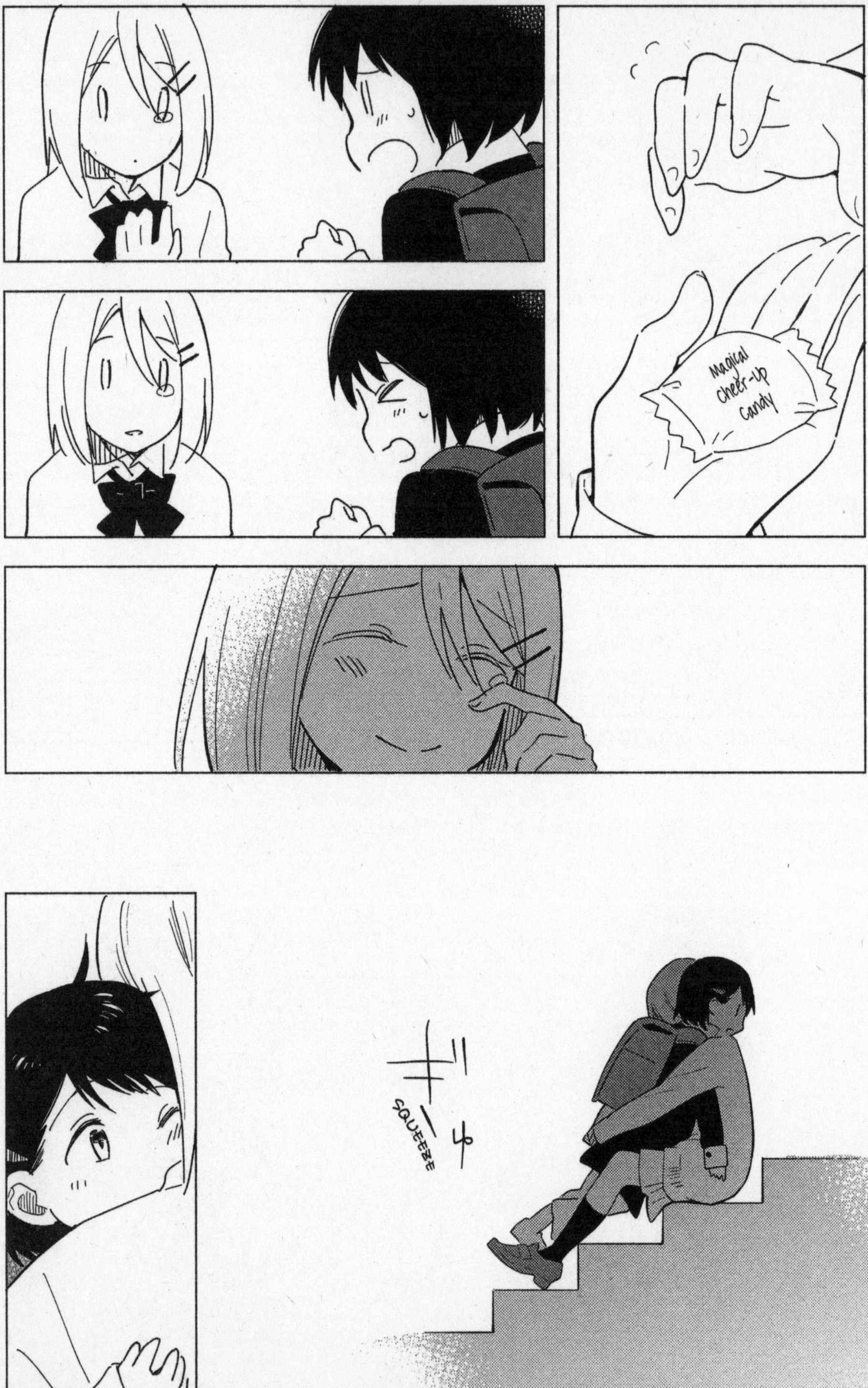
Magical cheer-up candy
SQUEEZE

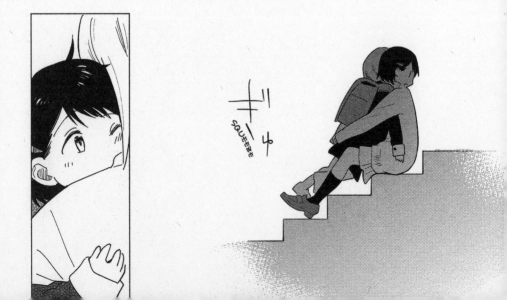

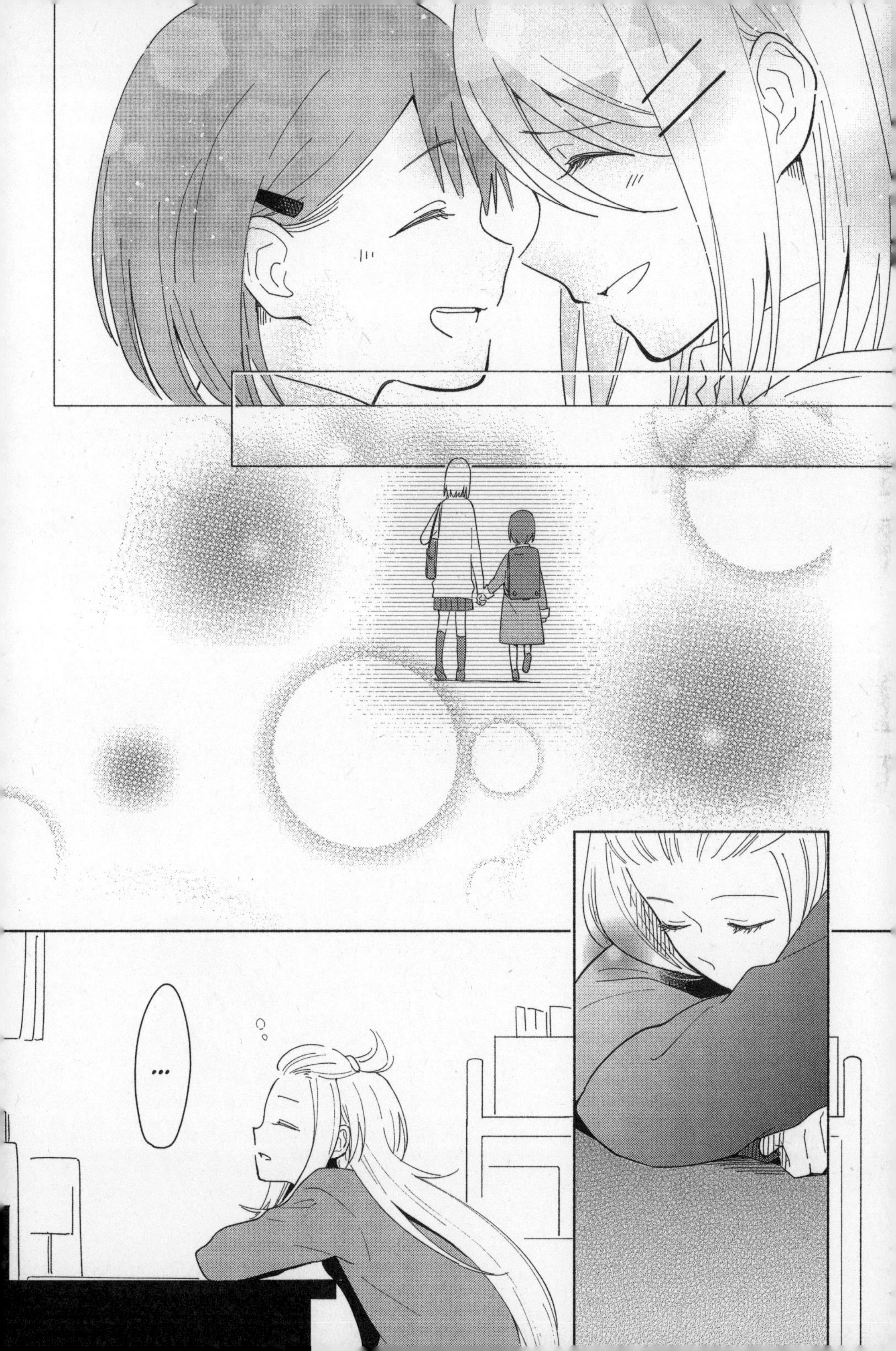
...

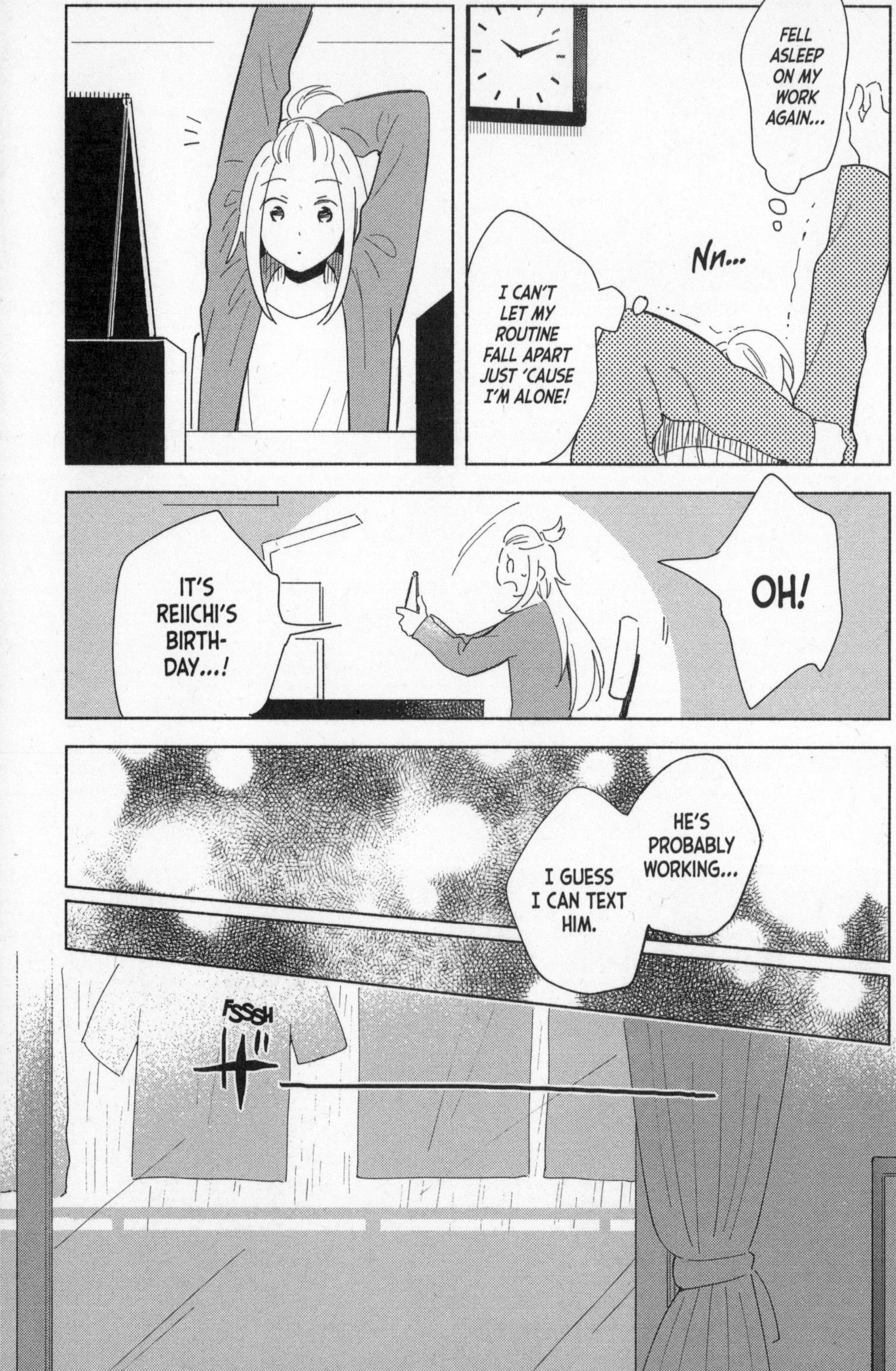
FELL ASLEEP ON MY WORK AGAIN...
Nn...
I CAN'T LET MY ROUTINE FALL APART JUST 'CAUSE I'M ALONE!
OH!
IT'S REIICHI'S BIRTH-DAY...!
HE'S PROBABLY WORKING...
I GUESS I CAN TEXT HIM.
FSSSH

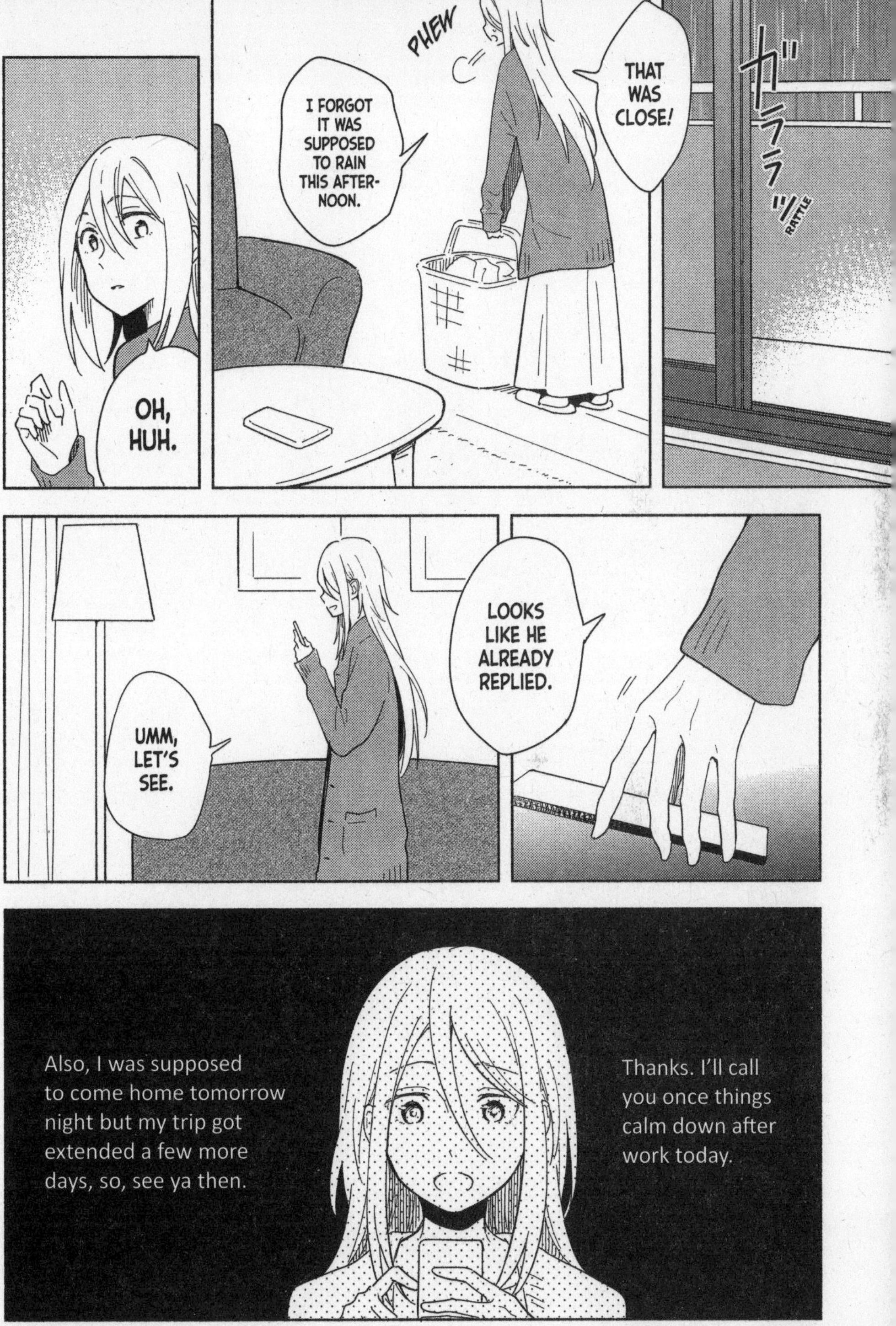
ガラララッ
RATTLE
THAT WAS CLOSE!
PHEW
I FORGOT IT WAS SUPPOSED TO RAIN THIS AFTER-NOON.
OH, HUH.
LOOKS LIKE HE ALREADY REPLIED.
UMM, LET'S SEE.
Thanks. I'll call you once things calm down after work today.
Also, I was supposed to come home tomorrow night but my trip got extended a few more days, so, see ya then.

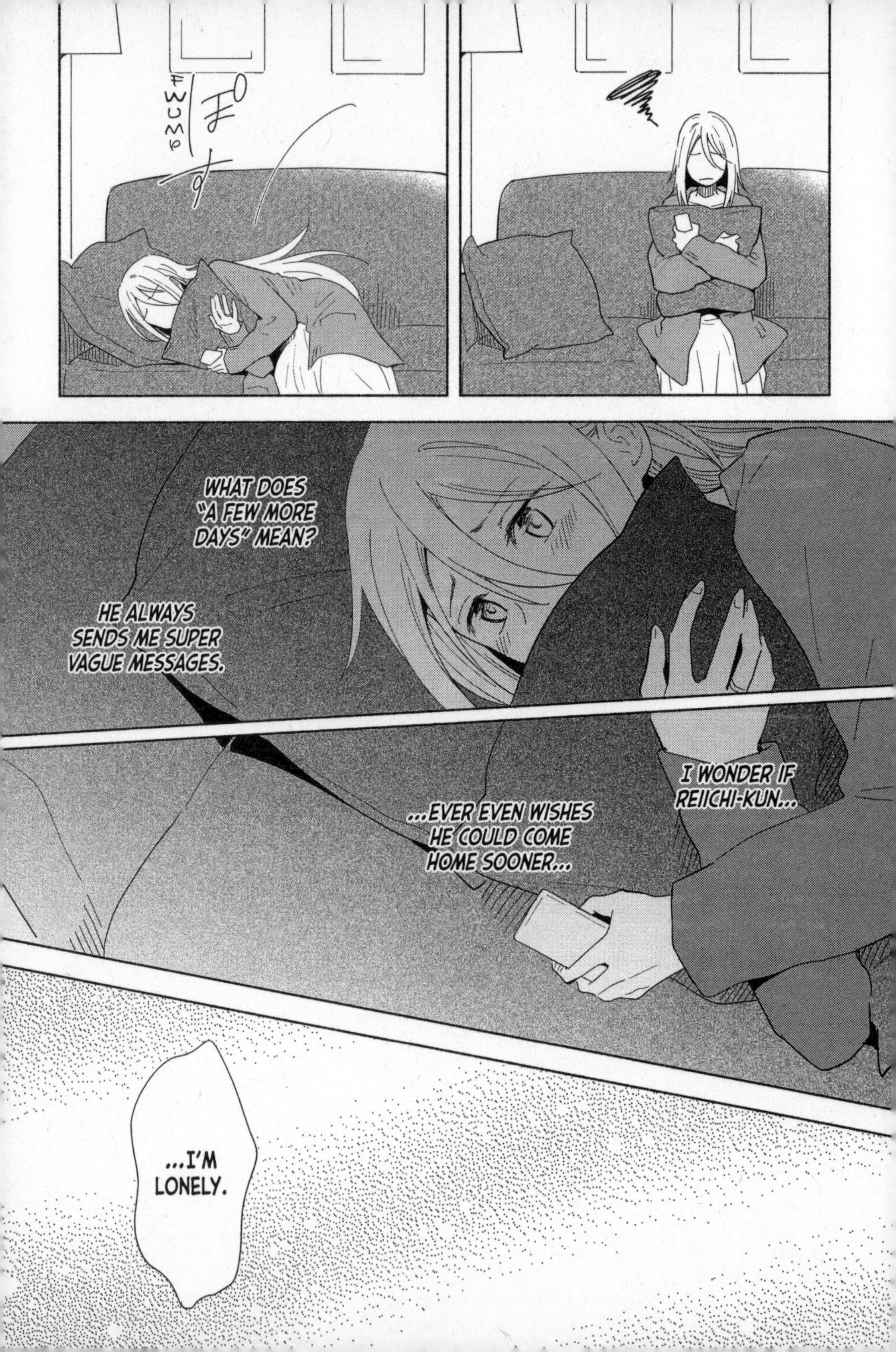
FWUMP
WHAT DOES "A FEW MORE DAYS" MEAN?
HE ALWAYS SENDS ME SUPER VAGUE MESSAGES.
I WONDER IF REIICHI-KUN...
...EVER EVEN WISHES HE COULD COME HOME SOONER...
...I'M LONELY.

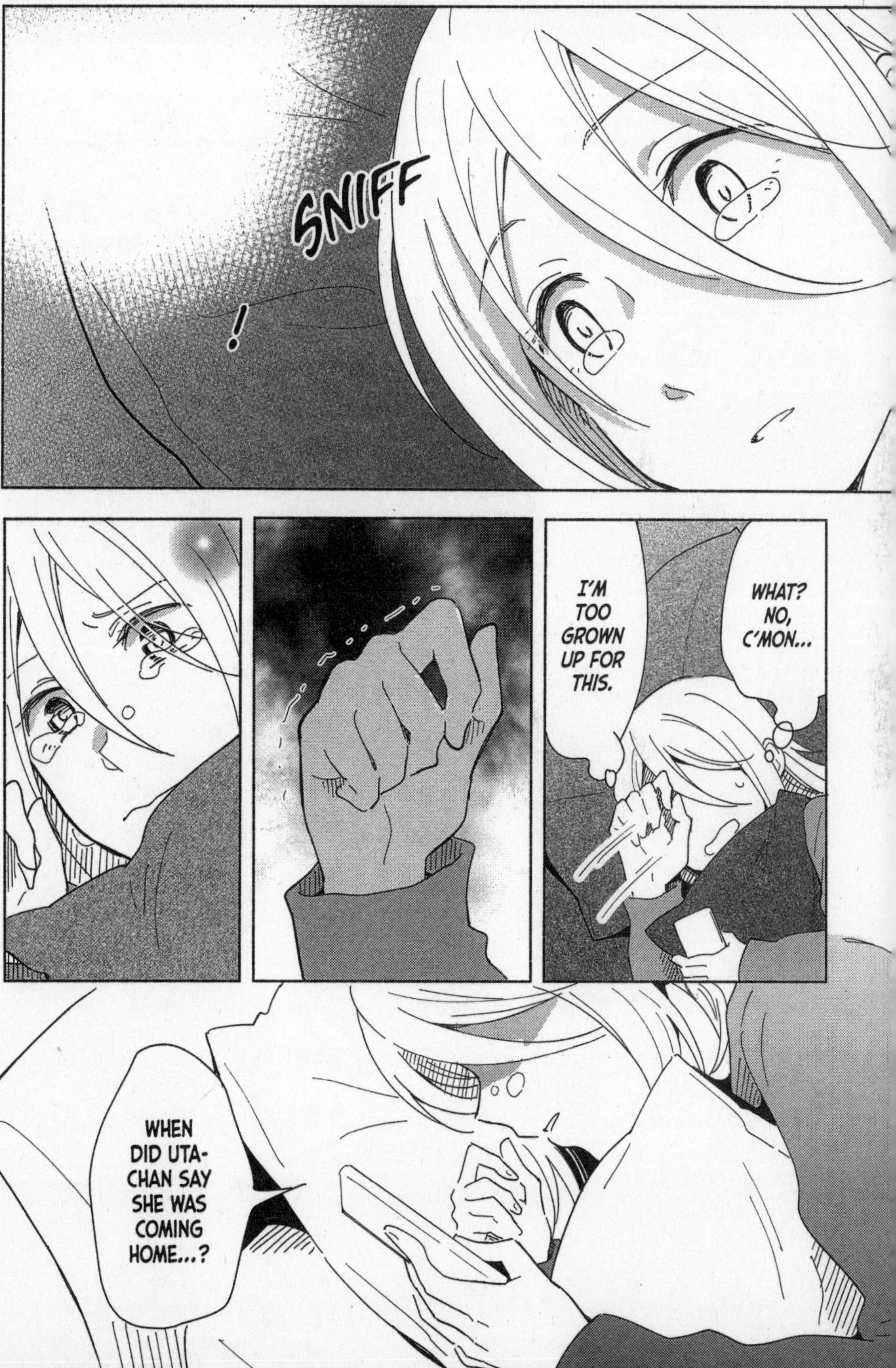
SNIFF
!
WHAT? NO, C'MON...
I'M TOO GROWN UP FOR THIS.
WHEN DID UTA-CHAN SAY SHE WAS COMING HOME...?

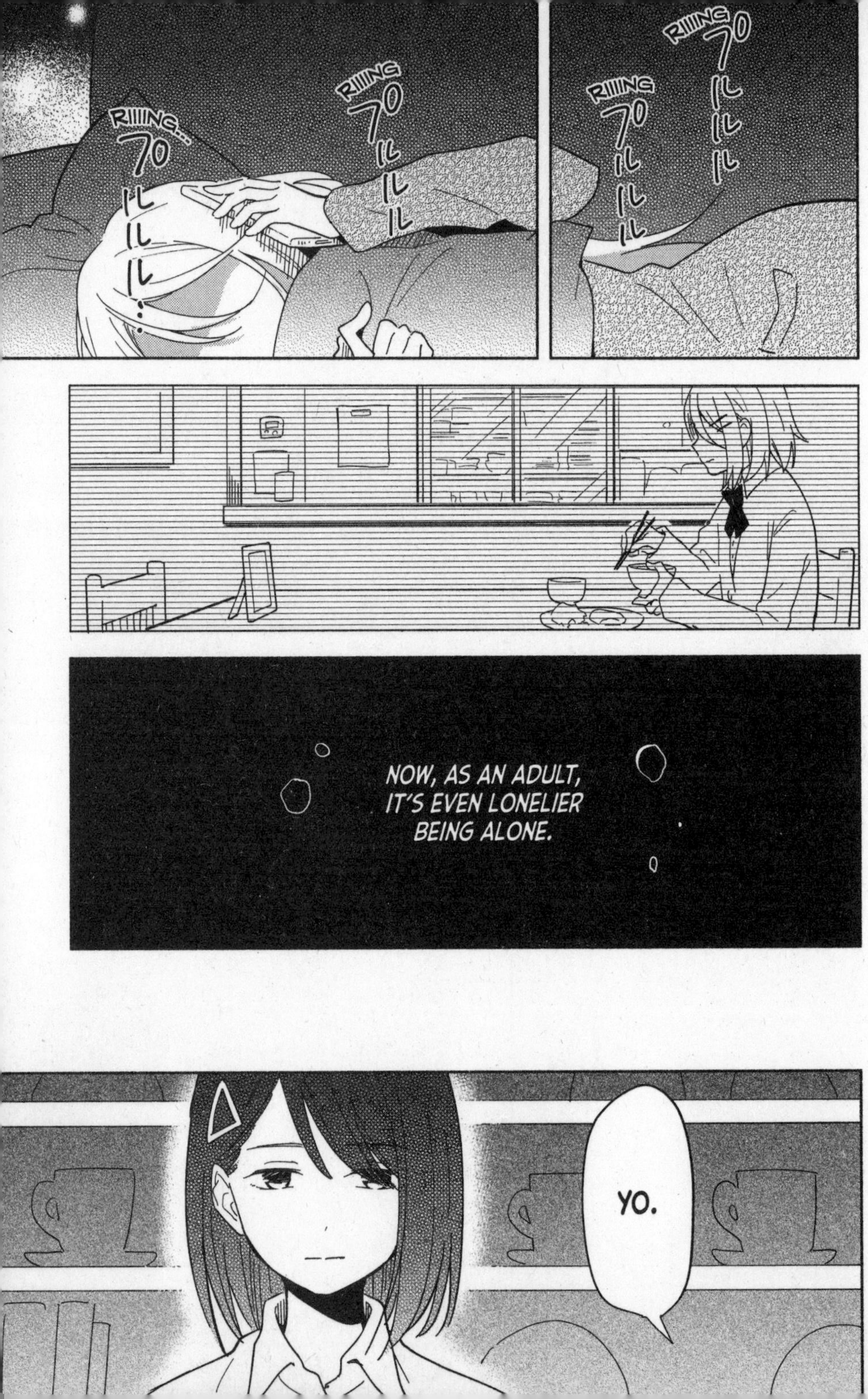

RIIING
プルルル
RIIING
プルルル
RIIING
プルルル
RIIING...
プルルル…
NOW, AS AN ADULT, IT'S EVEN LONELIER BEING ALONE.
YO.

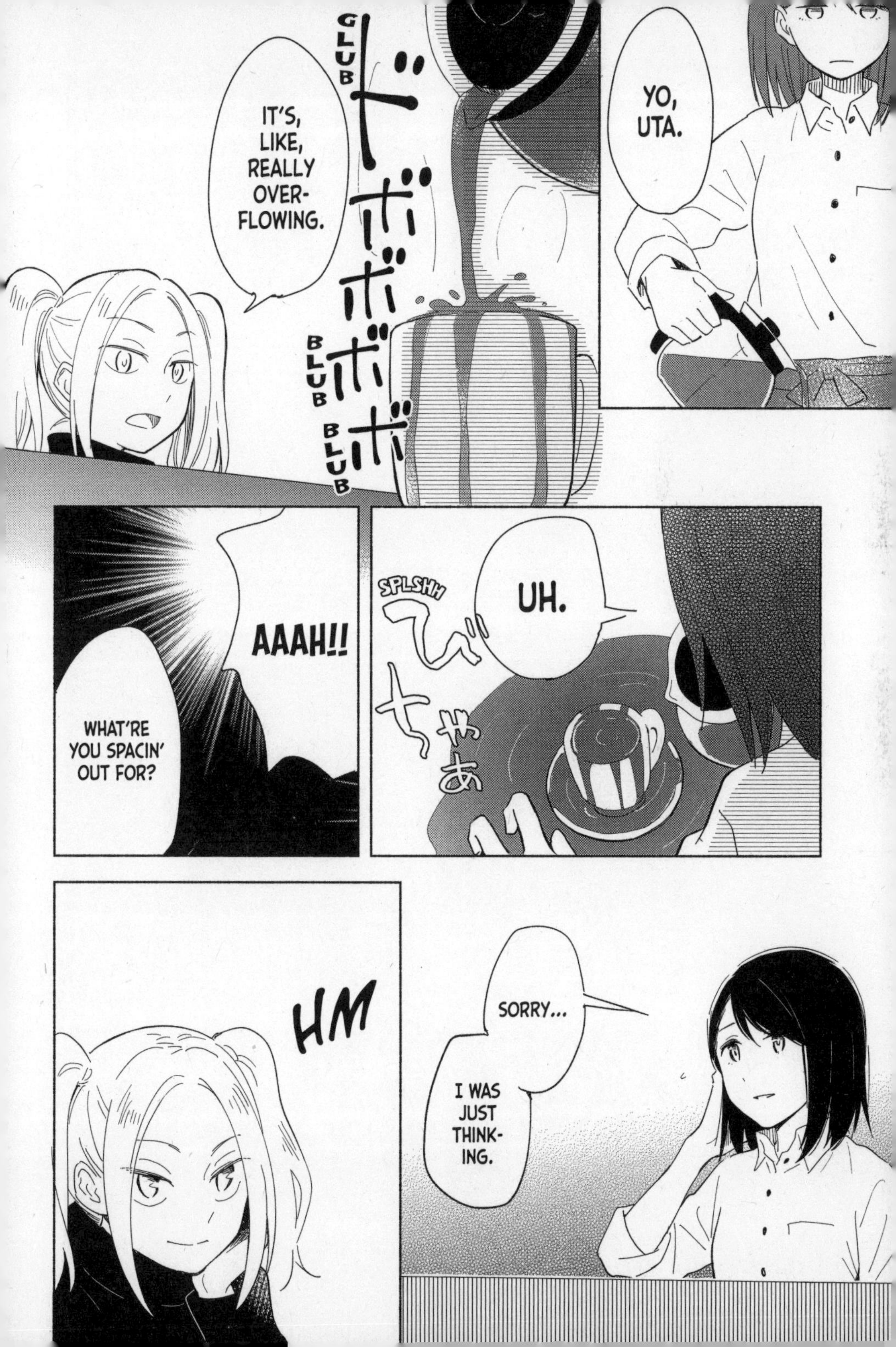
YO, UTA.
GLUB
BLUB
BLUB
IT'S, LIKE, REALLY OVER-FLOWING.
UH.
SPLSHH
AAAH!!
WHAT'RE YOU SPACIN' OUT FOR?
SORRY...
I WAS JUST THINK-ING.
HM

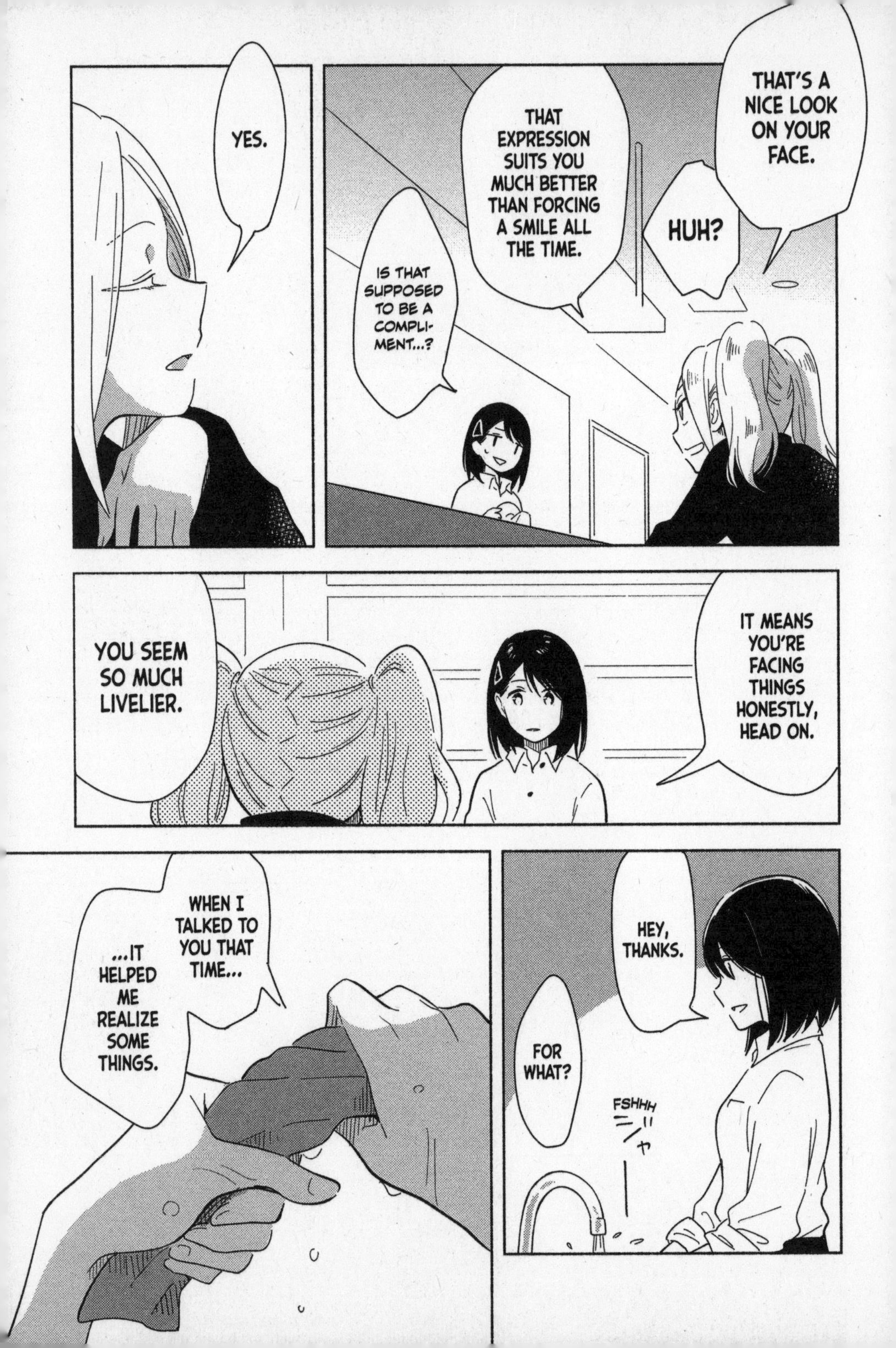
THAT'S A NICE LOOK ON YOUR FACE.
HUH?
THAT EXPRESSION SUITS YOU MUCH BETTER THAN FORCING A SMILE ALL THE TIME.
IS THAT SUPPOSED TO BE A COMPLI-MENT...?
YES.
IT MEANS YOU'RE FACING THINGS HONESTLY, HEAD ON.
YOU SEEM SO MUCH LIVELIER.
HEY, THANKS.
FOR WHAT?
FSHHH
ジャー
WHEN I TALKED TO YOU THAT TIME...
...IT HELPED ME REALIZE SOME THINGS.

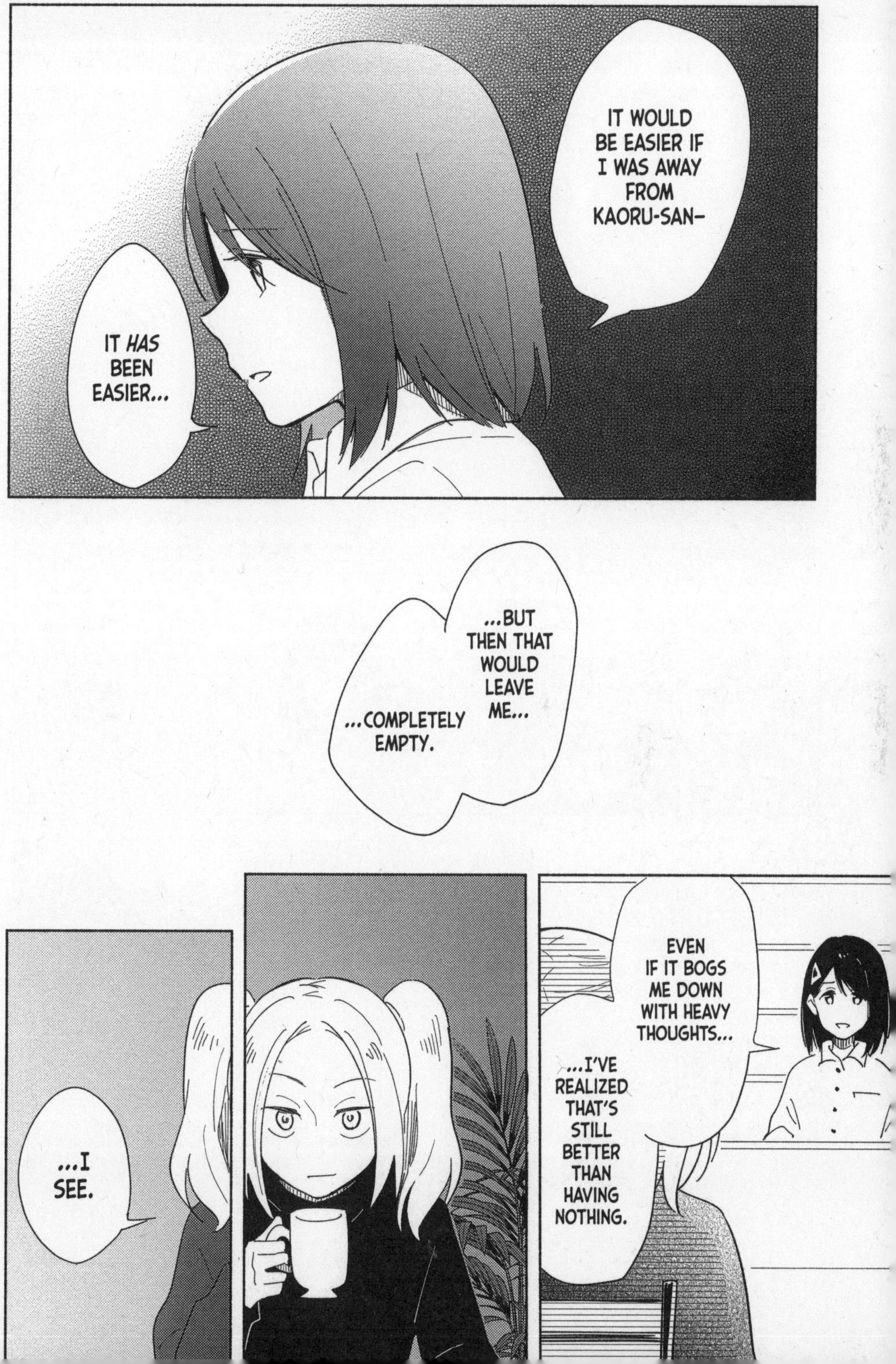
IT WOULD BE EASIER IF I WAS AWAY FROM KAORU-SAN–
IT *HAS* BEEN EASIER...
...BUT THEN THAT WOULD LEAVE ME...
...COMPLETELY EMPTY.
EVEN IF IT BOGS ME DOWN WITH HEAVY THOUGHTS...
...I'VE REALIZED THAT'S STILL BETTER THAN HAVING NOTHING.
...I SEE.

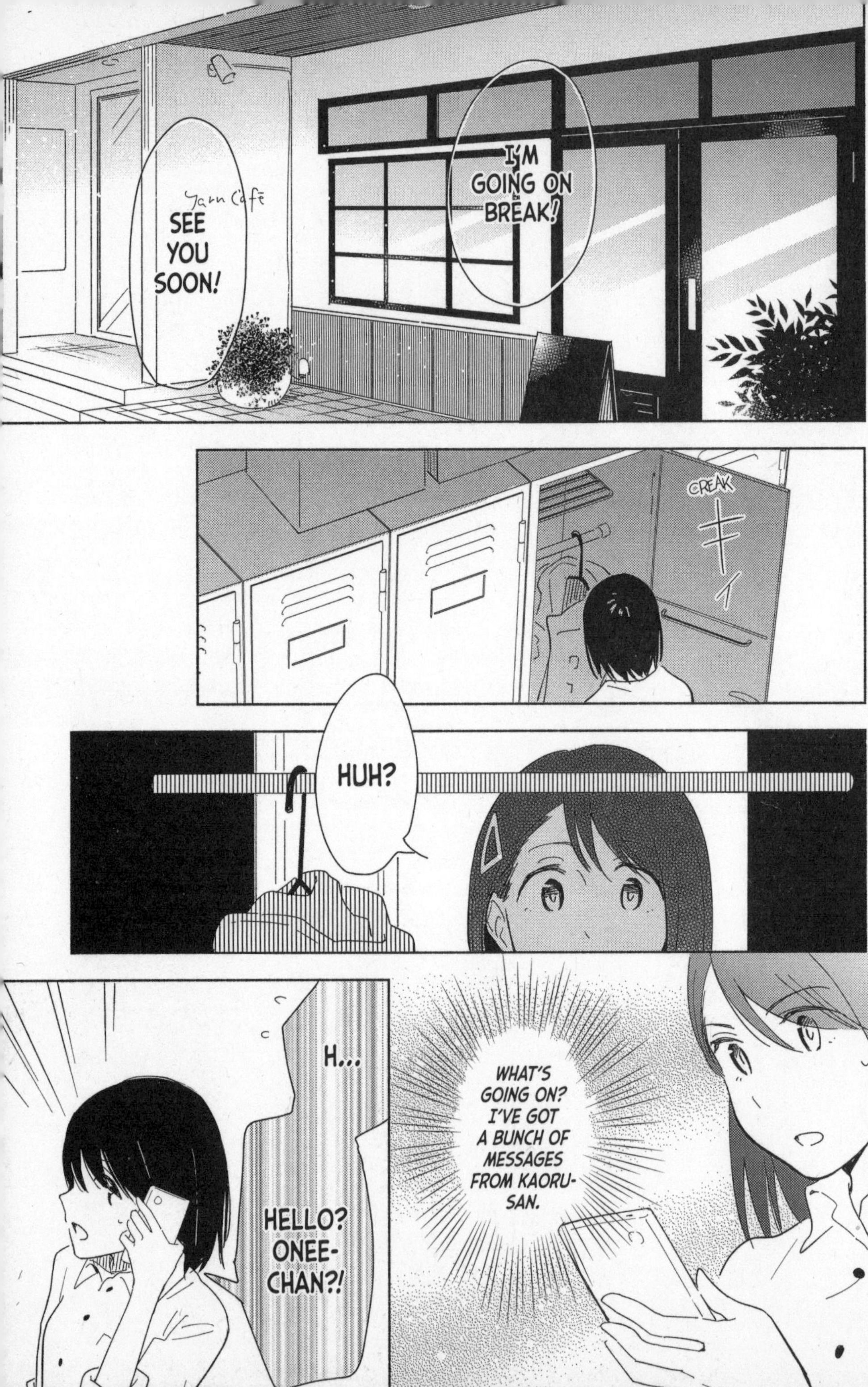
I'M GOING ON BREAK!
Yarn Café
SEE YOU SOON!
CREAK
キイ
HUH?
WHAT'S GOING ON? I'VE GOT A BUNCH OF MESSAGES FROM KAORU-SAN.
H...
HELLO? ONEE-CHAN?!

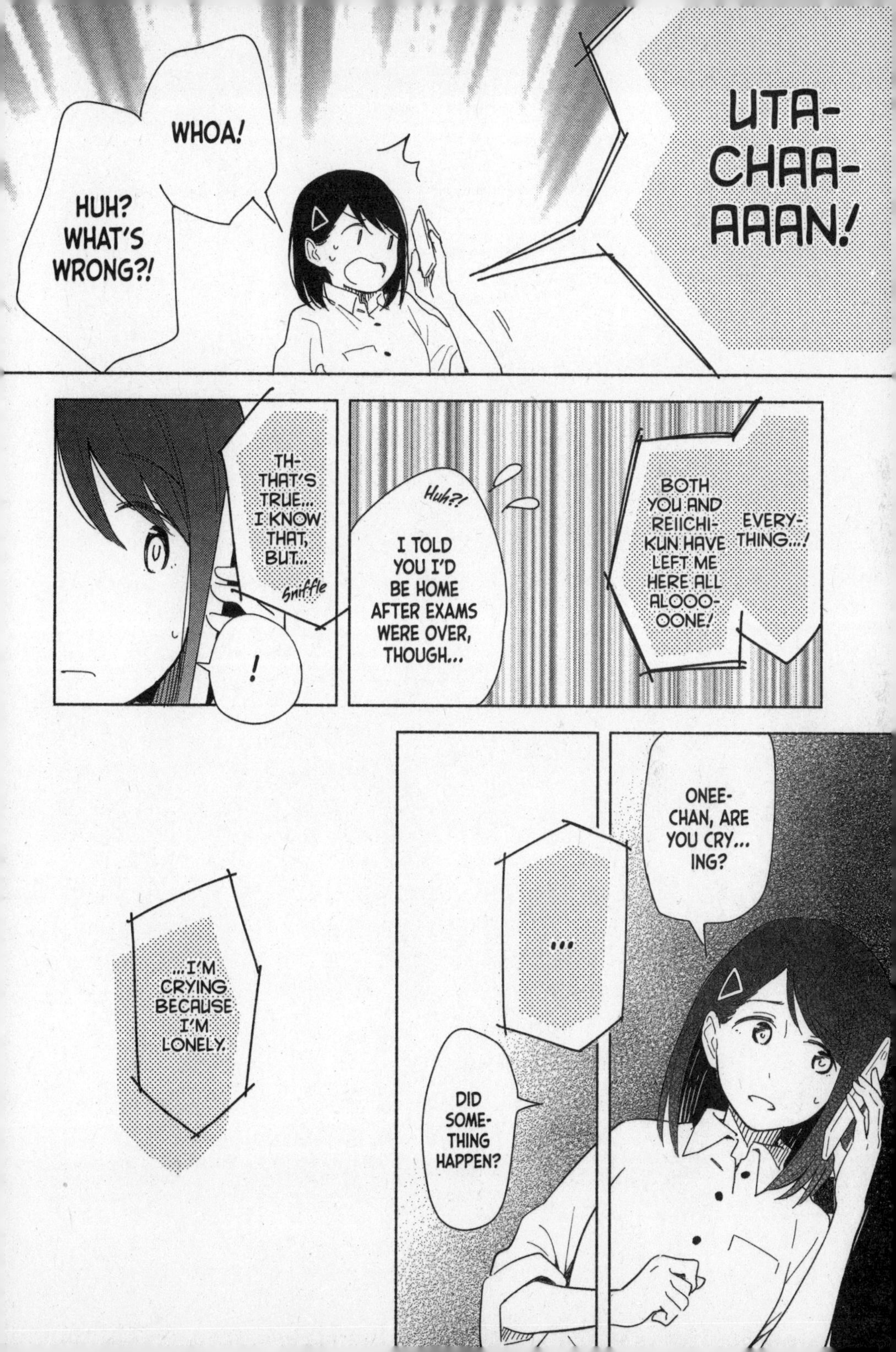
UTA-CHAA-AAAN!
WHOA!
HUH? WHAT'S WRONG?!
EVERY-THING...!
BOTH YOU AND REIICHI-KUN HAVE LEFT ME HERE ALL ALOOO-OONE!
Huh?!
I TOLD YOU I'D BE HOME AFTER EXAMS WERE OVER, THOUGH...
TH-THAT'S TRUE... I KNOW THAT, BUT...
Sniffle
!
ONEE-CHAN, ARE YOU CRY... ING?
...
DID SOME-THING HAPPEN?
...I'M CRYING BECAUSE I'M LONELY.

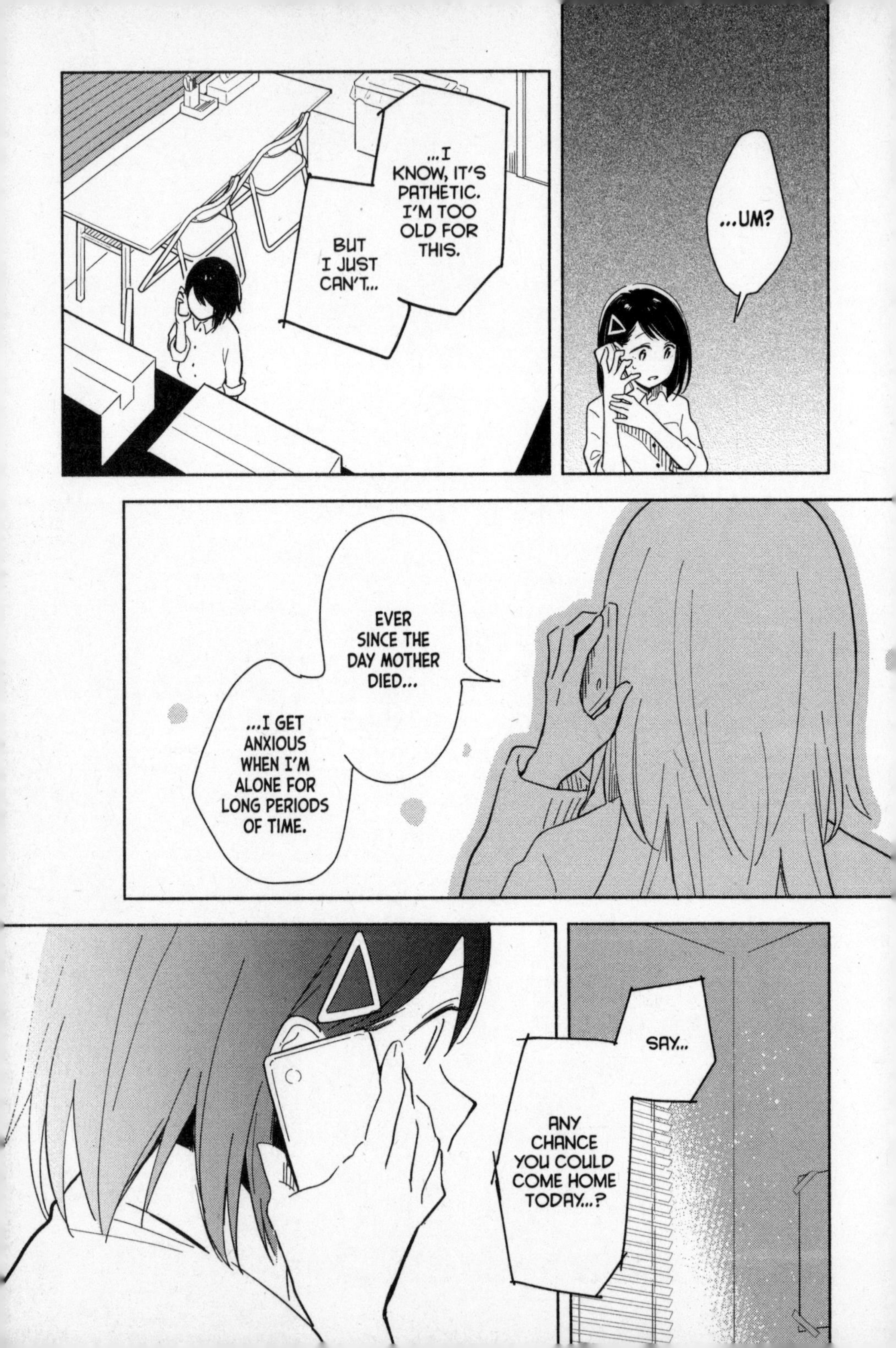
...UM?
...I KNOW, IT'S PATHETIC. I'M TOO OLD FOR THIS.
BUT I JUST CAN'T...
EVER SINCE THE DAY MOTHER DIED...
...I GET ANXIOUS WHEN I'M ALONE FOR LONG PERIODS OF TIME.
SAY...
ANY CHANCE YOU COULD COME HOME TODAY...?

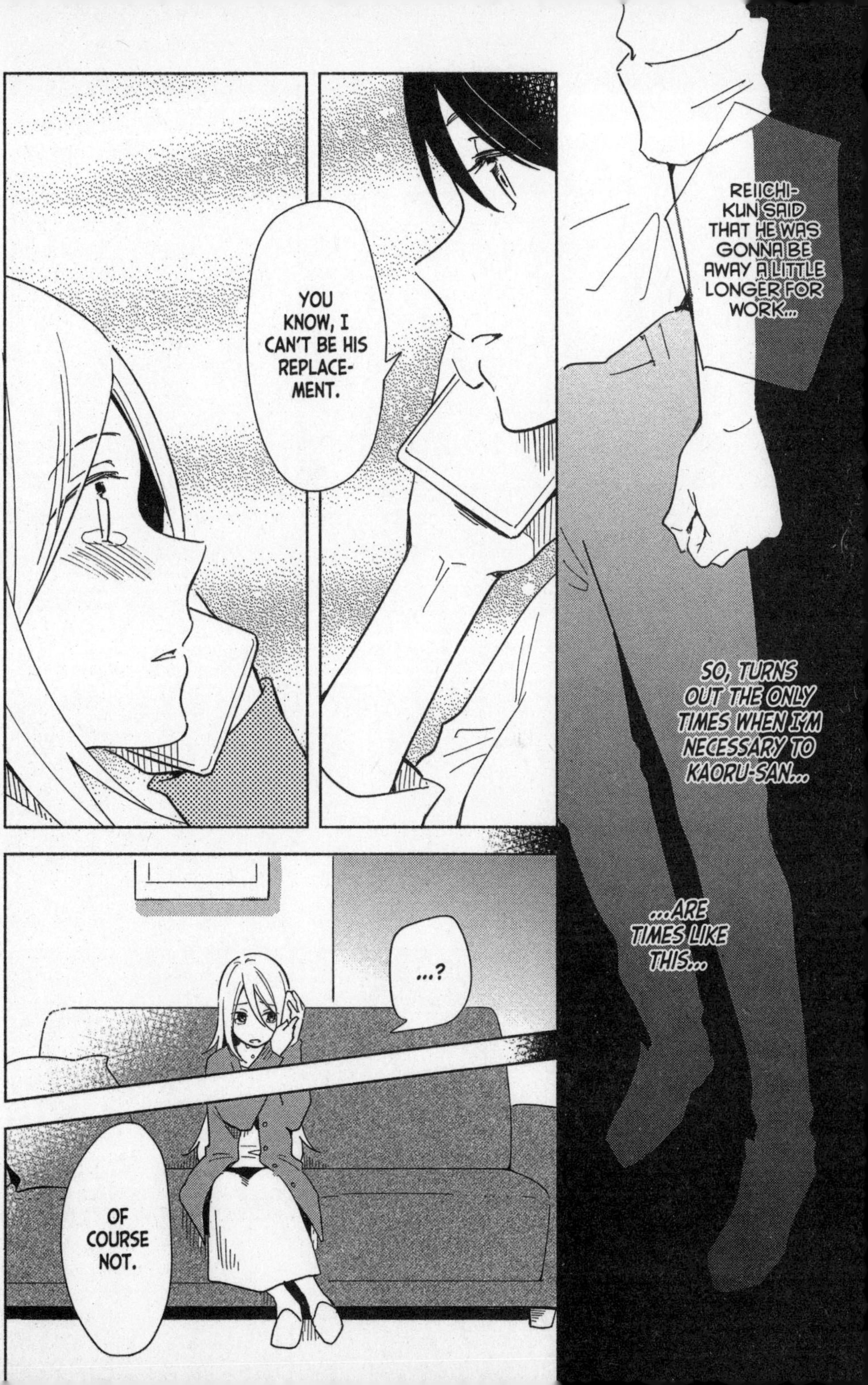
REIICHI-KUN SAID THAT HE WAS GONNA BE AWAY A LITTLE LONGER FOR WORK...
SO, TURNS OUT THE ONLY TIMES WHEN I'M NECESSARY TO KAORU-SAN...
...ARE TIMES LIKE THIS...
YOU KNOW, I CAN'T BE HIS REPLACEMENT.
...?
OF COURSE NOT.

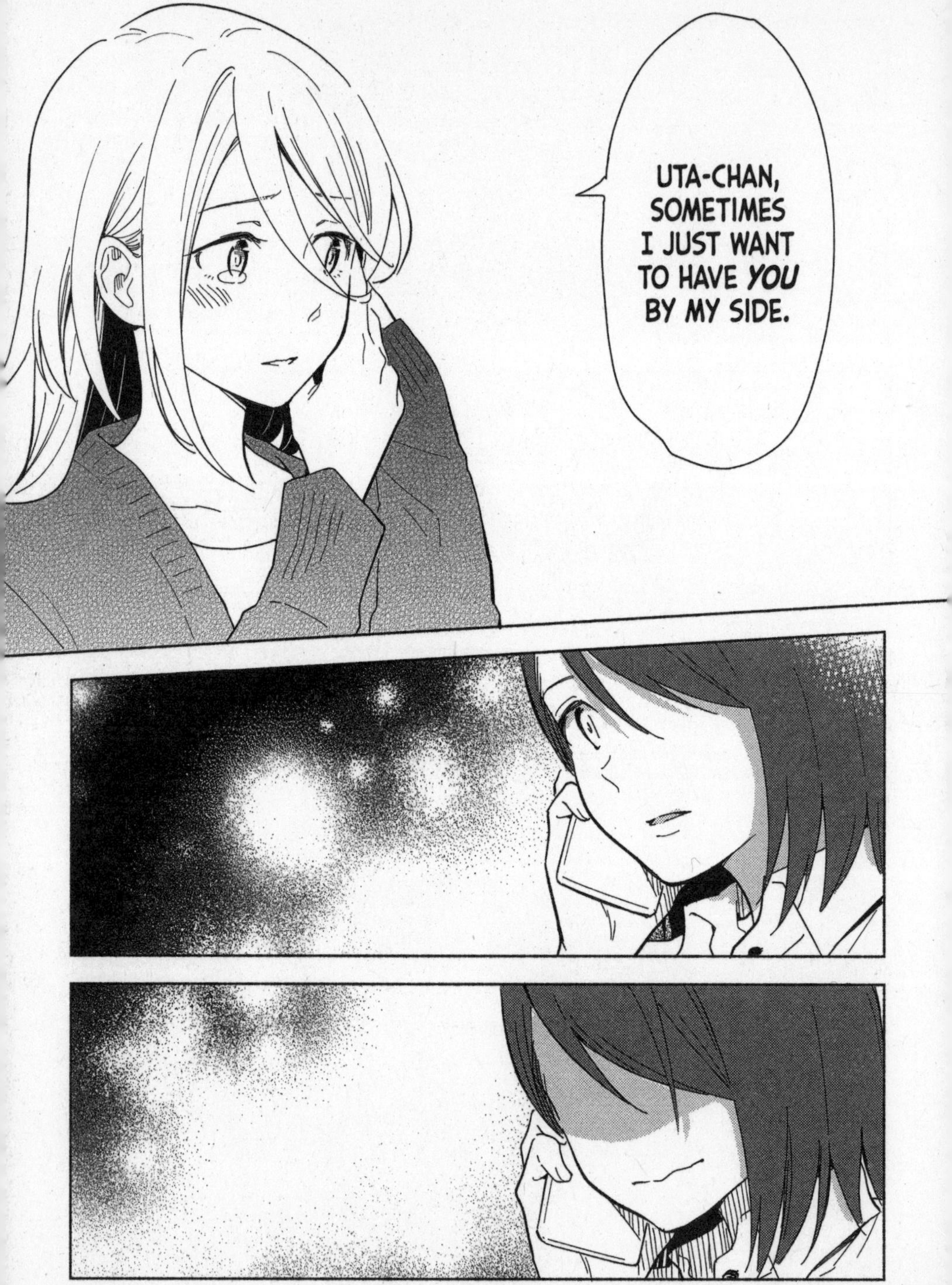
UTA-CHAN, SOMETIMES I JUST WANT TO HAVE *YOU* BY MY SIDE.

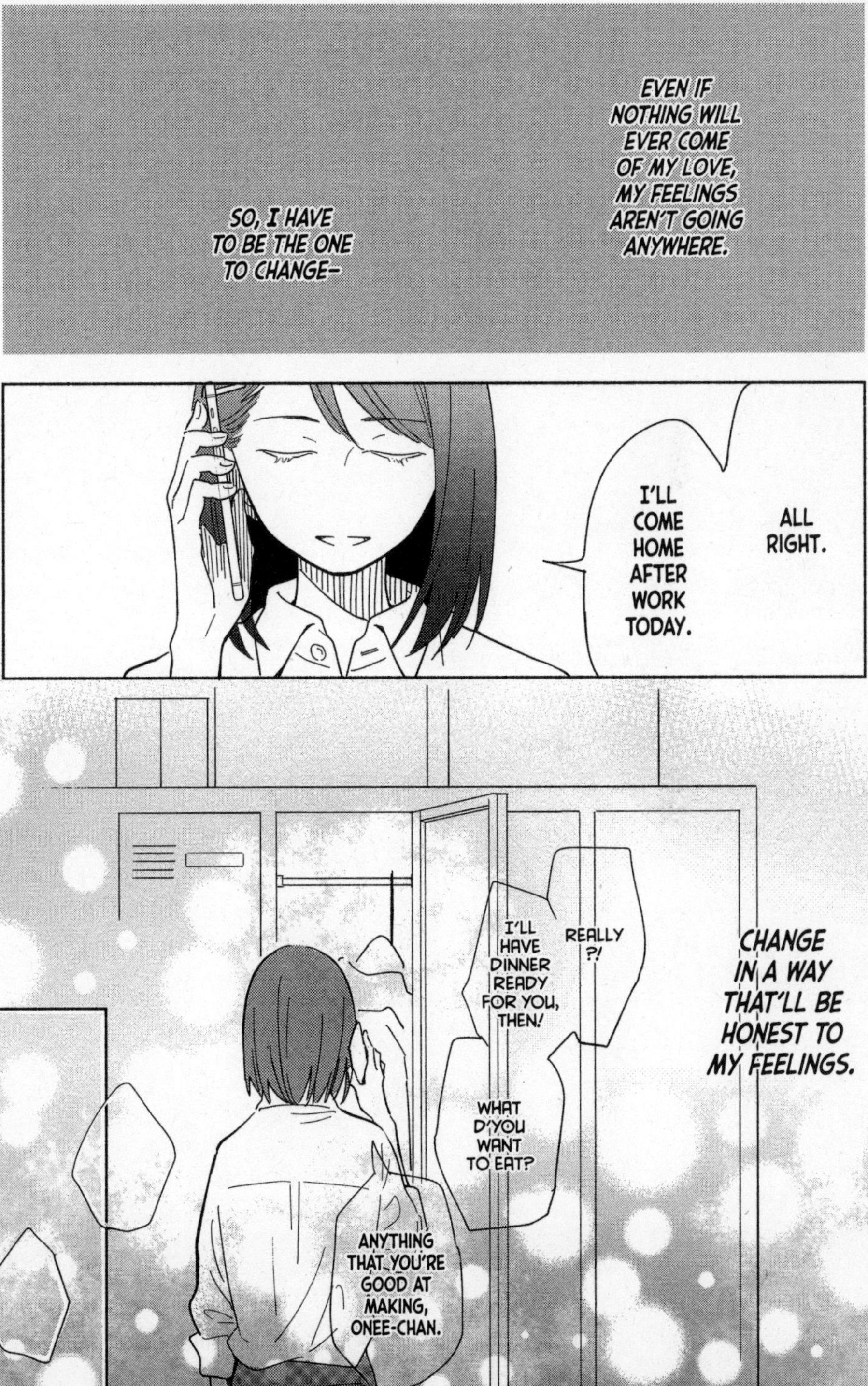
EVEN IF NOTHING WILL EVER COME OF MY LOVE, MY FEELINGS AREN'T GOING ANYWHERE.
SO, I HAVE TO BE THE ONE TO CHANGE–
ALL RIGHT.
I'LL COME HOME AFTER WORK TODAY.
CHANGE IN A WAY THAT'LL BE HONEST TO MY FEELINGS.
REALLY?!
I'LL HAVE DINNER READY FOR YOU, THEN!
WHAT D'YOU WANT TO EAT?
ANYTHING THAT YOU'RE GOOD AT MAKING, ONEE-CHAN.

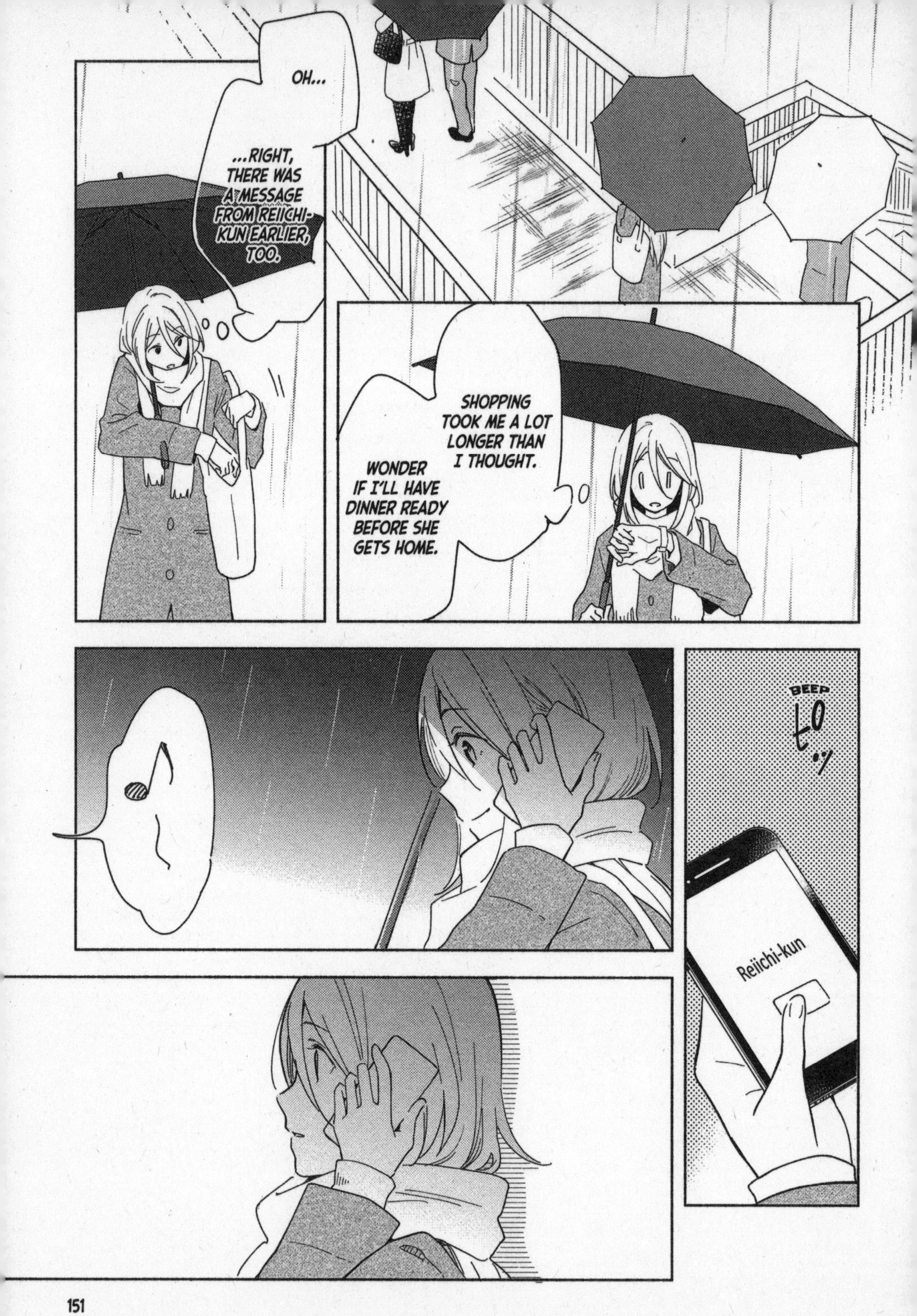
SHOPPING TOOK ME A LOT LONGER THAN I THOUGHT.
WONDER IF I'LL HAVE DINNER READY BEFORE SHE GETS HOME.
OH...
...RIGHT, THERE WAS A MESSAGE FROM REIICHI-KUN EARLIER, TOO.
BEEP
Reiichi-kun

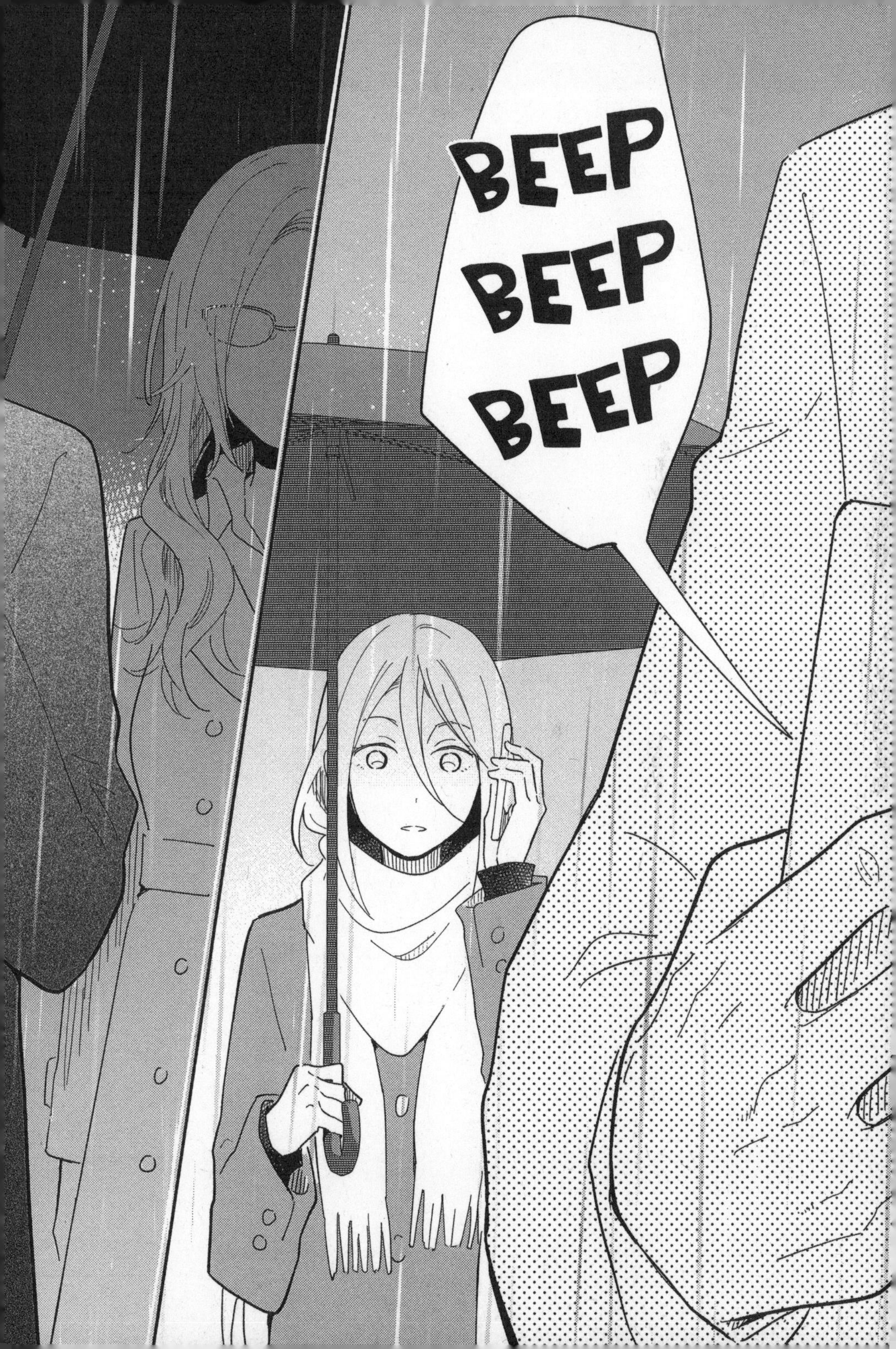
BEEP
BEEP
BEEP

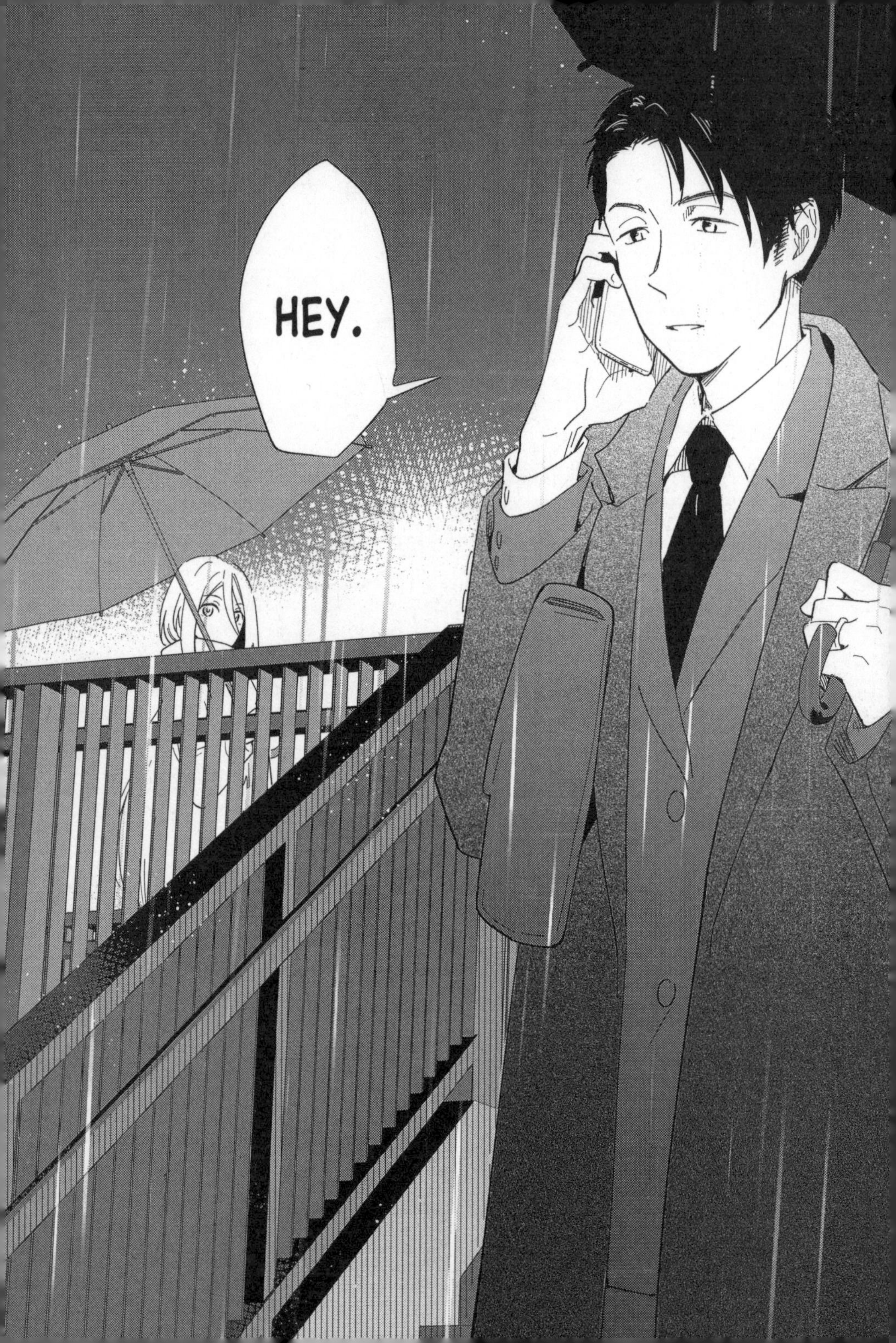
HEY.

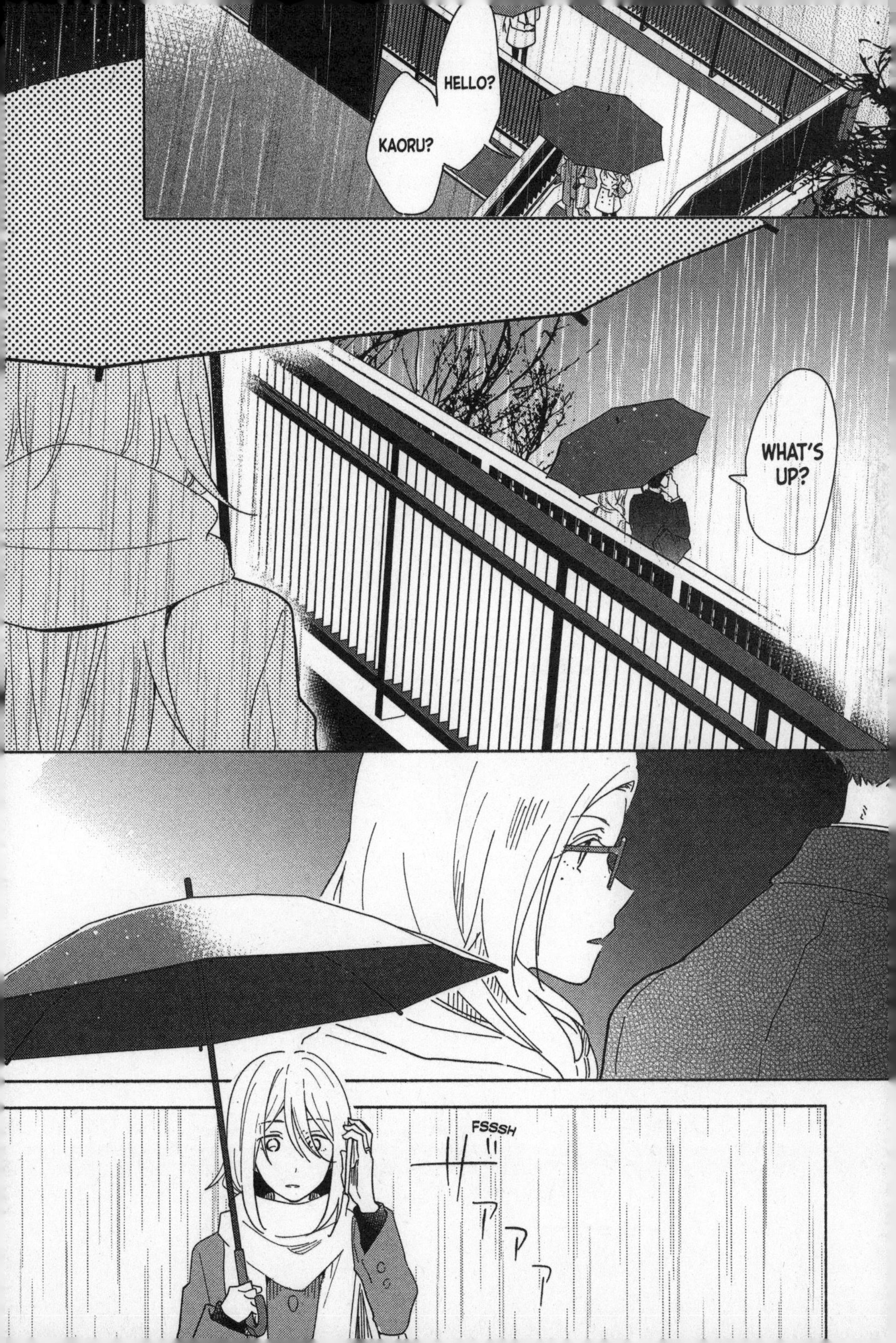
HELLO?
KAORU?
WHAT'S UP?
FSSSH

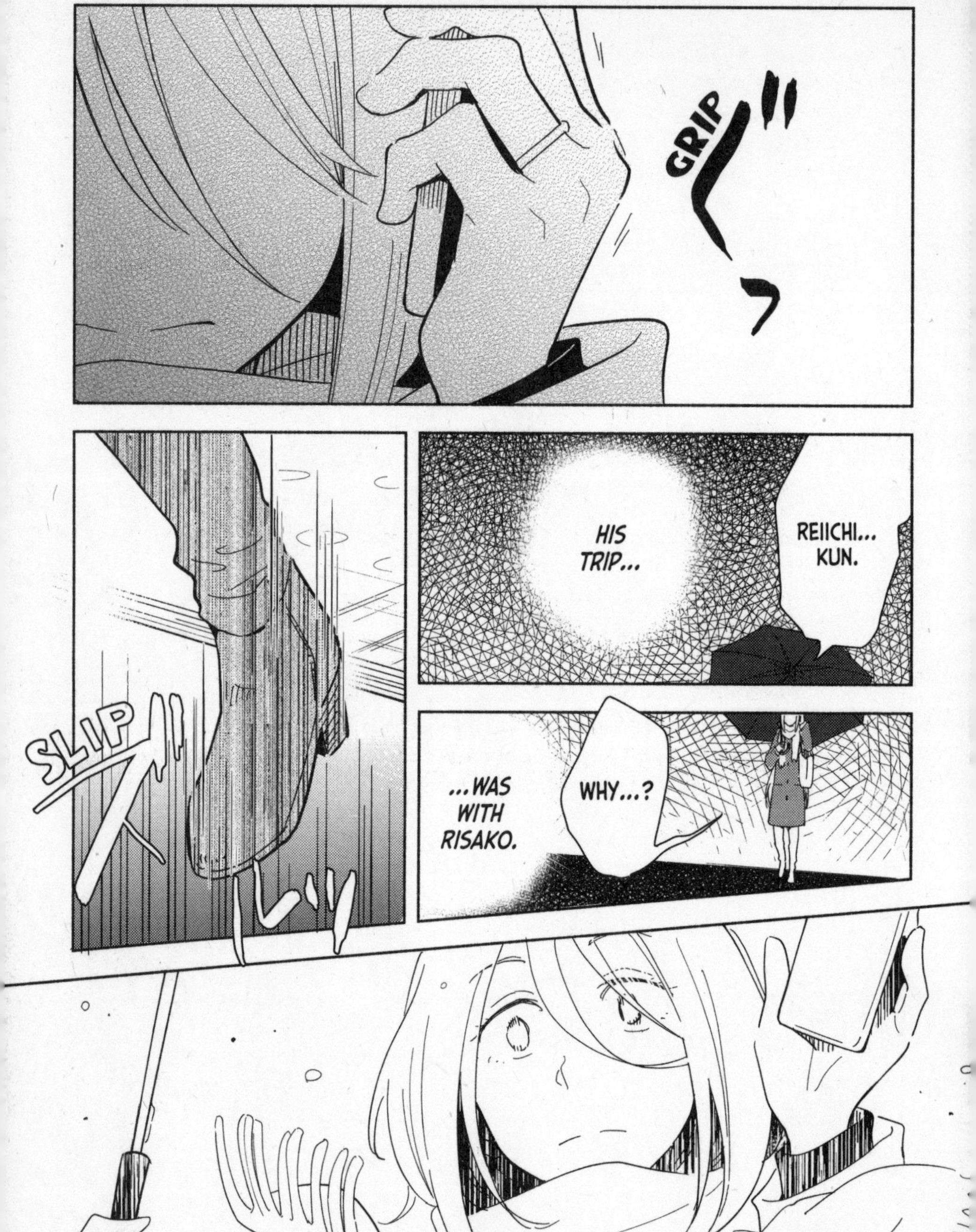
GRIP
REIICHI... KUN.
HIS TRIP...
WHY...?
...WAS WITH RISAKO.
SLIP

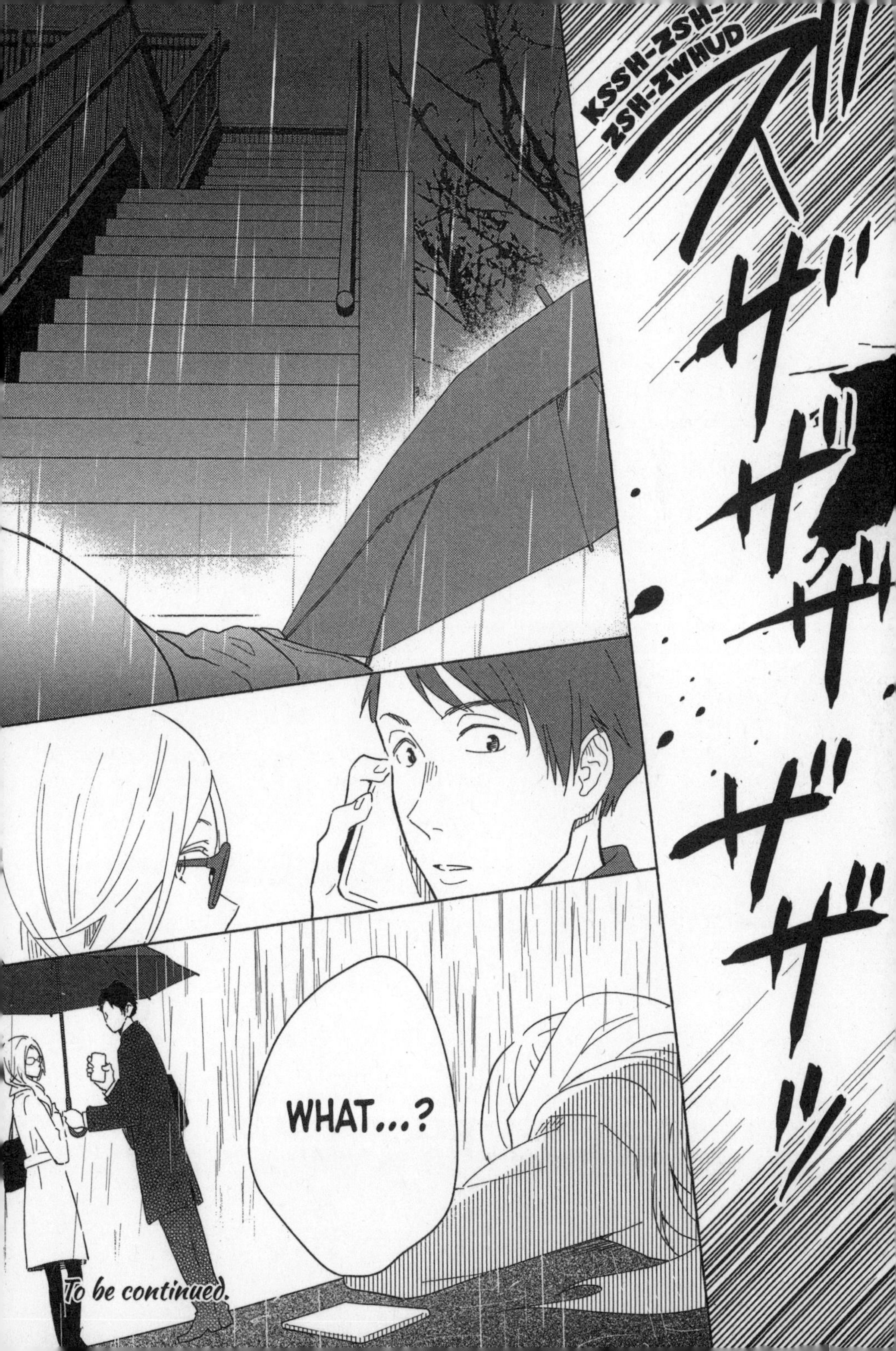
KSSH-ZSH-ZSH-ZWHUD
WHAT...?
To be continued.

If I Could Reach You

Bonus Story

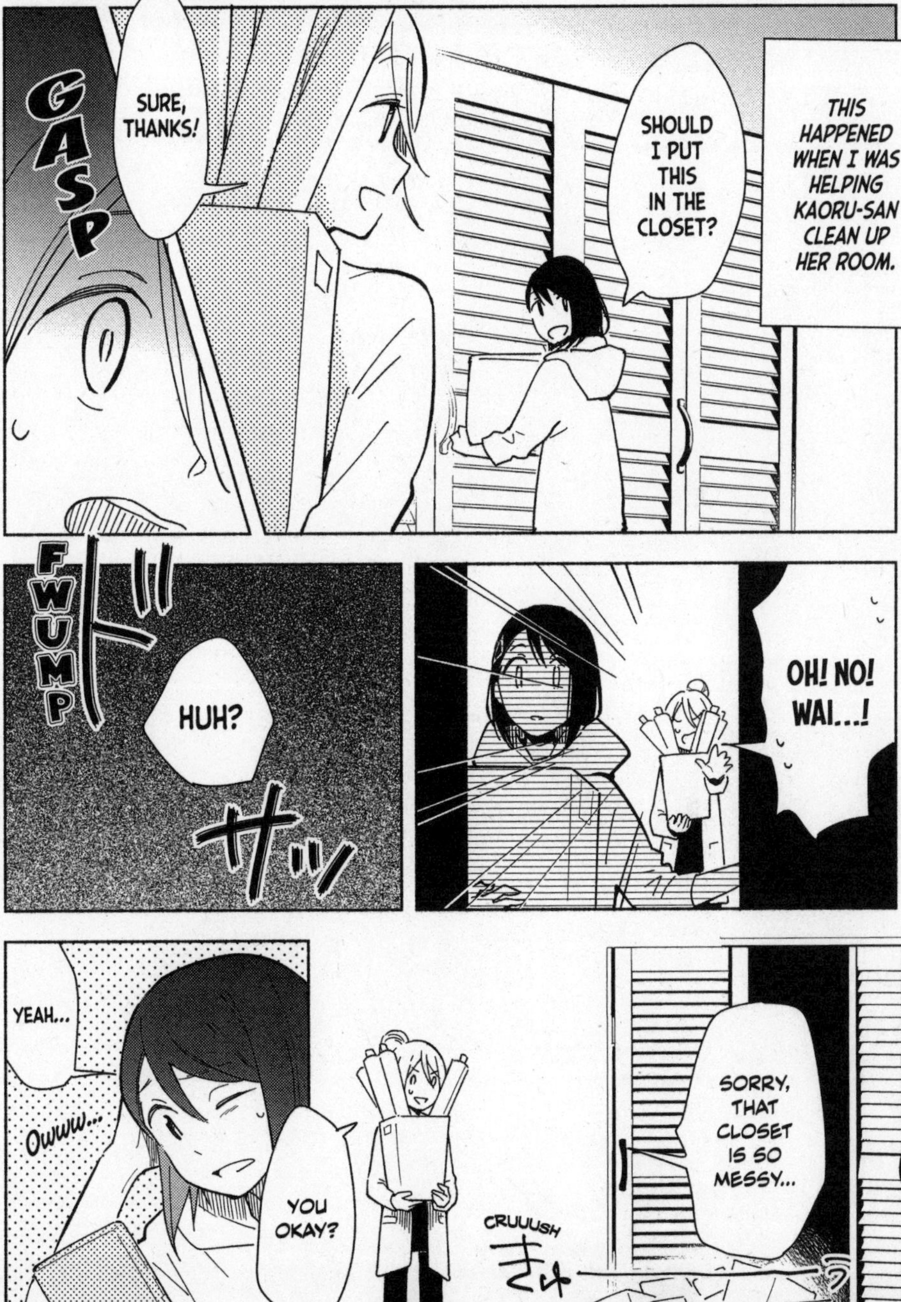
THIS HAPPENED WHEN I WAS HELPING KAORU-SAN CLEAN UP HER ROOM.
SHOULD I PUT THIS IN THE CLOSET?
SURE, THANKS!
GASP
OH! NO! WAI...!
FWUMP
HUH?
SORRY, THAT CLOSET IS SO MESSY...
CRUUUSH
YOU OKAY?
Owww...
YEAH...

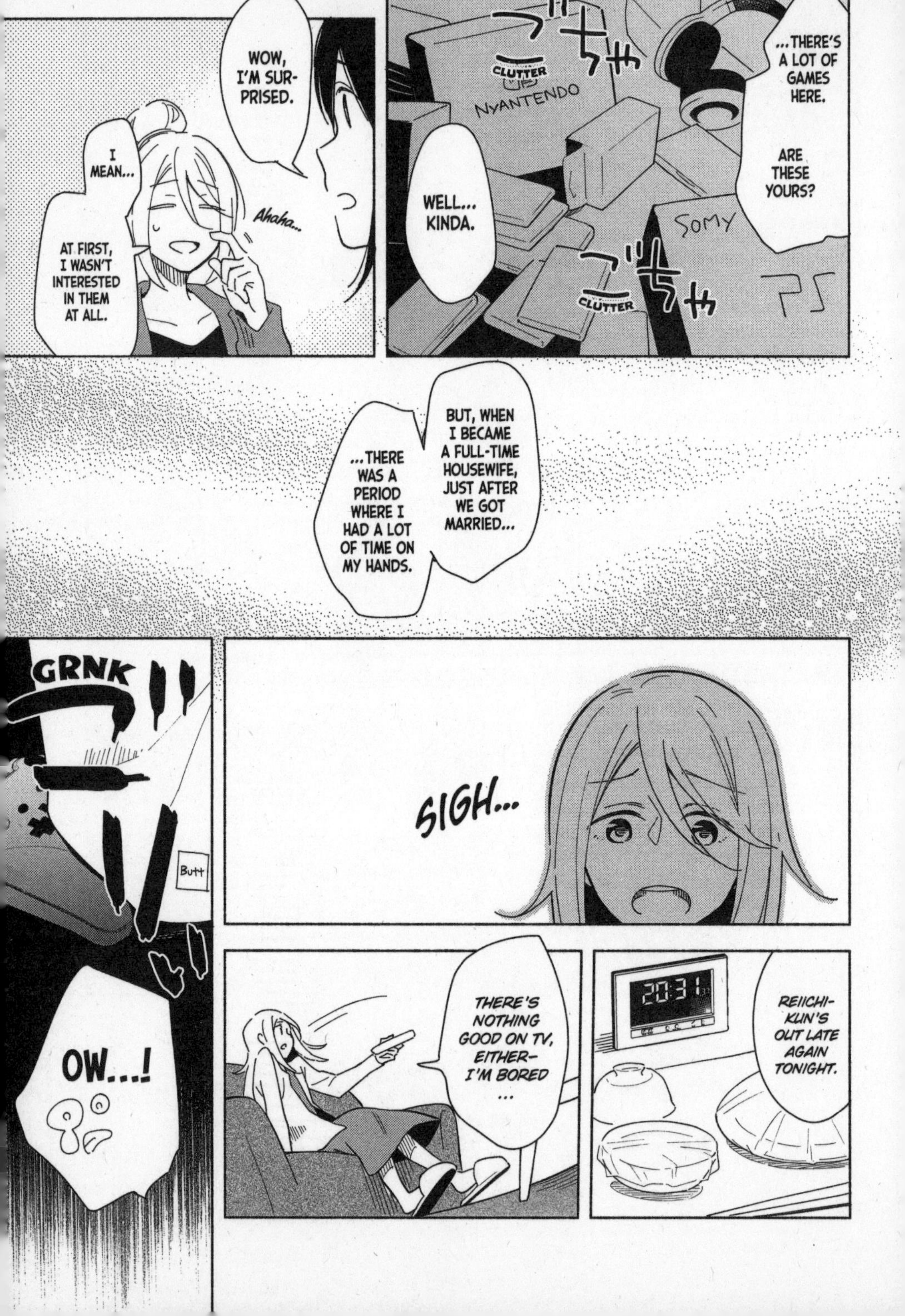
...THERE'S A LOT OF GAMES HERE.
ARE THESE YOURS?
CLUTTER
NyANTENDO
SOMY
PS
CLUTTER
WELL... KINDA.
WOW, I'M SURPRISED.
I MEAN...
Ahaha...
AT FIRST, I WASN'T INTERESTED IN THEM AT ALL.
BUT, WHEN I BECAME A FULL-TIME HOUSEWIFE, JUST AFTER WE GOT MARRIED...
...THERE WAS A PERIOD WHERE I HAD A LOT OF TIME ON MY HANDS.
SIGH...
REIICHI-KUN'S OUT LATE AGAIN TONIGHT.
20:31
THERE'S NOTHING GOOD ON TV, EITHER— I'M BORED ...
GRNK
Butt
OW...!

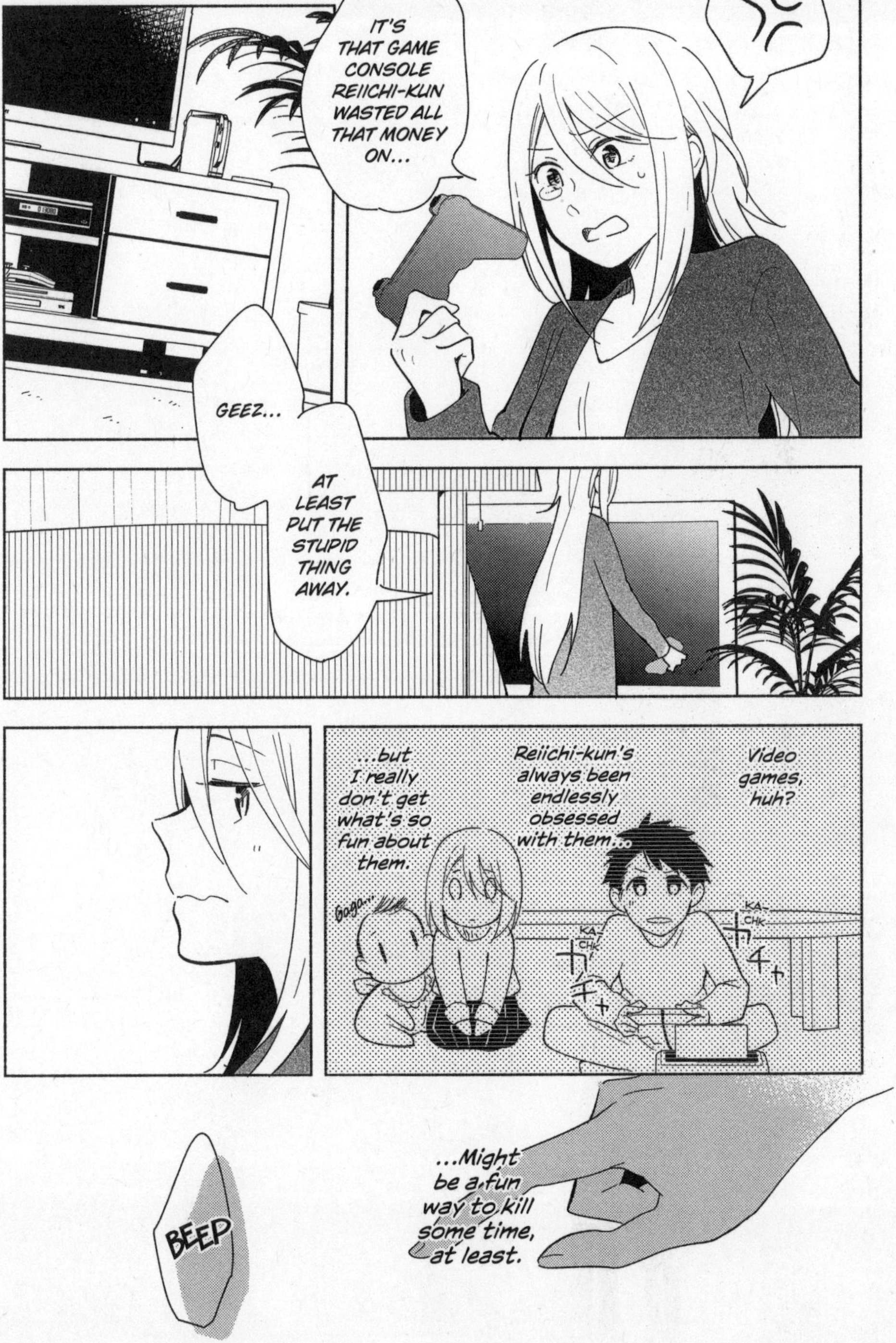
IT'S THAT GAME CONSOLE REIICHI-KUN WASTED ALL THAT MONEY ON...
GEEZ...
AT LEAST PUT THE STUPID THING AWAY.
Video games, huh?
Reiichi-kun's always been endlessly obsessed with them...
...but I really don't get what's so fun about them.
KA-CHK
KA-CHK
Gaga...
...Might be a fun way to kill some time, at least.
BEEP

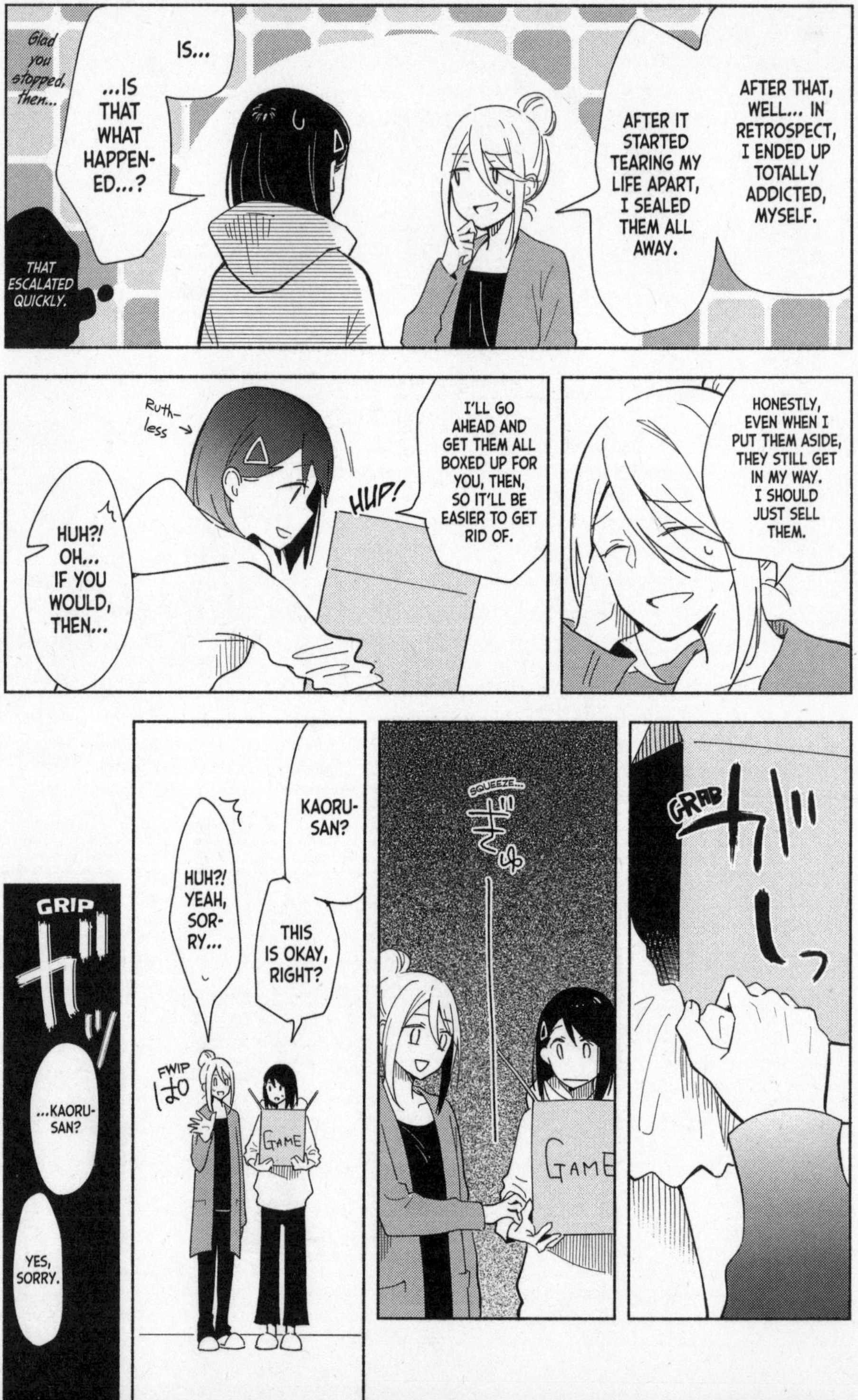
AFTER THAT, WELL... IN RETROSPECT, I ENDED UP TOTALLY ADDICTED, MYSELF.
AFTER IT STARTED TEARING MY LIFE APART, I SEALED THEM ALL AWAY.
IS...
...IS THAT WHAT HAPPEN-ED...?
Glad you stopped, then...
THAT ESCALATED QUICKLY.
HONESTLY, EVEN WHEN I PUT THEM ASIDE, THEY STILL GET IN MY WAY. I SHOULD JUST SELL THEM.
I'LL GO AHEAD AND GET THEM ALL BOXED UP FOR YOU, THEN, SO IT'LL BE EASIER TO GET RID OF.
HUP!
Ruth-less
HUH?! OH... IF YOU WOULD, THEN...
GRAB
SQUEEZE...
GAME
KAORU-SAN?
THIS IS OKAY, RIGHT?
HUH?! YEAH, SORRY...
FWIP
GAME
GRIP
...KAORU-SAN?
YES, SORRY.

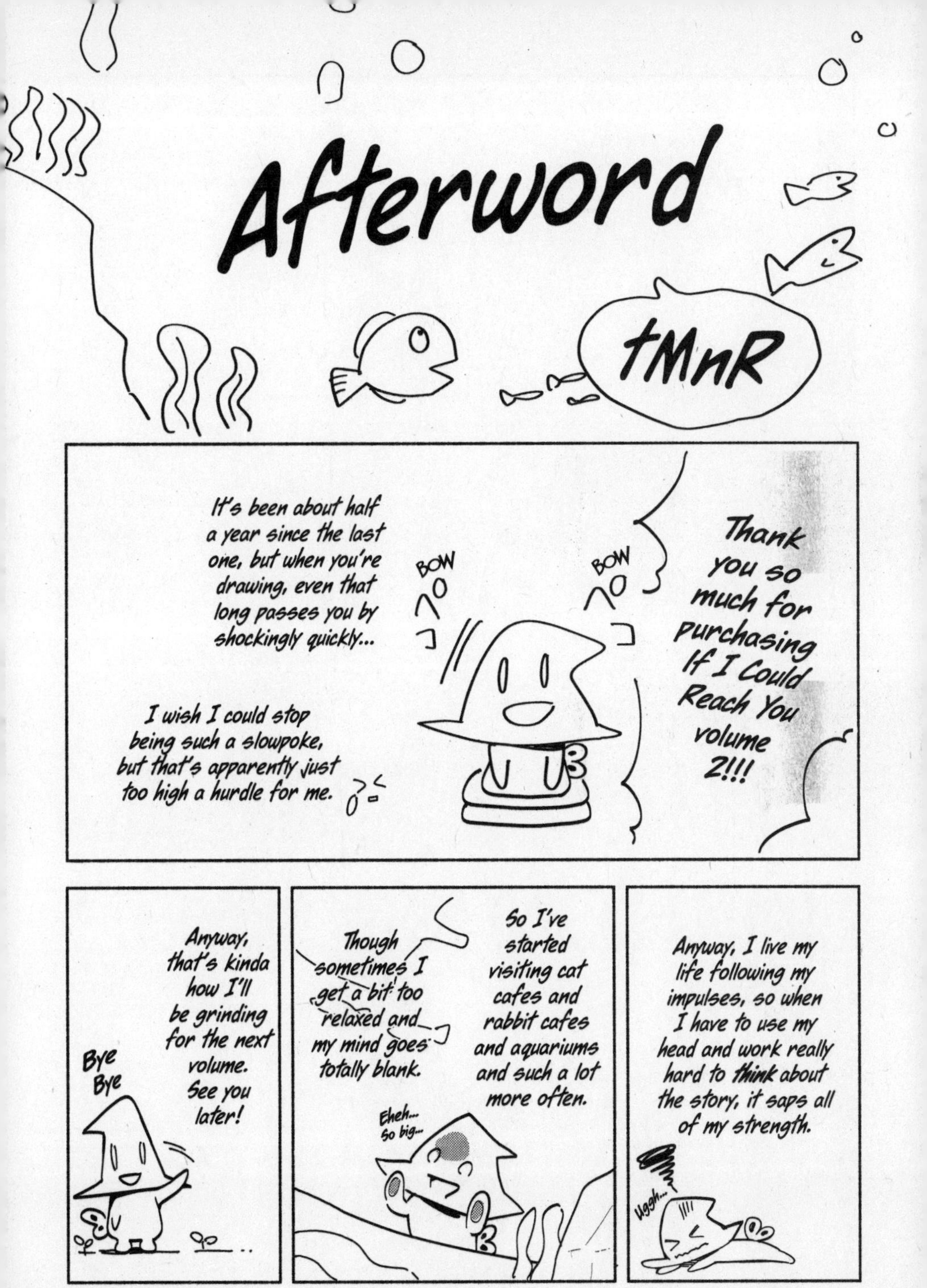
Afterword
tMnR
Thank you so much for purchasing If I Could Reach You volume 2!!!
BOW
BOW
It's been about half a year since the last one, but when you're drawing, even that long passes you by shockingly quickly...
I wish I could stop being such a slowpoke, but that's apparently just too high a hurdle for me.
Anyway, I live my life following my impulses, so when I have to use my head and work really hard to think about the story, it saps all of my strength.
Uggh...
So I've started visiting cat cafes and rabbit cafes and aquariums and such a lot more often.
Though sometimes I get a bit too relaxed and my mind goes totally blank.
Eheh... so big...
Anyway, that's kinda how I'll be grinding for the next volume. See you later!
Bye Bye

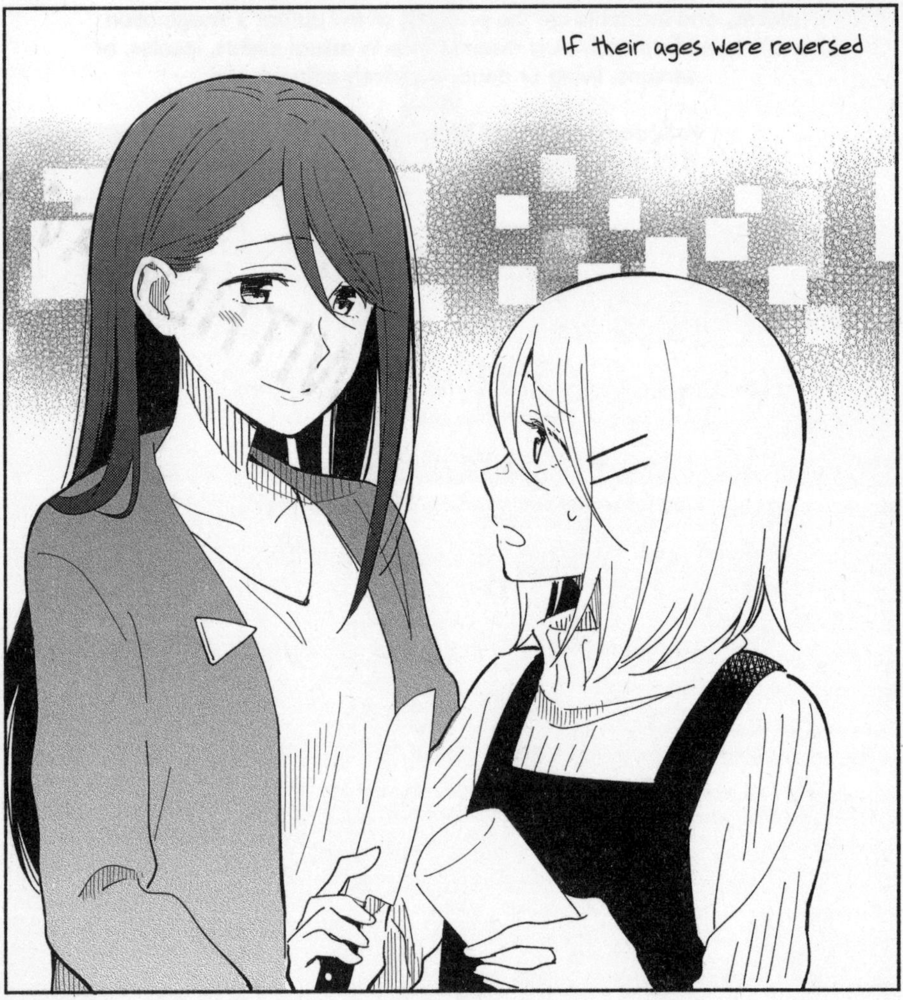
If their ages were reversed

Special Thanks

Editor Saito-san
Kawatani Design-san
Everyone Else Involved
A-chan
and my Dearest Readers...

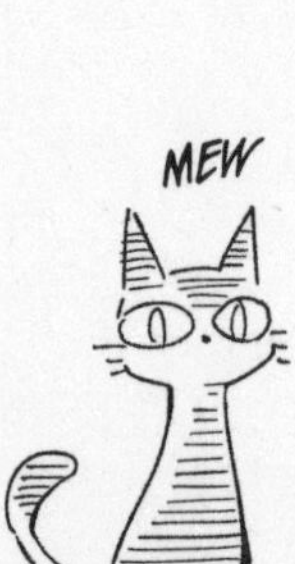
MEW

If I Could Reach You 2 is a work of fiction. ...products ...blance ...l, is en

...rade Paperback Original

...copyright © 2017 tMnR
...pyright © 2019 tMnR

Published in the United States by Kodansha Comics, an imprint of
Kodansha USA Publishing, LLC, New York.

Publication rights for this English edition arranged through
Kodansha Ltd, Tokyo.

First published in Japan in 2017 by Ichijinsha Inc., Tokyo
as *Tatoe Todokanu Itodatoshitemo*, volume 2

ISBN 978-1-63236-888-1

Printed in the United States of America.

www.kodanshacomics.com

9 8 7 6 5 4 3 2 1
Translation: Diana Taylor
Lettering: Jennifer Skarupa
Editing: Haruko Hashimoto
Kodansha Comics edition cover design by Phil Balsman

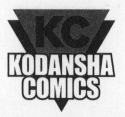

Publisher: Kiichiro Sugawara
Managing editor: Maya Rosewood
Vice president of marketing & publicity: Naho Yamada

Director of publishing services: Ben Applegate
Associate director of operations: Stephen Pakula
Publishing services managing editor: Noelle Webster
Assistant production manager: Emi Lotto